A Sudden Terror

A Sudden Terror

THE PLOT TO MURDER
THE POPE IN
RENAISSANCE ROME

Anthony F. D'Elia

HARVARD UNIVERSITY PRESS

CAMBRIDGE, MASSACHUSETTS

LONDON, ENGLAND

2009

Library of Congress Cataloging-in-Publication Data

D'Elia, Anthony F., 1967–

A sudden terror : the plot to murder the Pope in Renaissance Rome / Anthony F. D'Elia.

p. cm.

Includes bibliographical references and index.

ISBN 978-0-674-03555-3

1. Paul II, Pope, 1417–1471—Assassination attempt, 1468.
2. Conspiracies—Italy—Rome—History—To 1500.
3. Leto, Giulio Pomponio, 1428–1497.   4. Platina, 1421–1481.
5. Buonaccorsi, Filippo, 1437–1496.   6. Humanists—Italy—Rome—Biography.
7. Papacy—History—1447–1565.   8. Humanism—Italy—Rome—History—To 1500.
9. Renaissance—Italy—Rome.   10. Rome (Italy)—History—1420–1798.   I. Title.

BX1309.D45 2009

945′.63205092—dc22   2009019751

Reginaldo lumini vitae latinitatisque

Hunc libellum tibi "dedicavi, quod et summus philosophus es et

. . . [quod] nos non verbis tantum, ut vani philosophi solent, sed doctrina et exemplo instruxi[sti], unde falsum a vero bono seiungeremus quo et in vita felices et in morte beati aevo frueremur sempiterno."

PLATINA

Contents

A Sudden Terror

Carnival to Lent

Glaring at me with contorted eyes, Pope Paul turned to the bishop and said: "This one must be compelled by torture to confess the truth, for he knows the art of conspiracy well."

—BARTOLOMEO PLATINA, A HUMANIST AT THE PAPAL COURT

*T*HE YEAR WAS 1468. On Fat Tuesday, the last and most extravagant night of carnival in Rome, Pope Paul II sat attentively watching the races from his throne high above the boisterous crowd, when suddenly a scuffle broke out. The papal guards had stopped someone who was loudly insisting on speaking with the pope urgently about a matter of life and death. The man, his beard and dark eyes barely discernible under his hood, was dressed like a philosopher. Seeing that he had captured the pope's attention, the "philosopher" broke free of the guards and intoned: "Holy Father! You are in great danger!" The pope sat up, leaned forward, and beckoned the stranger to approach and explain. What he heard made him tremble and turn pale.

The cloaked informant asserted that an organized gang of miscreants was circulating in the crowd, not with the intent of cutting the purses of hapless revelers, but with a far more sinister aim: to murder the pope. An army of four hundred to five hundred criminals, he said, lay hidden in the ancient Roman ruins next to the pope's family palace. There, they awaited the signal to rise up, overwhelm the papal guard, and kill the pontiff.[1] The conspirators planned to overthrow papal rule and destroy the power of the priests. After issuing his warning, the stranger gave no further details that we know of, but slipped away. A "sudden terror" came over the pope.[2] As he looked down at the crowds of drunken revelers, he saw assassins everywhere. The masks and grotesque faces now seemed malignant and menacing. Paul was convinced that his life was in danger. But why would anyone want to murder the pope?

Pietro Barbo, the future Pope Paul II, had been born into a wealthy Venetian merchant family and trained for a career in commerce, but when his uncle became Pope Eugene IV in 1431, Pietro turned to the Church, against the wishes of his widowed mother. The ambitious young cleric was awarded a cardinal's hat when he was only twenty-three.[3] "Flattering by nature and falsely kind, if necessary," the young cardinal often resorted to tears to get his way if imploring repeatedly did not work. Because of this habit, his predecessor Pope Pius II (1458–1464) used to call Pietro "most pious Mary."[4] A popular cardinal, he once boasted that if elected pope, he would buy each cardinal a beautiful villa, to escape the summer heat. Pietro Barbo got his wish in 1464, when he became Pope Paul II. No villas were forthcoming. Instead, the new pope tricked the cardinals into signing a document affirming papal supremacy in all matters. He summoned each cardinal separately to a private room, locked the door, and demanded his signature. With his right hand Paul held forth the pen, while he covered the document with his left, to prevent the cardinal from reading it. The famously learned Cardinal Bessarion tried to escape but was dragged back and threatened with excommunication. Bessarion, too, finally signed.

Pope Paul II loved macaroni so much that he would eat the pasta even between meals.[5] Despite his love of rich food, he remained rather thin and severe-looking, unlike many of his obviously well-fed fellow clergymen. He had been called the handsomest cardinal in fifty years.[6] Paul was so fastidious about his looks that he wore rouge in public.[7] He had wanted to take the name Formosus (meaning "beautiful"), but after the cardinals protested that Formosus was also the name of a notoriously corrupt medieval pope, Barbo settled for Paul II.[8] The pope had an entire room dedicated to his beloved parrots. He kept a well-trained pet by his side during public audiences. The bird would admonish commoners: "Now, you are not telling the truth." Then, at the pope's command, the parrot would begin to screech: "Take him away, for he is not telling the truth!" At this, the commoners reddened and became so embarrassed before the assembled audience that they immediately fell silent and wished for nothing more than to remove themselves from the scene.[9]

The pope could also be generous, though. Carnival ushered in a week of merriment and unbridled pleasure, the last gasp for gluttony and excess before the forty lean days of Lent, when everyone had to fast in preparation for Easter. Before Paul ascended the papal throne, carnival in Rome had consisted of little more than some bull fighting and subdued revelry on the outskirts of the city. This pope changed all that. He turned the Roman carnival into a real party. He hosted sumptuous banquets for civic magistrates and citizens, at which delicate fish, choice meat, and many kinds of wine were served. After each feast he showered coins on the crowds outside his window, to demonstrate his benevolence toward the Roman people. Like other Renaissance cities, Rome used primarily the florin as currency, for the Medici bank in Florence had a virtual monopoly over European finance in the fifteenth century. Each year from 1468 through 1470 Paul spent between 329 and 376 florins on carnival banquets and other acts of liberality.[10]

To give some notion of the scale of the outlay, some comparisons will be helpful. In 1449 a slave wet nurse could be hired for seventeen florins a year. The Venetian artist Titian paid assistants in his workshop four florins a month in 1514. An apprentice banker lived on twenty florins a year, and a schoolteacher in early sixteenth-century Rome made twenty-five to thirty florins a year.[11] Paul's expenditure of hundreds of florins on carnival celebrations was, therefore, extravagant. The purpose of such elaborate festivities was to win over the Roman people, as Paul made clear in two medals he issued for carnival. On one medal was inscribed, "A public banquet for the Roman people," and on the other, "Public joy."[12] He did his utmost to make himself beloved by the Roman citizens and members of the papal government.

Paul II encouraged everyone to participate in the carnival celebrations. Gem-studded swords at their sides, cardinals in full military regalia rode on horseback through the streets, accompanied by an elaborate retinue. The cardinals' palaces were converted into casinos. The nephew of the future Pope Innocent VIII lost fourteen thousand florins to Cardinal Riario at one sitting. Such a fortune could have bought eight palaces in Florence at the time.[13] The Roman diarist Stefano Infessura was aghast at the cardinals' behavior: "This year at carnival all the cardinals rode on sumptuous triumphal floats, accompanied by trumpeters on horseback, and sent masked revelers through the city to the homes of other cardinals, accompanied by boys who sang and recited lascivious and pleasing verses and by clowns, actors, and others, dressed not in wool or linen, but in silk and gold and silver brocade. A great deal of money has been spent, and the mercy of God has been converted into luxury and the work of the Devil. There is no one who is not shocked by this."[14] Extravagance, especially during carnival, was a hallmark of Paul's papacy.

A major feature of the entertainment he offered to the citizens consisted of the public humiliation of those living on the margins of Roman society. For the carnival celebrations of 1468 the pope sponsored eight races. First the Jews ran, then the prostitutes, the elderly, children, hunchbacks, dwarves, and finally donkeys and oxen. They had all been forced to take part in the contest; the jeers of the crowd, the lashing and cudgeling, the pelting with rocks, drove the runners through the awful gauntlet, down the slippery, torchlit cobblestone streets. Many of these wretches stumbled and fell to the ground, bruised and filthy. The sight elicited such mirth "that people could not stay on

Carnival in Rome (1650), by Johannes Lingelbach, Kunsthistorisches Museum, Vienna. © Erich Lessing / Art Resource, New York. Paul hosted sumptuous banquets during carnival and from his window threw silver coins down to the masked revelers.

their feet but collapsed, breathless and exhausted."[15] Pope Paul II, having taken pains to move carnival to the center of Rome and greatly expand the races, enjoyed watching the suffering and humiliation of these helpless contestants. It was his idea to force the Jews of Rome, among others, to run, and he personally gave a gold coin to the winner of each race. Before Paul's pontificate, Jews had been forbidden to participate in the celebrations, but they were nevertheless compelled to pay a special tax to fund the festivities. Paul is often rightly seen as anti-Semitic. He did, however, lower the tax exacted from 1,230 florins to 555.[16] By forcing the Jews to run in the races, Paul also provided the Roman people with an outlet for their aggression, by promoting a safe enemy, a scapegoat against which the Christian majority could bond together. Later in the sixteenth century, after the Jews had been isolated in ghettos, carnival became an especially dangerous time for Jews, almost as bad as Easter, when, in order to protect them from Christian rage, the authorities forbade them to leave the ghetto.[17] Many Romans, some powerful, some powerless, had a motive to kill this eccentric and arrogant man.

In the catacombs the early Christians had buried their dead, and during times of persecution they used the confusing underground labyrinth of tunnels as a refuge in which to hold Mass and escape the pagan authorities. But these gloomy caverns of the dead had been largely abandoned and forgotten ever since Christianity had become legal under Constantine the Great in 313 CE—that is, until the 1460s, when a small group of humanist confederates began to frequent the catacombs. They were members of the Roman Academy, linked by a shared enthusiasm for classical literature and pagan antiquity. The group regularly met at the house of Pomponio Leto on the Quirinal Hill, conversed in classical Latin, composed Latin poetry, and pored over classical texts together. They held dinner parties and celebrated the anniversary of the founding of ancient Rome. The humanists also exchanged homoerotic poetry and probably acted on their illicit desires. They enjoyed dressing up in togas, and invented classical names for themselves. This group of effete poets would at first glance hardly seem to fit the bill as conspirators and would-be murderers.

When the humanists of the Roman Academy first ventured into the catacombs, they had to dig their way in, carry torches, and retrace their footsteps to find their way out again. The bones of Christian martyrs littered the narrow tunnels, which were lined on either side

Footraces (detail, 1476), by Francesco Cossa, Palazzo Schifanoia, Ferrara. © Erich Lessing / Art Resource, New York. Paul increased the number of races during carnival and forced Jews, prostitutes, hunchbacks, and donkeys to run.

with tombs, like couchettes on an overnight train. Hidden in these deep underground caverns, the humanists felt well protected from church authorities. Here the friends could lose themselves completely in their devotion to antiquity and each other. Among their many scandalous activities, they performed secret pagan rites and mock religious ceremonies, at which Pomponio was called Pontifex Maximus—the "High Priest"—a title reserved for the pope.

Nostalgia for the lost culture of antiquity left the humanists disillusioned with the present. Every corner in Rome reminded them of the Eternal City's glorious past. After fifteen hundred years the ruins of pagan antiquity, including the Forum, the Pantheon, the Colosseum, and the ubiquitous obelisks, were still more solid, sophisticated, and magnificent than anything built since. Renaissance architects struggled to match the ancient Roman brilliance, and they were judged by how close they came. While standing in the midst of ancient ruins, Pomponio Leto was sometimes moved to "floods of tears at the sign of better times."[18] Anything the ruins left to the imagination classical literature explicitly revealed. During the thirteenth century, humanist scholars had begun recovering the lost literature of antiquity. Most of the works in the modern canon of classical texts were discovered or reconstructed during the Renaissance. The humanists of the Roman Academy had the writings of more classical authors at their disposal than any other scholar had since the days of antiquity. As a consequence, they had a much richer, truer conception of classical antiquity, and in many respects a completely different one, than their medieval predecessors had. The deeper knowledge of classical antiquity in the Renaissance led to a more critical approach to the past and inspired new ways of thinking about style and language.

In premodern Europe educated people all spoke Latin; it was the language of learning, of law, medicine, government, diplomacy, and the Church. Medieval Latin was clumsy; it may not have been elegant, but it worked. When Cicero's speeches were recovered in the early Renaissance, intellectuals suddenly saw both the extent of Latin's decline in their own day, and the potential the language held to reach new heights of eloquence and express sophisticated thought. Rather than passively appreciating Cicero's Latin, however, as we might read or hear Shakespeare performed, humanists tried to make the lost language their own; they imitated Cicero and used his words and sentence structures in their writings and speech. They spoke to each other in classical Latin and composed Latin dialogues to recapture the living Ciceronian language.

The recovered literature of classical antiquity served as a rhetorical model, but it also contained rich information about the life, politics, and history of the ancient world. Cicero and the Roman historian Livy, among others, served as sources on ancient republicanism. Cicero offered theories of liberty, and Livy heroic tales of the Roman Republic, the days when individuals thought nothing of sacrificing themselves for political freedom. Reading and living these texts inspired the humanists of the Roman Academy to imagine a different Rome: one that was not ruled by the pope and controlled by the Church. "Excited by the stories of the ancient Romans and wanting Rome to return to this earlier time," the Milanese ambassador reported in 1468, "the humanists of the Roman Academy decided to free the city from its subjection to priests and conspired against the person of the pope."[19] Earlier attempts had been made to restore the republic. In 1434, Romans rebelled against Pope Eugene IV, Paul's uncle, forced the pope to flee in disguise, and formed a republic. Too frightened to return, Eugene remained in exile for nine years. In 1453 Stefano Porcari led a conspiracy to kill Pope Nicholas V and reestablish the republic. He almost succeeded but wound up dangling from a rampart of the Castel Sant'Angelo, the papal dungeon where twenty humanists would be tortured and imprisoned for over a year for a similar crime in 1468.

Pomponio Leto, Bartolomeo Platina, and Filippo Buonaccorsi (Callimachus) were singled out as the leaders of the conspiracy. They were the best of friends. With their classical knowledge and dedication to learning, they had much in common. In his popular cookbook Platina represents them joking merrily with each other, leaning over a bubbling pot of soup to be served at a dinner party. It was their friendship, perhaps, that attracted them to the teachings of the philosopher Epicurus, for whom the absence of pain was, along with a community of friends, the highest pleasure. But for the humanists the joys of social life included the sexual. Callimachus, a Tuscan who, like other humanists, had come to Rome to serve as secretary to a cardinal, wrote love poetry to younger members of the academy. He praised their beardless youthful beauty and described the pleasures of their embrace. Pomponio, the beloved mentor and head of the academy, was similarly inclined. At the time of the conspiracy, he was under arrest in Venice on a charge of sodomy stemming from the love poetry that he had written about two youths, students in his care. Back in Rome it was alleged that "unnatural" vice had driven the humanists to murder the pope.

Pomponio was a professor of rhetoric at the University of Rome who was known for his pagan beliefs and devotion to the genius of ancient Rome. At a time when everyone in Europe, apart from the oppressed minority of Jews and Muslims, was a Roman Catholic, the assertion that the humanists were pagans had serious repercussions. Pomponio tried to defend himself, but without success, especially after it came out that he had not fasted—indeed, had even eaten meat—during the forty days of Lent. Platina, who would later write a damning life of Pope Paul II, worked for Cardinal Gonzaga and had extensive contact with church government. He had started life as a mercenary and had served in two armies for four years before finding his true passion in classical literature. His love of Plato's philosophy was cited as clear evidence of pagan leanings.

The humanists had been suspected of harboring ill will toward the pope for some time before the mysterious philosopher's revelation on Fat Tuesday. Platina had already been imprisoned once three years earlier for challenging the pope's autocratic rule and for threatening to call a church council to depose him. Callimachus, who was overly fond of drink, often attacked the clergy in his drunken diatribes, and he had recently handed out fliers predicting the imminent death of the pope. An anonymous astrologer had similarly foretold that the pope would become ill and die within days. By some bizarre coincidence, Paul II was in fact seized shortly thereafter by a violent chill.[20] Like most people of his time, Pope Paul took astrology very seriously.

The appearance of Halley's Comet in 1456 prompted all manner of astrological predictions and calls for prayer to ward off the ill fortune that the flaming ball of fire might portend. With their expert knowledge of the stars and admittedly outlandish ideas about the movement of planets, astrologers were the necessary forerunners of modern astronomers.[21] Most universities, in fact, had chairs of astrology until quite recently. The Church never regarded astrology and magic as nonsense, as modern skeptics do. These were deceptive sciences, effectual but demonic, for they tried to manipulate Nature for personal gain to reveal its secrets. Astrologers claimed to divulge knowledge that only God possessed; their belief that stars determined character threw into question the Christian doctrine of free will. The Magisterium of Mother Church alone could pronounce on the proper use of magic and had a monopoly on all things spiritual. Portents, horoscopes, witchcraft, and magical spells were taken very seriously in this world, where the reasons for even the simplest changes in weather were unfathomable.

Once the pope had decided that the humanists had been plotting to kill him, he could discern numerous reasons for which they would desire his death. Everything made sense: their reading of pagan literature had corrupted their morals to the point of homosexual excess, and the same literature had instilled in them a longing to revive the glorious republic of ancient Rome. Still, they were a small group of scholars without the accomplices or financial backing to carry out such an audacious plan. They must have had outside help. Who could have abetted them? The papacy did not lack for critics. Both the king of France and the Holy Roman emperor Frederick III attempted to control the Church within their own realms, and Paul's autocratic imperialism had alienated and enfeebled the cardinals, the princes of the Church. In the course of the interminable border disputes, the king of Naples repeatedly threatened to invade Rome—Pope Paul was even forced to flee the city on one such occasion in the summer of 1468. The lord of Rimini, Sigismondo Malatesta was continually battling the papacy over territorial claims. Sigismondo was so notoriously treacherous that he had formed an alliance with the Ottoman Turks. He must have been involved in the humanists' plot. Sigismondo's own secretary wrote that his lord wanted to go to Rome to kill the pope, since he despised Paul so much.[22] Moreover, the humanists were directly linked to an even more sinister and powerful figure, an enemy of the Christian faith who desired nothing more ardently than to have the pope's head.

The Turkish sultan, Mehmet II, was the bane of Europe. He was in essence the founder of the Ottoman Empire, which would last until the end of World War I. His lightning victories, and his cultural pretensions, prompted even Christian writers to compare him to Alexander the Great. In 1453 Mehmet had captured and sacked Constantinople when he was only twenty-one years old. The brilliant civilization of Byzantium, heir to Greek culture, was finished. A few squabbling monks remained, and voices in Europe called for renewed Crusades, but Constantinople would never be taken back. It became the capital of the Ottoman Empire; the Muslim crescent was affixed to the high dome of the sixth-century Hagia Sofia, perhaps the greatest church ever built. Islam replaced Christianity. But Mehmet was not content with such a splendid conquest. He overwhelmed Greece and Bosnia, and Ottoman marauders terrorized parts of the Veneto in Northern Italy. He continued his ruthless march, every day drawing closer to the greatest prize, Rome.

Ottoman spies had been slipping into Italy for years, often with the assistance of local inhabitants. But why would European Christians have considered lending support to a Muslim Turk who intended to conquer their native land and force it to change religions? For some rulers who allied themselves with the Turks collaboration was purely a matter of political survival; others were driven by commercial interests. The colorful Florentine merchant Benedetto Dei spent time at the court of the Grand Turk. Dei used his influence with the sultan to gain key commercial advantages in Ottoman lands for Florence over its hated rivals the Venetians and to turn the sultan against them. Others who came to the assistance of the Turks believed that the expansion of the Ottoman Empire was unstoppable and wanted to ensure their place with the victors. The Greek refugee George of Trebizond was one. He had had a prophetic vision about an Ottoman victory and offered his services to the sultan.

The humanists of the Roman Academy also had their reasons for "wanting to seek out the Turk," in the words of the Milanese ambassador. Islam was one of the three great religious and intellectual traditions of the West. Many Italian humanists had studied Hebrew, and it is not surprising that some were interested in Arabic and the Islamic tradition. Pomponio Leto planned to go East to study Arabic. Callimachus, the purported ringleader of the conspiracy, was later implicated in a plot to deliver the Greek island of Chios to the Turks. The sultan, Mehmet II, was a charismatic ruler and an avid admirer of the Italian Renaissance. It was well known that he supported numerous Italian artists at his court and that he had also had Italian humanists as tutors. Winning the patronage of such a prince would have tempted any humanist to betray his homeland and religion. Had the humanists succeeded, they would have been amply rewarded. They would have also enjoyed a religious and cultural tolerance not found in Christian Europe, where the Roman Church regularly condemned pagans and sodomites to be burned at the stake as heretics. Although notoriously cruel to his enemies, the sultan was remarkably tolerant of difference, whether cultural, sexual, linguistic, or ethnic. The humanists perhaps knew that under such a potentate they would have to hide neither their pagan beliefs nor their homoerotic desires.

Platina often dined at the palace of his great patron Cardinal Gonzaga. During the Renaissance, the formal meal for invited guests was breakfast. Dinner was reserved for family or close friends. Gonzaga's household was small to moderate in size for that of a cardinal—only eighty-two people, including stewards, cooks, servants, stable hands, a tailor, and a barber.[23] The young cardinal, who had brought Platina to Rome seven years earlier, had already saved the ill-starred scholar once, in 1465, after Platina had threatened to call a council to depose the pope. Had it not been for his patron's intervention then, Platina would have continued to languish forgotten in the cold, damp papal prison.

On the evening in question, three years later, after a delightful dinner, Platina was relaxing in the cardinal's bedchamber, and perhaps admiring Gonzaga's goldfinch; he particularly enjoyed watching the way the bird ate while holding its food in its claws, as if they were hands. This night, however, was not like others. Armed guards had already broken down the door of Platina's house, smashed the windows, and seized his servant to learn the scholar's whereabouts. Next, the men arrested Platina in the bedchamber at Cardinal Gonzaga's palace and dragged him before the pope. Disheveled and pale, the pope glared at him and asked: "Are you also plotting with Callimachus against me?"

Surprisingly, the cardinal himself had been responsible for Platina's arrest. Gonzaga and other cardinals had heard rumors of a plot from their secretaries. Some of the churchmen chose not to believe them and dismissed it all as a "silly fantasy," but Gonzaga and another cardinal looked into the matter further. When they learned that "the Vicar of Christ was soon to suffer a violent death," the cardinals thought it prudent to tell the pope, if for no other reason than to establish their own innocence in the matter.[24] The pope reacted immediately. "Just as the pope was benevolent, pious, and merciful toward all," a contemporary biographer wrote, "so too did he show himself to be fierce and relentless against insolent and rebellious subjects."[25] Paul sent an armed guard out to arrest those he considered the greatest threat, the humanists of the Roman Academy. Twenty of these men of letters were arrested and thrown into the papal dungeon, the Castel Sant'Angelo.

Pomponio later described the moment in a poem:

> Everywhere floggings and torments await us;
> We are to be dragged up by the butcher's rope.[26]

The strappado was the most commonly used method of torture in early modern Europe, probably owing to its cruel simplicity. The victim's arms were tied behind his back by the wrists; the rope was then thrown over a beam in the ceiling and the victim was hoisted up. When interrogators wished to increase the pain, they would loosen the rope, let the victim fall, then haul him up short after about six feet. This sudden jerk would tear apart the shoulder muscles and ligaments and produce excruciating pain. Sometimes additional weights were attached to the legs. A normal interrogation included four drops. In 1513 Niccolò Machiavelli had weights attached to his legs and was dropped six times in the Bargello jail of Florence. In a sonnet he addressed to Giuliano de' Medici, he wrote: "I have, Giuliano, had thick leather straps around my legs with six hoists of the rope on my shoulders: of my other miseries I do not wish to speak, for this is the way poets are to be treated!"[27] Machiavelli was accused of participating in a republican plot against the Medici rulers of Florence.

The humanists arrested in 1468 claimed they were innocent, but of course that was to be expected. Only physical coercion could make them tell the truth. According to Roman law, the testimony of servants was credible only when obtained by torture, because, it was believed, they would naturally defend themselves and their masters. Centuries of anti-Catholic propaganda have offered us grim images of the torture chambers of the Inquisition and its ingenious methods for extracting information and punishing heretics. Yet all premodern governments routinely used torture, as do many modern states. Through

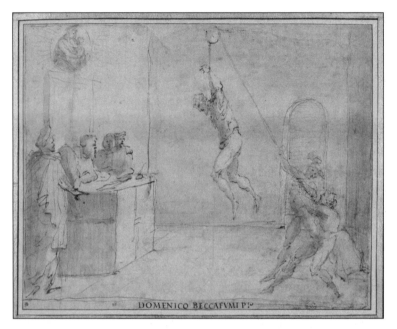

Torture on the Strappado (ca. 1500), by Domenico Beccafumi, the Louvre, Paris.
© Réunion des Musées Nationaux / Art Resource, New York. The strappado was
the most common method of torture in Renaissance Italy.

a clever dodge of casuistry, the Church never executed anyone. Instead, the thousands of people that the Catholic Church condemned
were officially handed over to local secular governments, which duly
followed the Church's recommendation and executed the prisoners.
The seriousness of the charge against the humanists meant that torture was an inevitable part of the legal process. They were accused of
an act of high treason, of plotting to murder the most Holy Father, the
Vicar of Christ.

Platina's right shoulder never would heal properly. The papal guards
pushed, shoved, and stripped him down. They bound his wrists to-

gether tightly behind his back with coarse rope. They threw the cord over a beam and slowly raised him up to the high ceiling. He could already hear his shoulders popping and his ligaments tearing. Cries of pain drowned out his protests of innocence. Then the drop. "The cries of the tortured humanists," Platina later wrote, "resounded so loudly that you would have taken the Castel Sant'Angelo for Phalaris' bull."[28]

The humanists endured repeated applications of torture; one later died from his wounds. Details about the plot began to emerge. The conspirators had planned to assassinate Paul after carnival on the first day of Lent, while the pope was smudging worshippers' foreheads with ashes at the Church of San Marco.[29] The plan of attack, an ambassador reported, was as follows: "Forty men in three groups, disguised as drunken revelers, were to provoke a fight with the pope's guards as a distraction. Then, two hundred armed men were to jump out from hiding places in nearby ruins, come in from the other side of the palace, and cut anyone they might meet to pieces. If this went badly, most of the cardinals and bishops and even the rest of us, who were completely innocent, would be killed. Others said that it was to happen during carnival, when everyone was permitted to wear a mask."[30]

In the end the plan failed, but many questions remained unanswered. The pope himself interrogated Platina and Pomponio; the other ringleader, Callimachus, had escaped. What could have driven them to even consider so evil a plot? Perhaps pagan literature, with its celebration of sodomy and other vices, was to blame; or perhaps the humanists had fallen under the spell of the Turkish sultan, the protector of Islam. But how could they have believed this generous, popular pope to be a tyrant?

CHAPTER TWO

The Price of Magnificence

You have a heroic stature and such a beautiful body, a balanced harmony of limbs, a sweet, decorous complexion, and such gracious eyes that you appear superhuman. In a most beautiful body there must be a most beautiful mind.

—Francesco Filelfo, letter to Pope Paul, September 15, 1464

THE NEWS of Paul's election to the papacy in 1464 was greeted with great rejoicing. The Romans went wild; joyous celebrations broke out on every street, and the people unanimously acclaimed Paul "a true father of the fatherland, a founder of peace, and a lover of justice."[1] From the start Paul signaled that his pontificate would be more magnificent and more regal than those of earlier pontiffs. He would enlist ceremony and extravagant festivities to assert and promote papal rule over Rome and the rest of Christendom.[2] Paul was crowned in front of Saint Peter's not with a new tiara (as popes generally were) but with the ancient one that was said to have belonged to Pope Sylvester (314–345) and had not been used since. Here was a strong imperial message harking back to the ancient glory of the papacy. After the coronation came the *possesso* ceremony, during which the new pope was led in procession from Saint Peter's to the Lateran Palace across the city. Not since antiquity had the Romans seen such a magnificent triumph. The pope rode on a white horse adorned with crimson and silver as far as Chiesa Nuova; from there he had himself carried to the Lateran in a litter. Twenty-three thousand florins were spent on the procession and the banquets for the cardinals and bishops at the Lateran.[3] Machiavelli would criticize Paul's successor,

Sixtus IV (1471–1484), for spending twenty thousand florins, which "would have seemed extravagant even for a king," on his inaugural banquet.[4] If the total income of the papacy in 1480 was 210,479 florins, and the papacy had far less revenue in 1463, it would mean that Paul spent more than a tenth of the yearly budget in one day.[5] Such extravagance was to be expected from a cardinal who thirteen years earlier had celebrated his being created bishop of Vicenza with a full triumphal entry into the city, in the style of a Roman emperor. He spent twenty florins on his baldachin and the caparison for his horse alone.[6] The pope was generous and known for lavish expenditures, but also for hoarding gold and silver. One contemporary biographer remarked: "Everyone openly believed that there had never been a richer pope. He used to say that he amassed such wealth for the welfare of the Church, especially against the Turks."[7]

The new pope continued to add to his already famed collection of precious cameos, coins, medals, statues, and priceless gems. Lorenzo de' Medici, Federico Gonzaga, and other princes of the Renaissance had similar collections, but none as rich as the pope's, which was renowned throughout Italy.[8] Paul used his hobby to bolster his power. He not only made contacts through displaying the collection to important visitors but also rewarded faithful cardinals and allies with gifts of precious gems.

Most dramatically, Paul incorporated some of his prized gemstones into his notorious tiara. Although he had chosen to wear an ancient tiara for his coronation, Paul commissioned a lavish new triple crown, an ostentatious ornament that has come to symbolize the papacy. On making the new tiara, a contemporary related, Paul "used so much gold and so many gems that he surpassed all his predecessors in expenditure." It was a "triple gold-embossed, twisted tiara . . . to which he added such a great mass of gems, large pearls, and different stones distinguished for their quality and size that it cost more than 180,000 thousand florins. Several stones were bought for twenty-two thousand

Bust of Pope Paul II, by Bartolomeo Bellano, Palazzo Venezia, Rome. © Alinari / Art Resource, New York. "Such a beautiful body, a balanced harmony of limbs, a sweet, decorous complexion, and such gracious eyes that you appear superhuman" (Francesco Filelfo).

florins, some for fifteen thousand, others for twelve thousand, and the rest for five thousand."[9] Platina further specifies: "It had diamonds, sapphires, emeralds, topaz, large pearls, and every kind of precious gem. Wearing this majestic tiara, Paul would appear in public like another Aaron. He wanted to be seen and admired by all."[10] The tiara represented the highest Christian priesthood, founded on that of the Prophet Aaron, the first high priest of the Old Testament. Paul's triple-crown design was based on a description in the ancient historian Josephus of the tiara worn by the Prophet Aaron. The tiara also symbolized the pope's direct link with God and the supremacy of the pope over all other rulers in secular matters.[11] Most popes commissioned a new tiara—but not one this ostentatious—and they wore it on only one occasion, during the part of the coronation ceremony that took place outside Saint Peter's Basilica. Wearing the crown inside the basilica was traditionally seen as taboo, because the pope was the humble servant of Christ at the altar. Starting at Easter in 1465, Paul wore his new tiara on most ceremonial occasions even within the basilica. In a laudatory poem of the time, a poet played on the dual meaning of *regnum* as "tiara" or "kingdom": "Looking to decide matters from the majesty of a supreme throne, O Paul, you founded a kingdom [or "made a tiara"] equal to none, and adorned it with gems from the Red Sea; as if to prophesy the future."[12] The popes still wear a tiara based on the same design today. Paul's personal taste for extravagant display thus became an enduring aspect of the Renaissance papacy.

The gem-studded tiara evoked awe in the crowd, but some thought such a luxurious display unfitting for a Christian pontiff. After seeing Paul's tiara, a member of the Fraticelli, a radical sect dedicated to poverty, exclaimed: "When I came to Rome and saw Pope Paul II's tiara, I was shocked to see so many bright gems, shiny stones, and brilliant diamonds. I thought the pope's head was on fire. I asked myself whether we should call this a show of religious piety, humility, and modesty or its ruin and destruction."[13] Another member of the sect attacked Paul by name, called Rome the whore of Babylon, and predicted that divine judgment was imminent.[14] This splinter group of the Franciscan order had been around since the thirteenth century. In 1323 Pope John XXII had declared its doctrine of apostolic poverty heretical, but this pronouncement only redoubled the members' vitriol against the corrupt Church. The heretics held out and grew in numbers. By 1466 Paul had had enough of their defiance and criticism of his luxurious ostentation. He had dozens of the leaders of the Fraticelli, both male and female, arrested at a gathering in Assisi. They were imprisoned in the Castel Sant'Angelo and tortured. Their "confessions" under torture revealed the extent of their perversity, for instance, in what they called the ritual of *barilotto* ("drinking barrel"). In their churches they would engage in wild mass orgies while invoking the Holy Spirit. A baby born from this intercourse was then burned as a sacrifice; its ashes were mixed with holy wine and drunk by all, to the accompaniment of the Eucharist.[15] The heretics were imprisoned in the Castel Sant'Angelo from 1466 to 1471.[16] In the 1460s several cardinals wrote treatises against them defending the ownership of property and the wealth of the papacy and the cardinals.

Outspoken critics of clerical wealth in the fifteenth century were numerous. Apart from the Fraticelli, others, such as the humanists Lorenzo Valla and Platina, decried the greed, indulgence in luxury, and corrupt practices of the Renaissance clergy and longed for the moral purity and humility of the virtuous Christians of antiquity.[17] After praising the pastoral devotion of early Christian bishops, for example, Platina remarks in his life of Pope Antherus (235–236 CE): "Today most bishops do the opposite; considering their own advantage, or rather pleasure, they always look upon a richer bishopric as a source of plunder. They don't ask how large the flock is or how to feed them, but inquire how much the see brings in every year. Little mention is made of the care of souls, but much of increasing revenues, so that they may support more horses and more lazy and stupid servants in their homes."[18] Platina, however, saved his sharpest criticism of clerical extravagance for his life of Pope Paul II. The first imprisonment of the humanist in the Castel Sant'Angelo overlapped with that of the Fraticelli, and the heretics may have influenced him on this issue. Platina wrote: "Paul collected ancient statues and displayed them in his palace. Like the pagans, he coined an infinite number of gold, silver, and brass medals bearing his image and laid them in the foundation of his palace. In this, Paul was imitating the ancient pagans rather than Peter, Anacletus, and Linus" (the first popes).[19] Paul was interested in the material, not the literary, culture of antiquity. In an early draft of the same passage, Platina had written: "In this, Paul was imitating Tiberius rather than Peter; Claudius rather than Anacletus; Nero rather than Linus."[20] The original comparison is much more cutting than the final version. Instead of imitating the virtuous popes of the past, Platina says, Paul emulated three of the worst Roman emperors, each of them, as Leonardo Bruni wrote in his popular *History of the Florentine People,* known for "cruelty, madness, and wicked behavior."[21] Comparing popes to Roman emperors had become commonplace, and it was hardly problematic, at least if they were good emperors. Nevertheless, Platina found it necessary to temper his criticism, even though he was writing after Paul had died, and for the benefit of Sixtus IV, a pope who bore his predecessor little love.

The Politics of Festival

As cardinal, Paul built one of the largest palaces in Rome, in 1455.[22] He spent fifteen thousand florins on the work of engineers and architects. The building was made of solid stone: no wood was used, except for the roof, and iron grates covered the windows.[23] Over the years he continually renovated the palace, which stood at the end of the Via del Corso, in the area he later transformed into the festive center of the city. As pope, Paul remained in the palace but significantly enlarged it.[24] (Only after he died did the Vatican Palace become the primary residence of the popes, as it is today.) In the palace on the Via del Corso Paul entertained cardinals and civic magistrates, and from one of the balcony windows he watched the numerous events of the most festive time of the year, carnival. Paul helped make Roman carnival into the elaborate feast it would soon become in his native Venice. Rather than play it safe after the conspiracy of 1468, Paul promulgated a statute in 1469 to sanction all the changes he had made to the Roman carnival.[25]

The propagandistic purpose of these elaborate spectacles was demonstrated most vividly in 1466. For the anniversary of the founding of Rome (April 21), the Roman commune held a triumph in honor of Paul, to celebrate his military victory over the counts of Anguillara. Count Everso, a feudal lord from the Roman countryside, had been asserting his autonomy from the papacy since the days of Pope Nicholas V (1447–1455). Everso formed alliances with enemies of the papacy and supported any challenge to papal rule. He had backed Tiburzio's rebellion in 1460 (discussed in Chapter 3) and would have lost his life but for the clemency of Pius II. Nevertheless, during Paul's pontificate Everso's two sons continued their father's antipapal policy. Wanting to deal once and for all with the Anguillara problem, in June 1465 Paul sent a small army to crush the brothers. Two cardinals led the papal forces, joined by Federico da Montefeltro's mercenaries. Within two weeks the war was over. Contemporaries were quick to praise the pontiff's lightning victory over the rebels.[26] Cardinal Ammannati-Piccolomini compared Paul's victory over the counts of Anguillara to Hercules' strangling of the fire-breathing monster Cacus: "Our age praises Paul as liberator. Just as the ancients celebrated Hercules' triumph, so did we stage a festival." Exuberant celebrations took place in towns all over Italy, up to the foothills of the Alps, as "people rejoiced and gave thanks to God, for they could now travel safely to the Holy City without fearing to pass through Anguillara territory."[27] Of course,

Palazzo Venezia, Rome. © Alinari / Art Resource, New York. Paul built one of the largest and most sumptuous palaces in Rome in 1455.

the celebrations were hardly spontaneous. They were government-sponsored affairs in which the carefully crafted message was made abundantly clear.

For the celebrations in Rome, the pope himself funded a masquerade based on pagan history and mythology that included a lengthy procession of giant floats. The feast began when from his window the pope released a large flock of birds, which were then hunted down to great applause. Trumpets cleared the way for armed giants surrounded by wild men, who continually threw firecrackers. They were followed by a naked winged Cupid, who sang the praises of the pope, while taking aim at him with flaming arrows. A hundred and sixty youths in white tunics escorted the kings and queens who had been humbled by the Roman Empire. Cleopatra and Caesar wheeled past; Mars, Bacchus, and the gods of Mount Olympus feasted at banquet tables. The military standards of ancient Rome were proudly displayed; consuls and senators processed with suitable dignity. The goddess Diana rode by on a white horse, followed by thirty golden-haired nymphs wearing gold-embossed white tunics and carrying horns and bows. Actaeon shadowed Diana, and twenty well-armed Amazon warriors followed the train of virgins. At this point the procession stopped before the pope's window, and Diana declared that there was no place in the world that would not gladly submit to the pope's rule *(imperium)*, so just and holy. She pledged herself and all her virgins: "Oh most kind prince, do not disdain to count us among your holy subjects."[28]

Criticism of Paul's displays of magnificence was inevitable. In 1466 one unemployed scholar, Giannantonio Campano, praised the pope but also offered a backhanded critique: "You are resplendent and illustrious. Even if this is most worthy of the highest pontiff, people are not lacking who interpret the matter otherwise. They ascribe it not to the splendor of the curia and the majesty of so great a see, but to a certain superficial refinement and pleasure. You wish Rome and your people to be happy and refreshed with public shows and games, as great princes usually do when their empires are flourishing. But do you think that there are no detractors to disapprove of your games and festivals? . . . Whatever we do in life, we are at the mercy of the crowd, who think differently or, rather, perversely."[29] Campano, who had enjoyed the patronage of the previous pope, Pius II, chose this odd strategy in an attempt to win Paul's favor and to obtain a commission to write the history of his pontificate. Not surprisingly, Campano failed to gain a position or a commission at the curia. Paul chose other writers, less ambiguous in their praise, Canensius and Gaspar of Verona, to tell his story.

Another more forthright critic was Cardinal Ammannati-

Piccolomini. Significantly, Pius II had also served as his benefactor, to such a degree that the cardinal adopted that pope's surname. In 1468 he wrote in a letter: "Pope Paul, you have a great yearning for eternity; you want to be spoken of in centuries to come. For this reason you not only had coins minted in your image but placed them in the foundations and walls of buildings, so that when they fall down after a thousand years, monuments to your name might spring up. . . . A zealous imitator of ancient *vanitas*, you bestow secular games and banquets on the Romans . . . so that your pontificate will not fall silent after you. Pardon me, Paul, this is neither true praise nor viewed as a priest's duty. It is vanity. No wise man approves of coins, inscriptions, and the lewd diversions of the people, for they are sins."[30] Such criticism did not dampen the pope's enthusiasm for extravagant display—indeed, if anything it prompted him to flaunt his tastes—but it surely contributed to Paul's animosity toward the humanists.

Near the end of his papacy, in March 1471, Paul staged a celebration that surpassed even his earlier extravaganzas, in honor of the arrival of the legendary and magnificent Duke Borso d'Este of Ferrara. For this occasion the pope postponed carnival and then prolonged the festivities for an entire month. Fountains flowing with wine, festoons of flowers, and triumphal arches were erected throughout the city; the sweet sounds of musical instruments could be heard on every street. The duke, adorned with gold and gemstones, entered in a sumptuous cavalcade; eighty men, each with four hunting dogs, marched in white, green, and red uniforms; fifty knights dressed in gold, silver, and velvet brocade carried golden trumpets. Another, no less elaborate, procession also greeted the duke, this one led by the Roman senator Giovanni Battista, who was dressed as a triumphal Roman emperor, adorned with gold, and followed by a hundred patrician counselors. One hundred and seventy-five mules, with silver collars and decked out in white, red, and green, were followed by another seventy-five bearing the duke's wardrobe. Numerous trumpeters and grooms brought up the rear of the procession. The duke, in an attempt to match the pope's generosity, gave four thousand florins to the Romans in tips alone. The pope had wild bulls set loose, and the duke staged a mock battle with his knights. Paul concluded the celebrations with a great hunt, for which occasion he had a bronze medal coined, depicting a forest with hunters chasing wild boar, goats, and stags and displaying the motto "Solum in feras pius bellatur pastor," meaning, "The pious shepherd wages war only with wild beasts."[31] If Pope Paul II was the "pious shepherd," were the "wild beasts" the humanists that he had so viciously tormented? Four months later, on July 26, 1471, the pope died.

These lavish festivities were part of the imperial imagery that Paul adopted for his papacy. Like the Roman emperors, he distracted the people with bread and circuses. Paul promoted and financed such popular festivities to a much greater extent than any previous pope had. Abounding in mythological symbol and deliberately imitating ancient Roman triumphs, they smacked of pagan culture. So why did Paul, who routinely indulged in imperial display and vied with the pagan Romans in staging grandiose popular spectacles, react so violently in 1468 against the humanist scholars, themselves taken with the culture of pagan antiquity?

Carnival was traditionally a time when the world was turned upside down and morality went on holiday, when authority was openly criticized and clerics ridiculed.[32] The questioning of authority occasionally led to violence and open revolt. Clerics and secular officials, however, mostly saw this challenge to the status quo as a safety valve. Ridicule of the establishment both reinforced the existing authority through negative example and reaffirmed a strong sense of community. In the sixteenth century, Venice in particular made use of carnival as a means of reasserting civic unity and government control after the populace had had a chance to let off steam. Similarly, Paul, by expanding, centralizing, and funding carnival celebrations in Rome and introducing new elements, openly branded public entertainment with his papal endorsement. In his carnival arrangements, papal rule extended beyond the political into the social and cultural realms. The humanists' criticism and flaunting of authority, Callimachus' drunken anticlerical outbursts and handing out fliers against the pope, were no mere harmless carnival custom, but a destabilizing threat to the choreographed spectacle of Paul's supremacy—and to his life.

The Triumph of Papal Monarchy

From the window of his tiny cell high up in the Castel Sant'Angelo, Platina watched the Holy Roman Emperor confer knighthood on 125 Germans on the great bridge that stretches across the Tiber River in front of the dungeon fortress.[33] It was a new bridge, for the original had collapsed during the Jubilee of 1450, when the mule on which Cardinal Barbo, the future Pope Paul II, was riding blocked the path and created a traffic jam. A crowd returning from Saint Peter's forced way onto the small bridge; hundreds were either trampled or drowned in the Tiber.[34] The conferral took place during Frederick III's second visit to Rome, from December 1468 to January 1469. In 1452 an earlier rebel, Stefano Porcari, had used Frederick's first such visit, to harangue the people and call for imperial support against papal rule. An uprising ensued, which was quickly put down, and Porcari was sent in exile to Bologna. Perhaps recalling this incident, Paul increased the number of papal forces in Rome during the emperor's stay.[35]

The emperor hardly commanded the same respect as some of his predecessors. Pope Leo III had crowned Charlemagne as the first (Holy) Roman emperor on Christmas Day 800 CE, after Charlemagne had saved the papacy from the incursions of the barbaric Lombards in Northern Italy.[36] Subsequent popes crowned all emperors. Nevertheless, throughout the Middle Ages, emperors tried to assert their control over Northern Italy against an expanding papal state. The rivalry led to widespread violence, as feuding political parties allied themselves with either the Guelfs, who backed papal power, or the Ghibellines, who had imperial leanings. Even after the collapse of the Ghibellines in the thirteenth century, Dante and Petrarch looked north for an imperial cure for the sick woman of Italy, as Dante called her. Not surprisingly, promoters of papal rule presented the relations between emperors and popes as anything but equal. In a laudatory poem about Paul's reign, Leodrisio Crivelli wrote that emperors held it as law that they must "seek their golden insignia from the holy hands [of the pope]." Crivelli then supported his assertion with contemporary examples: "We recently saw how Emperor Sigismund took his vows kneeling before Pope Eugene IV amid great applause; what glory for the clergy! . . . No less, august Frederick, who rules over the lands of Austria, accomplished everything by the decision of Pope Nicholas V. The scepters of power are given to you and your care, O Most Holy Paul."[37]

As we have seen, for Frederick's visit no pomp and splendor were spared. The papal master of ceremonies, Agostino Patrizi, recorded in great detail the elaborate celebrations and procession that Paul had organized for Frederick.[38] The emperor arrived at night. Cardinals Bessarion and d'Estouteville met him at the northern gate of the city, the Porta del Popolo, welcomed him with a speech, then escorted him through the sumptuously decorated streets, first to the pope's titular church, San Marco, then to Saint Peter's. Three thousand torches lit the procession; the emperor rode with the cardinals under a white silk baldachin embroidered with gold.[39] The emperor was escorted inside the basilica, where he knelt and prayed at Saint Peter's tomb. Only when he rose from his prayer did he behold the pope in full splendor seated on a high, richly decorated throne. The emperor immediately knelt, before approaching the throne and kneeling again; he then kissed the pope's feet. Paul smiled, bent down, and allowed Frederick to embrace and kiss both his knees. A green silken throne was brought out for the emperor and placed next to the pope's, but lower, so that the seated emperor's head was level with the pope's feet.[40]

Beyond the fulfillment of a vow to undertake a pilgrimage, Frederick had other purposes in visiting the Eternal City. It was unavoidable that he and the pope should discuss the war with the Ottoman Turks, but the two agreed only on the need to explore the subject further at a congress of the ambassadors of all the Christian rulers. Frederick's immediate goal, it seems, was to obtain the right of succession to the throne of Hungary and Bohemia for himself and his son. But Matthias Corvinus, the current Hungarian ruler, was a papal favorite and would not be denied the throne. In the end, the emperor achieved little, apart from the granting of two new bishoprics, the pope's blessing for the order of Saint George, and an agreement to commence the canonization process for Margrave Leopold of Babenberg.[41]

Frederick's disappointment, however, was Paul's gain. The pope may have spent 6,000 florins (3,690 of his own money) on banquets, processions, and festivities during the emperor's visit, but all the ceremonies publicly demonstrated the ascendancy of the papacy over the Holy Roman Empire.[42] Quite apart from the choreography, Frederick expressed an almost embarrassing deference toward the pope. After they both exited the Lateran on New Year's Eve, "in complete devotion Frederick rushed with his servants to help the pope onto his horse and he himself tried to slide the pope's foot into its golden stirrup. The pope smiled at the emperor, and they rode their horses under the same canopy through the streets and squares of the city. The people's joy was so great throughout the city that our times had seen no grander spectacle."[43] The sources confirm the clear message that the pope no longer had need of the Holy Roman Emperor and was in fact becoming an independent imperial power.

Patrizi, the papal master of ceremonies, concludes his account by saying: "The kindness that the pope showed the emperor was great and was considered all the greater since papal authority was in no way less than in earlier times, but its power was far superior. For through the diligence of the pontiffs, especially our Paul, the Roman Church, with God willing, has increased in wealth and empire to such an extent that it is to be compared with the greatest kingdoms. But the authority and the power of the Holy Roman Empire has diminished and eroded to such a point that scarcely anything remains beyond its name."[44] The pope, Patrizi stressed, nevertheless treated the emperor as an equal, his constant deference to the pontiff notwithstanding. Although an imperial visit recalled the old rivalry, the tables had now turned in the pope's favor, and Paul used the event to promote a potent image of his superior status.

Rise of the Cardinals

During Paul's pontificate, France constituted a much greater threat to the papacy than did Germany. Right after the humanists were arrested, in fact, a rumor circulated that the king of France and Ferrante of Naples were behind the plot.[45] Such speculation was not unfounded, in light of recent relations between France and the Holy See. After the Council of Basel in 1438 King Charles VII of France and the French clergy had made a formal declaration, known as the Pragmatic Sanction of Bourges. It asserted the supremacy of a council of cardinals over the pope, and the French clergy's right to administer church property and benefices in France without papal interference. Although the pope did not consider the proceedings of the Council of Basel legitimate, the Pragmatic Sanction was a powerful affirmation of conciliarism. Advocates of conciliarism argued that a council of cardinals had greater authority than a pope. Conciliarists looked to the precedent of the Council of Constance, which had deposed three claimants to the papacy and elected a new pope in 1417.

After becoming the king of France, Louis XI tried to assert control over church affairs in his realm. He had sworn absolute obedience to the previous pope, Pius II, but as one of the king's councilors argued, this bound Louis only to Pius, not to Paul. Louis in fact delayed the customary profession of obedience to the pope until 1466 and then asked for the right to appoint twenty-five bishops in exchange for it. Louis furthermore petitioned Paul to make one of the king's loyal subjects a cardinal, and in return promised to suppress the Pragmatic Sanction. The pope consented, and the king made the declaration. The Parliament of Paris, however, refused to ratify the king's pronouncement against the sanction, and the University of Paris appealed for a council to be convened.[46] The Pragmatic Sanction was more than a mere protest—it became a tool in the political battle between the pope and the other European princes in the Renaissance.

Although Pius II had condemned conciliarism in the 1460 bull *Execrabilis,* the idea still had its supporters. The Milanese ambassador, in his dispatch on the 1468 conspiracy, specifically described the humanists involved in the plot as "some poets, who are secretaries to cardinals."[47] The implication is that the cardinals, as members of church councils, of course stood to gain the most from a conciliarist (more democratic) Church.[48] Cardinals had in fact already tried to curtail the pope's power.

At the conclave of 1464, before the votes were cast that resulted in Paul II's election, the bishop of Torcello, Domenico de' Domenichi, delivered a lengthy disquisition on the state of the Church and the need to confront the Turks, limit the influence of secular princes, and restore the majesty of the College of Cardinals. The cardinals wanted to make sure that the new pope, whoever he might be, would resolve these matters. On the first day of the conclave they drafted a document called the Election Capitulation, and all except one swore to observe it. Among other restraints, the capitulation bound the next pope to pursue a war against the Turks, to reform the curia, and to summon a General Council within three years. The document also placed restrictions on the number and age of new cardinals, papal nepotism, and appointments to new and old benefices. Furthermore, whatever decisions the pope made were to be approved by the College of Cardinals: the cardinals would meet twice a year in council, to monitor and if necessary reprimand the pope or remind him of his promise. Through these measures they would severely limit the papal monarchy, and conciliarism would triumph, by turning the Roman Catholic Church into an oligarchy. Subject to the approval of the College of Cardinals, the pope would have been reduced to being first among equals. As Cardinal Barbo, the future Paul II had signed the capitulation and sworn to abide by it even after his election.[49] But that had been Cardinal Barbo. Pope Paul II had other plans.

A bull to confirm the capitulation was supposed to appear three days after the coronation. Instead, the new pope, after consulting legal experts, declared the capitulation nonbinding, withdrew his oath, and forced the cardinals to sign a new document reaffirming the principal of papal monarchy. After Cardinal Bessarion was dragged back and threatened with excommunication, only one cardinal, the elderly Carvajal, stuck by his refusal to sign. Paul locked the document with all the signatures up in a chest; no one was allowed to see what he had actually signed. Cardinal Alain of Avignon told Paul that the pope had used his twenty-four years' experience as a cardinal as preparation for destroying the College of Cardinals.[50] Cardinal Gonzaga predicted that a council would humble the new pope. In France it was rumored that another schism was unavoidable.[51]

Paul thus tried to destroy conciliarism at the outset of his pontificate, but the movement continued to be a constant concern for him, and the threat that a council of cardinals would be called to curtail the pope's power played an important part in the events of 1468. If Paul limited the real power of the cardinals, he nevertheless tried to compensate by enhancing their sense of grandeur, in granting them, for example, the privilege of wearing red hats and purple cloaks and caparisoning their horses in purple, which had formerly been reserved for the pope. He also raised the salaries of needy cardinals and allowed them to sit on raised seats in churches and assemblies.[52] "So great was [Paul's] kindness," Platina wrote, "that he would visit sick curial officials who were of some importance, give them medicine, and encourage them back to health." Platina intimates that the action was insincere by asserting that Paul visited only officials "of some importance." In the original version of Platina's life of Paul, the word "kindness" was qualified by the phrase "whether true or false," which the humanist later deleted. In the final version Platina again calls the pope's motives into question, by stating that "Paul saw to it that he was made executor of the sick men's estates, which he distributed as he saw fit; and if something was of interest to him, he would buy it with money from the auctioned estate."[53] In the eyes of his biographer, Paul was a "deceiver and a dissembler," another phrase Platina edited out of the final version of his life of Paul.[54] Platina, whose body was broken by torture in the papal prison, might understandably have had a jaundiced view of Paul. Others also, however, had cause to loathe the pontiff.

A Reformer and His Critics

From the start of his pontificate, Paul was not popular in official circles. The former friendly cardinal was now seen by some to be a distant, cold, and cruel pope.[55] Ambassadors complained of the additional bureaucracy needed because of Paul's suspicious nature. Paul insisted, for example, that the chancery accept only original documents, not notarized copies, as was common practice.[56] He allowed few audiences. It was three times harder to obtain one with Paul than it had been under Pius II, according to one ambassador. Paul's inaccessibility was due in part to his habit of working at night. (A German ambassador had to wait until 3:00 AM for an audience.) For this reason, the humanist Callimachus nicknamed the pope the "Firefly."[57]

Business delays and inefficiency meant that fewer dispensations were awarded, and the resultant reductions in income caused widespread dissatisfaction on the part of curial officials.[58]

One of Paul's first acts, as part of a financial reform of papal bureaucracy, was to reduce drastically the number of abbreviators. Abbreviators were clerks charged with condensing papal bulls into shorter briefs, composing letters, and performing other secretarial duties. With their Latin skills and command of the language, humanists were ideal for the job. In cutting back the college of abbreviators, Platina asserts, Paul called the humanists "useless and ignorant; he took away the belongings and positions of those whom he should have been soliciting with honors and rewards."[59] Commenting on Paul's action, a contemporary source, Egidio, thought it "most unworthy of the highest priest." Egidio continues:

> Paul had engaged in commerce, where everything is sold for a price, but after being ordained, he retired from the merchant's, or rather shady speculator's, profession. Those who trade in sacred matters and use altars and shrines for lucre are completely deluded. It is fitting for rulers not to take the belongings of their subjects; but it behooves a priest not only not to take another's property, but to distribute his own liberally. This business made every one of that order [abbreviators] hostile; they hurled every kind of abuse at him in speech, proclamation, and writing. Many accused him of pride, several attacked his character, some reproached his temerity, and certain fellows threatened a council. For these reasons, many were thrown into prison and tortured.[60]

Rather than seeing the discharge of the abbreviators as a sincere attempt at financial reform, Egidio ascribed it to the pope's stinginess, more befitting a Venetian merchant than a Roman pontiff.[61] Let us recall that in his youth the pope had been trained for a career in commerce.[62]

Antimercantile sentiment also attached to Paul's identity as a Venetian. After Paul alluded to Ammannati-Piccolomini's lowly origins, the cardinal asked the pope whether his nobility was any more genuine, being "Venetian and mercantile, gained from long voyages."[63] Venice and Rome were perennially at loggerheads over which was culturally and religiously superior. After dismissing the humanists from their jobs, Egidio says, Paul then sold those same jobs to others at a profit. Venality in the sale of offices was to be a hallmark of the Renaissance papacy. Sixtus IV, Alexander VI, and later Leo X were the most shameless sellers of offices, but this quick fix for getting out of debt was already gaining ground during Paul's pontificate.[64] Reform may have been one motive for Paul's cutbacks in the college of abbreviators, but there was also profit to be made in the resale of the positions the humanists had held.

The most salient feature of this episode, however, was the threat to call a council. Our contemporary observer, Egidio, emphasizes this point: "Although the name 'council' is always suspect to pontiffs, and feared, it was more feared especially at that time, when skilled, erudite, and elegant men were proposing it." After losing his position in the papal government, Platina told the pope that he would bring the matter to the ecclesiastical court, the Rota. At this, Platina writes: "Paul glared at me with contorted eyes and said, 'So, are you referring me to judges? As if you did not know that all laws repose in my breast? This is my decision: that they should all leave their posts and go where they wish; I care nothing for them; I am the pope, and I am permitted to revoke or approve others' acts at my discretion.'"[65] Platina certainly conveys the image of a tyrannical pontiff wholly uninterested in justice. After this exchange, the pope refused to see the humanists. Trying to gain access to him, Platina writes, was like attempting to "roll an immovable stone."

The humanists spent twenty nights encamped in vigil outside Paul's antechamber. When this ploy failed, Platina wrote a letter to the pope in which he threatened to call a General Council.[66] "Rejected and insulted by you," Platina declared, "we will encourage kings and princes to call a council to force you to explain why you have robbed us of our livelihood."[67] Platina was immediately arrested for treachery, chained in fetters, and examined under torture. He was convicted of two offenses. The first charge was that he had written a libel against the pope, which Platina deflected by defining libels as anonymous, whereas he had clearly written his name on the letter. His letter was therefore not a libel. The next charge was that he had mentioned a council. Platina replied that this was no crime, "for the holy fathers established the fundamental beliefs of Christianity in councils, . . . and among the Romans both private and office-holding citizens had to give an account of their time in office and the life they had led before it."[68] Such arrogance and harsh criticism of the pope must have still rankled in Paul's mind three years later, when he heard rumors of a plot to murder him. Platina would later delete a sentence from his life of Paul that acknowledged as much: Paul "remembered old quarrels and avenged injuries."[69] In 1464, for his insolence in threatening to call a church council to chastise the pope and to reinstate the unemployed abbreviators, Platina, in addition to undergoing torture, spent four months in prison (October 1464 to February 1465), mostly without heat in the dead of winter. Paul wanted Platina's head, but Cardinal Gonzaga saved the humanist's life by calling Platina a madman.[70] Pomponio, Paolo Marsi, young Lucio, and other humanists were also imprisoned in harsh conditions.[71]

Paul was interested in dramatically curtailing the influence of his predecessor Pius II, the humanist pope. Platina, during his first prison stay in the Castel Sant'Angelo in 1464–65, had, tellingly, written a laudatory biography of Pius. Pius had hired the humanist abbreviators who lost their jobs, many of whom were later implicated in the 1468 conspiracy.[72] Paul undertook two decisive acts—the dismissal of numerous humanist abbreviators and the arrest and imprisonment of the humanists in 1468—that together ensured the brutal elimination of the remnants of Pius' legacy. The magnificence of Paul's papal monarchy demanded no less, for the pope had to have complete loyalty and subservience at any cost.

Paul's targeting of the humanists in 1468 was similarly due in part to the very real threat of conciliarism. After his arrest, Platina was questioned under torture about whether he had "sent a letter from Pomponio to the emperor or some Christian prince in order to start a schism or call a council."[73] He denied it, but the accusation reveals how seriously the pope took the threat to call a council. In the same year, 1468, a Milanese ambassador reported that King Louis XI and Charles the Bold, Duke of Burgundy, were trying to extort concessions from Paul through the threat of a council. The Parliament and the University of Paris at the same time reissued their call for a council, as did the Hussite king of Bohemia.[74] When two years earlier, in the summer of 1466, the Venetians had raised the issue of a council, Paul, turning livid, threatened to excommunicate them and to place the entire city under interdict. Among the other consequences of an interdict, priests were forbidden to administer the sacraments, a terrible situation in a society as religious as that of Renaissance Italy. During the humanists' imprisonment in 1468, the warden Rodrigo Sánchez de Arévalo wrote a treatise for them to read, in which he affirmed the legitimate election of Paul and condemned conciliarism.[75]

Pope Paul II emerges from these accounts as a crazed megalomaniac, who lavished money on senseless luxuries, yet inflicted misery on the humanists out of parsimony, and who claimed absolute dominion over others within and outside the Church. Although he was an eccentric man whose excesses were criticized at the time, his vision of an authoritarian papacy whose power could be bolstered by extravagant spectacle has endured to the present day. In fostering such a magnificent and, some would say, tyrannical paradigm for the papacy, Paul inevitably made enemies. The question was how far they would go in their opposition to him.

CHAPTER THREE

Lessons of Rebellions Past

The Romans are a contentious people.

—VESPASIANO DA BISTICCI

*A*T FIRST no one took notice of the Benedictine monks who had slipped out the door of the pope's palace. It was June 4, 1434. Pope Eugene IV, the future Pope Paul's uncle, had had trouble with the unruly Romans since the start of his pontificate three years earlier. There had already been one rebellion in 1431, when the previous pope's family, the Colonna, had provoked a popular uprising, because Eugene was trying to rescind the privileges that Pope Martin V had granted to his family. Eugene managed to quell this revolt, but the Colonna came back with much greater force in 1434 and rallied the Romans to their cause. Now the rebels surrounded the pope's palace and held him prisoner. Some called for his execution, while others wanted to trade the valuable hostage. Pope Eugene feared so greatly for his life that he decided to risk a daring escape in disguise. The "monks" mounted scrawny mules and slowly made their way to a small fishing boat on the Tiber, where a strapping pirate named Valentino nervously awaited their arrival. A few passersby had noticed the docked boat, and some stopped to watch what might ensue. At last, the pirate spied the monks making their way down the hill. One of them, a large, well-fed fellow, looked somehow familiar. The growing crowd of Romans moved closer to inspect the unconvincing-looking monks, at which the pope became visibly anxious; he tried to urge his mule on with a few well-placed kicks, then slapped the beast, and finally shouted at it. By then the bystanders had recognized the pope and sounded the alarm. Valentino sprang from the boat, ran to the first mule, snatched up the pope, and whisked him bodily onto the boat—just in time, for the mob of Romans that had gathered on the banks of the Tiber began pelting the monks and the boat with stones and dispatching arrows, spears—anything that came to hand—in their direction. Valentino yelled to Eugene to lie low, as the crew began rowing furiously out to sea. The pope grabbed a shield, lay flat on the muddy bottom of the boat, and winced at the sound of rocks smashing against metal.

The crowd showed no signs of relenting. Men shouted out offers of bribes if the pirate would dock. An armed fishing boat blocked the pope's path of escape. But Valentino held fast and headed straight for the vessel, as the crewmen loosed arrows at the boat from their crossbows. The dilapidated fishing boat of the Romans didn't stand a chance. The Romans on the old craft lost their nerve and gave way when they saw the pirates making dead for them. Thus the pope made it safely to Ostia, where another pirate, Vitellius, was waiting with a ship to take him to Pisa, the port of Florence.[1] The pope would not return to Rome until 1443. During those nine years the Church was based in Florence.

Roman rebellions had plagued every Renaissance pope. The conspiracy of 1468 was not the first attempt to expel the papacy and revive the ancient Roman Republic. It was, however, the least successful. Pope Paul had learned from the troubles of his predecessors to take the threat of conspiracy very seriously. Wanting to avoid the dangers to which earlier popes had been exposed, and the humiliation his uncle in particular had faced, Paul courted the favor of the Roman people with lavish acts of generosity, as we have seen, and acted swiftly when rumors of a rebellion reached his ear.

In 1417 Martin V (1417–1431), newly inaugurated pope, had ended years of schism and definitively moved the papacy back to Rome. Throughout most of the fourteenth century, the papacy had resided at Avignon, in France, held hostage, it was said, by the French monarchy. When the papacy had first returned to Rome in 1377, Romans initially welcomed Pope Gregory XI with great rejoicing.[2] Many, however, still opposed the papacy. Gregory eventually prevailed over this opposition in 1378, but he died shortly thereafter. The next pope, the Neapolitan Urban VI, managed to alienate both the Romans and the French cardinals, who elected an alternate pope.[3] Thus began the Great Schism, at the height of which three different men claimed to be pope. The chaos ended in 1417, when, as we have seen, a council of cardinals deposed all claimants and resolved the dispute by electing Oddo Colonna as the sole pope, Martin V.[4] The Colonna were the most powerful family in Rome. They were moreover the mortal enemies of another powerful family, the Orsini. Rome was divided into Colonna and Orsini neighborhoods. The new pope's family connections helped him get elected and assured a successful reassertion of papal power in Rome. Martin spent his pontificate renovating Rome and enriching the church coffers, but also his family and friends.

Pandone dei Pandoni was an unlikely republican rebel. He was nicknamed Porcellio, "little pig."[5] His long career consisted of an endless series of largely unsuccessful attempts to win patronage for his decidedly mediocre verse. If Renaissance humanists have a reputation for being insincere sycophants who changed opinions as often as they changed benefactors, for whom they produced cloyingly laudatory poems, it was because of humanists like Porcellio. He was one of the new scholar-poets who were trying to make a living from their erudition and their skill at composing classical Latin verse. Other humanists, most notably Leonardo Bruni and Poggio Bracciolini, found work as political advisers and administrators. Their eloquence in Latin would become a hot commodity in the fifteenth century, but Porcellio's talents were not in demand.

With the advent of Martin V as pope, Rome was reborn. Humanists acclaimed him as a "third Romulus" for restoring the "squalid and almost extinct city." He clamped down on violence in the countryside and the city, so that the "prosperity and peace of the ancient emperor Augustus seemed to return."[6] The arrival of a new pope brought new opportunities to seek patronage. Humanists came in droves to the Eternal City to find work, and for the most part they did.[7] Like many humanists, Porcellio tried to ingratiate himself with the pope and was able to gain some support.[8] In gratitude and as an effort to attract further favor, Porcellio dedicated a bizarre allegorical poem to his benefactor, entitled *Bos prodigiosus,* the *Prodigious Bull.* In the poem, Porcellio describes an immense plain filled with ruined pagan temples, and a statue of a woman in a tower pulled in a cart by two lions; above the ruins of sumptuous palaces a lone column stands tall and untouched. A bellowing bull wanders up to the column and decides to copulate with it. "He thrusts his pelvis forward and rubs his loins against the column and emits semen mixed with pure blood."[9]

The rest of the poem describes how the Romans and the Senate interpreted this prodigy. A few say that the people will be yoked to the carriage of some tyrant; others say that the violent times of Marius and Sulla will return. Finally, an old man asserts that the bull's semen mixed with blood on the column portends not war but peace. The city will never be subject to tyrants, he declares, for the pope has returned. The people accept this interpretation. In the coming days, voracious wolves are heard howling in the city, violent men defile temples, and holy images exude sweat; these and other portents all point to the justice and peace brought by the saving column. The poem ends with a prayer that the pope may live happily and that he may provide for the bard who has recited the pope's good deeds.

The lone standing column is obviously meant to be Martin V, whose family name, Colonna, means "column" in Italian; and the ruins signify the state of Rome before his pontificate.[10] These identifiers make it seem all the stranger that a bull should copulate with and ejaculate onto the column. Nevertheless, despite its bizarre indecorum, Porcellio's classically inspired panegyric must have been well received, for the poet was chosen to write the epitaph for the pope's tomb. Martin V died on February 5, 1431, and Gabriele Condulmer, the nephew of Gregory XII, became Pope Eugene IV (1431–1447).

From the start of Eugene's pontificate tensions manifested themselves. Portents confirmed what everyone feared. At the pope's first meeting with the cardinals a "sudden terror came upon everyone, and panic over the roof falling in led to a riot. All pushed their way through the doors, trampling one another along the way." At least one bishop died. At the same time a herd of cattle poured through the gates of Saint Peter's. "One bull entered the basilica and ran down a priest at the high altar, then gored a woman selling candles." A cow even repeated the sex act that Porcellio had immortalized in his poem dedicated to Martin V: "A cow approached a marble column near the Pantheon containing inscriptions of the Roman people, raised her hind legs, and rubbed herself up against it."[11] At this time Rome was hardly a booming metropolis. Sheep and cattle outnumbered people and grazed freely amid the ancient ruins.[12] Still, everyone agreed that these aggressive bovines were a bad sign.

The new pope was not Roman, like Martin, but Venetian, an aristocratic outsider who made the Romans uncomfortable. Eugene's first act was to start a feud with Martin's family, the Colonna. He immediately revoked their privileges and confiscated the properties that his predecessor had granted to his family; instead, the new pope gave powerful positions to their archenemies, the Orsini. In a final affront Eugene, following a rumor about Martin V's hidden treasure, had the deceased pope's chamberlain tortured.[13] Convinced that the new pope wanted to extinguish his family, Stefano Colonna, who had been the police captain for the Church, fled to the house of his relation Cardinal Prospero Colonna. They joined other powerful families and rallied the Roman people to take up arms against the pope. A civil war broke out. But papal troops easily expelled the belligerents from Rome.

After this loss, the Colonna conspired with the duke of Milan to attack the Castel Sant'Angelo, kill the pope, and expel the Orsini. One of the conspirators, a friar named Masius, was caught and confessed to everything under torture. He was defrocked and quartered in the Campo dei Fiori. His limbs were displayed on the four principal gates of the city as a warning to all. The pope immediately excommunicated the Colonna. Over two hundred people were arrested and put on trial for high treason; they were all condemned to prison or the scaffold.[14] Rome may have been sedated by this swift vengeance, but war raged in the countryside. Soldiers from Naples, Venice, Florence, and Milan clashed, and as usual the peasants suffered. Just as Eugene was gaining the upper hand, he was struck by a sudden illness, possibly caused by poison. The pope hastily reconciled with the Colonna and made peace.

Eugene now had to turn his attention to a group of cardinals who had called a church council in Basel. Their aim was to achieve ratification of their conciliarist view that a council of cardinals was superior to the pope and in fact could depose a pope. They took as a precedent the Council of Constance, which, as recounted earlier, had deposed three claimants to the throne of Peter. Eugene sought to dissolve the council by challenging its authority with three bulls, but the cardinals were too powerful. The king of France and the German emperor Sigismund supported the council, and there was a serious threat that Eugene would be deposed. Fortunately, Sigismund had come to Italy to be crowned Holy Roman Emperor, and only the pope could perform the ceremony; so they made peace, and the coronation took place on May 21, 1433. The peace, however, was short-lived.

Inquisition Scene (1710–1720), by Alessandro Magnasco, Kunsthistorisches Museum, Vienna. © Erich Lessing / Art Resource, New York.

The duke of Milan incited the dissatisfied mercenary general Niccolò Fortebraccio to turn against his former employer, Eugene, and besiege Rome. The duke also sent troops led by Francesco Sforza to invade the papal lands in the Marches and Tuscany, which were happy to revolt against what they saw as oppressive papal rule. Eugene was surrounded. In desperation, he revoked his three bulls condemning the council and formally recognized its authority. Conciliarism was victorious for the time being. Eugene tried to bribe the armies sent against him; Fortebraccio declined the inducement and continued his siege of Rome, but Francesco Sforza accepted the offer and with his brother's help set out against Fortebraccio, who now enjoyed the services of another famous mercenary captain, Niccolò Piccinino. Together Fortebraccio and Piccinino withstood Sforza's attacks and along with the

Milanese ambassadors and the Colonna stirred up the Roman people against the pope.

When Eugene's biographer Vespasiano da Bisticci observed that "the Romans are a contentious people," he was thus only stating the obvious. Rome was ripe for revolt. Marauders were continually plundering property, driving away cattle, and harassing and enslaving the Roman people. When the Romans complained about their slaughtered cattle, the pope sent them to the papal chamberlain, who happened to be his nephew, the dissolute Venetian noble Cardinal Francesco Condulmer. The cardinal told them that they worried too much about cattle, and that the Venetians lived a much more civilized life than the Romans, without any cattle.[15] Embittered by this answer, the Romans decided they had had enough, and on May 29, 1434, amid shouts of "To arms and to liberty," they rose up against the pope's magistrates, took his nephew the cardinal hostage, and proclaimed a republic. The conspirators dragged the pope to the Capitoline and forced him to renounce all claim to authority over the secular government of Rome. To a meeting with the mercenary general Niccolò Piccinino the rebels sent emissaries "insisting that he lead the army and promising to give him Rome."[16] (Twenty-six years later, in 1460, another generation of Roman conspirators would similarly beg support from a Piccinino, this time Niccolò's son Jacopo, and would promise to give Rome to him. Taking over Rome thus became a family affair for the Piccinino.)

Eugene was shocked by the turn of events. For the next six days, he lived like a prisoner. Somehow he had to escape Rome. He was, however, under close watch. The Romans knew that for the rebellion to succeed, they needed a hostage pope as security. Eugene was tempted to try to escape with a bishop, but he knew that he would not get far. Instead, he loudly informed the bishop that he "feared no violence and encouraged him not to worry." The servants reported the pope's words to the guards who, thinking the pope sincere, relaxed their vigilance.[17] On June 4, while some bishops sat outside his door pretending to await a prearranged audience, Eugene and a colleague slipped out disguised as Benedictine monks, as we have seen, rode on mules as far as the Tiber, and made their dramatic escape to Florence. Eugene would not return to Rome until 1443. He set up the papal court in Santa Maria Novella in Florence. But he was not totally safe even there: he narrowly escaped an agent that the duke of Milan sent to assassinate him in 1435.[18]

During the time Pope Eugene IV was hiding out in Florence, Rome remained free of papal rule, and the old republic was reestablished. Seven "governors of the Roman Republic" were appointed to preserve the newfound Roman liberty.[19] Porcellio applauded the rebels' actions and lamented the effect of the Church on Rome:

> O Rome, you have had empire and famous triumphs while old and
>   holy fathers have watched over you.
> But after the ancient curia of the Romans ceased,
> Honor ceased, glory ceased, and splendor and modesty.
> Laws and magistrates and the holy Senate are lacking
> Today, as are military glory and holy justice. Alas, what shame!
> You, who but a little while ago were the head of the world, and free,
>   have become enslaved to mad tyrants.[20]

It was time for the Rome of old to rise again. Only the Castel Sant'Angelo held out. There, the papal provost Baldassare Offida withstood all attacks and continuously fired cannons at the republicans, who had built two walls of defense. Offida went on the offensive and tricked the rebels: he had the guards inside the castle call out, "Long live the people and their officials," open the gates, and invite the Romans to take control of the fortress. Once they had entered, however, the gates closed, and the guards captured eight leaders of the republic. Cannons then demolished the defensive walls and sent the rebels fleeing in panic and despair.[21] All seemed lost. The Romans had no choice but to exchange the pope's nephew, Cardinal Condulmer, for the eight hostages. Francesco Sforza and Venice still threatened Rome. Only Fortebraccio remained with the Romans, but it was not long before he too deserted them. The Roman citizens had also turned against the republican leaders, who had ransacked parts of the city after plundering the papal palaces. Even Lorenzo Colonna and his small army could not halt the wave of crime after Rome's liberation. So when the pope, surely loath to return to the scene of his humiliation, sent his representative Bishop Giovanni Vitelleschi to lay claim to Rome again a few months later, all men of moderation welcomed a return to papal rule and order. The republic collapsed without any further fighting.

Porcellio, in a poem, lamented the wasted opportunity:

> The Roman youth drove out the rule of the pope
> and gave an empty name to liberty; for two days
> in May it remained, and a triumphant Rome rejoiced;
> but it ruled little in the empty name.
> Having held out three nights in an orderly fashion,
> the republic perished in October, and God became a monarch.
> From this came the first stain of evil, in one thousand four hundred
>   thirty-four.[22]

In hindsight, of course, it was easy for him to condemn the short-lived republican dream; but while he is critical of the empty rhetoric of liberty, his verse comes down particularly hard on the temporal power of the Church—"the republic perished and God became a monarch . . . from this was the first stain of evil." The institution of papal rule was the original sin that had tainted more than a thousand years of Christian history. For his involvement in the rebellion, whatever that might have been, Porcellio was tortured and imprisoned in the Castel Sant'Angelo.[23] His involvement in the rebellion may be explained by the fact that Porcellio's protector in Rome was Cardinal Colonna.

When Bishop Vitelleschi arrived to reclaim Rome for the papacy on October 25, 1434, cheers of "The Church! The Church!" greeted his arrival. A republican sympathizer described Vitelleschi, a former mercenary, as a "diabolical man"; he was certainly a cruel and tyrannical one. The humanist Lorenzo Valla, a contemporary, cited him as an example of "how barbarous the domination of priests often is."[24] Vitelleschi pursued the pope's enemies with great zeal—he executed many from the Colonna and other noble families and had their villas and the houses of the conspirators torn down. He razed Palestrina, Zagarolo, and other cities in Lazio. After capturing the leader Poncelleto, Vitelleschi had him dragged through the city, gouged with hot pincers, and drawn and quartered in the Campo de' Fiori. For his services the bishop was treated to a royal triumph. He rode on a steed arrayed in shining armor; twelve youths held a golden baldachin over his head; magistrates bore torches; citizens waved olive branches; and priests intoned hymns of thanks, as bystanders chanted, "Long live the Patriarch, the Father of the city!" In a further attempt to placate the overbearing bishop, in 1436 the Senate decreed that an equestrian marble statue of him be erected on the Capitoline Hill with the inscription: "Giovanni Vitelleschi, . . . third father after Romulus of the city of Romulus."[25] A year later, the pope marked his gratitude by promoting the bishop to cardinal. Vitelleschi's fortunes, however, changed suddenly in 1440. Presumably with the pope's approval, the provost of the Castel Sant'Angelo attacked him in an ambush, wounded him, and imprisoned him; two weeks later the cardinal was dead.[26] No one seemed to pay the incident much mind. Rome was in any case firmly back in papal hands.

Lorenzo Valla composed his famous discourse attacking papal power, *On the Donation of Constantine,* against Eugene IV in 1440, the same year Vitelleschi met his end. The immediate context was a territorial war between the pope and Valla's patron, Alfonso of Aragon, king of Naples.[27] In the treatise Valla proves that the document known as the Donation of Constantine was a medieval forgery. The document, supposedly written by Emperor Constantine, gives the entire Roman Empire to the popes, making them rulers of this world, not just spiritual authorities. Popes had theretofore used this document to justify their possession of Rome and the papal states. Valla brilliantly demonstrates that the language and certain historical inaccuracies date the document to about the ninth century, five hundred years after the time of Constantine. In his arguments, Valla goes beyond textual criticism and justifies rebellion against a tyrannical papacy. He praises the "just and equitable" demands of the 1434 rebellion against Eugene IV, and states that the popes "held Rome in continuous subjection by force of arms." He adds, "The Pope assiduously plots against the liberty of peoples."[28] Rather than liberating them, he says, the popes enslaved the populace. Furthermore, Valla argues that if we accept the donation as genuine, people are justified in assassinating the pope: "If the Romans were free to expel Constantine as they did Tarquin or to kill him as they did Julius Caesar, all the more will the Romans and the provinces be free to kill that man, whoever he may be, who has taken Constantine's place."[29] Many thinkers during the Renaissance saw Constantine's donation, whether authentic or forged, as the beginning of Christianity's decline, for riches and power bring corruption and greed.[30] The tyranny these engendered, such critics felt, justified violent rebellion.

Valla soon abandoned invective and other such direct tactics and reconciled with the next pope; in 1448 the humanist took up employment in the papal curia.[31] In his inaugural lecture at the University of Rome in 1455, Valla in fact particularly praised the Roman pontiffs for preserving Latinity and Latin literature during the Middle Ages. Still, humanists were rarely consistent, and although he held the high position of apostolic secretary, Valla expressed criticism of the papacy, albeit indirectly, when on the feast day of Saint Thomas Aquinas in 1457 he emphasized the simple virtue of the ancient Church.[32] Valla's debunking of the donation, however, was to have a long life. Supporters of papal power replied to Valla's polemic not so much with logical arguments as with staunch loyalty expressed by a firm belief in the authenticity of the donation.[33] Church leaders finally admitted that the donation was a forgery in the late sixteenth century, which was, paradoxically, when the papacy was reasserting autocratic rule in the face of the assaults of the Reformation. With or without acknowledgment of the authenticity of the donation, the popes would rule Rome for another four hundred years.

Pope Paul had more in common with his uncle than merely apprehension in the face of danger to his person. A later source uses the same words, in separate passages, to describe the mistrust each felt for men of letters: "He used to say that he loved men of learning and was generous toward them, not only because of their erudition but especially because he feared their indignation, since, when wronged, they were armed with weapons that could not be evaded."[34] The popes tolerated humanists out of fear that they would otherwise take up the pen against the papacy. More of a patron than his nephew would be, in 1431 Eugene reestablished the University of Rome; he employed the humanist Poggio Bracciolini; and in 1434 he appointed another humanist, Flavio Biondo, as apostolic secretary.[35] After the pope's death, Poggio nevertheless described Eugene's pontificate as a failure: "Rarely has a pontificate brought such great devastation to the lands of the Church and ruin to men. . . . Some found the cause of such great evils in the pope's love of war, others in his advisers, for they say that he himself wanted peace, but that he was driven to war by the persuasion of others. For my part, I saw many virtues in him, whether they were true or, as some contend, false. But whether you attribute the failing to the men or to the times, it is a fact that the subjects of the Roman Church never experienced such misfortune during any earlier pontificate." Platina similarly criticized Eugene for being too intent on war.[36] The greatest lesson Paul would have learned from his uncle's pontificate was the importance of keeping the Romans content and of avoiding any appearance of cruelty or avarice. In seeking to be more popular than the uncle who had aroused so much hatred, Paul therefore showered the populace with money, gifts, banquets, and entertainment.

The Conspiracy of Stefano Porcari

During Eugene IV's self-imposed exile in Florence, Stefano Porcari acted as mediator between the pope and the Roman people.[37] He tried to negotiate a compromise, but Eugene declined and sent Vitelleschi, as we have seen, to punish the rebels and to reinstate his rule through a brutal show of force. The experience confirmed the Roman noble Porcari's passionate belief: Rome had to rid herself of the tyrannical popes and reclaim her ancient glory as a virtuous republic.

Stefano Porcari had worked for two years (1427–28) as a juridical official in Florence. There he befriended Leonardo Bruni, Matteo Palmieri, and other humanists, who were applying their knowledge of ancient republicanism to governing Florence.[38] Porcari's speeches from this period are full of praise for the republican government of Florence and the ideals of civic humanism; indeed, the Roman admired Florence as a "sanctuary of the sweetest liberty." These orations must have been copied and circulated widely, for they survive in numerous fifteenth-century manuscripts.[39] Porcari read about the glories of the ancient Roman Republic in Livy and Sallust and conversed with the Florentine humanists about their longing to revive ancient virtues. By the time Porcari returned to Rome, his enthusiasm for the republic of ancient times had outstripped mere speculation to become a political conviction.

Eugene IV died in 1447, four years after returning to Rome. The next pope, Nicholas V, completely transformed the Eternal City. He repaired the roads and aqueducts; he renovated monuments and started extensive building projects. Nicholas commissioned translations and copies of numerous classical authors that would become the core of the new Vatican Library.[40] To generate revenue for the dilapidated city, he called a Jubilee in 1450, crowned Frederick III emperor, and brokered a long-awaited peace on the Italian peninsula in 1454.[41]

Already before Nicholas became pope, Porcari had started stirring up trouble. During the Vacant See (the time between the death of one pope and the coronation of the next) in 1447 Porcari delivered a harangue in which he declared that it was a shame the Romans had become enslaved to priests and that it was now time to throw off the yoke and recover freedom.[42] During a Vacant See, papal power is suspended and the secular government of Rome takes over; riots and violence against church rulers often took place during such periods.[43] Although Porcari succeeded in inspiring the crowd with his call for a revival of republican liberty, Neapolitan troops were at hand to prevent any further uprising. When Nicholas became pope, he tried to silence Porcari by promoting him to governor general of the seacoast and the Campagna. But Porcari soon returned, filled with greater revolutionary zeal than ever.

In the midst of carnival in 1452 preparations were being made for the imperial coronation of Frederick III. (During Nicholas's pontificate, carnival in Rome was limited to the traditional competitions and banquets in Piazza Navona and Monte Testaccio.) Carnival was, like the Vacant See, a time when protests against rulers could be voiced with some immunity.[44] Porcari took advantage of this license, and of the large crowds already gathered for carnival, to declare that Rome would regain its freedom when Frederick arrived. Porcari's eloquence set off a small riot in the center of Rome, which was quickly put down.[45]

Nicholas, once again reluctant to punish the talented nobleman, exiled him to Bologna, but with a generous stipend. Porcari was to check in regularly with Cardinal Bessarion, the papal legate.[46] But this of course was hardly much of a deterrent for the determined republican. From Bologna, he corresponded with his nephew, Battista Sciarra, who started assembling mercenaries and arms.[47] When suitable preparations had been made, Porcari feigned illness to avoid meeting with Bessarion and, after riding virtually nonstop on horseback for four days, arrived undercover in Rome.[48] His brother-in-law, Angelo di Maso, had gathered a large group of followers together for a sumptuous banquet at his house: "Porcari entered the room wearing a golden cloak, which made him look like an emperor. He had a handsome physique and a striking presence; he was so eloquent and beloved that no one could resist his words."[49] At this point Porcari delivered his most famous speech, in which he declared: "How long will we bear this lethal burden? Is it right that we are forced to serve the clergy and constantly mourn our life and times in darkness and in lamentation? In dire straits we live for an empire that wallows in extravagance, enriches itself with spoils and gold, and gorges itself on power that is built on our blood. Behold this barbarity! When will this age change? Are we not men? . . . We have been sullied by squalor and blood, and we have sufficiently atoned for the lies of foreigners."[50] Anger over the perceived foreign occupation of Rome by the clergy pervades his speech. Such complaints, nevertheless, should carry little weight, for Nicholas had previously restored the communal treasury and guaranteed that government offices would be given to Romans.[51]

To encourage his would-be accomplices, Porcari appeals to their manhood: "Are we not men?" Porcari may have been thinking of Cicero's etymology of "virtue" as coming from *vir* ("man"), which linked virtue with manliness.[52] In conclusion, Porcari shames his audience by recalling the love of liberty that prevailed in ancient Rome: "Once Roman offspring were happy with their children, who for love of liberty exposed their peerless souls to a beautiful death and chose to exchange their lives for glory."[53] Self-sacrifice for the fatherland, a virtue exemplified in Roman republican heroes, was an ideal that Porcari had also repeatedly invoked in his earlier orations, in Florence.[54] After the speech Porcari handed out a thousand ducats and promised to enrich his accomplices.[55] They applauded Porcari's speech and vowed to follow him.

The plan was to be carried out on Epiphany (January 6). After setting fire to the Vatican stables, the conspirators would seize Nicholas and the cardinals at Saint Peter's. Porcari planned to bring a golden chain to bind the pope. If they met with resistance, he warned, they would kill the pope. Meanwhile, his confederates would take over the Senate, gain control of the Castel Sant'Angelo, proclaim the liberation of Rome, and declare Porcari a tribune of the people.[56] They counted on a popular uprising in their favor, which in light of earlier revolts probably would have occurred. Porcari might have had a chance, but being exhausted by his trip, he delayed. Bessarion, suspicious about Porcari's absence, sent a warning to the pope, and some of the conspirators revealed the plot.[57] The pope sent his guards to Porcari's residence. Thirty conspirators fought their way out, including Porcari's nephew, Battista Sciarra, who cried: "For the people and for liberty!" during the ensuing melee.[58] Porcari fled out a back door and hid in his sister's house. Later he appealed to Cardinal Orsini, who tried to have him arrested, but Porcari escaped again and hid this time at his other sister's house.[59] Under torture, however, an accomplice revealed his whereabouts, and guards were dispatched. While they searched the house, Porcari lay hidden in a wooden chest, upon which his sister and another woman sat chatting. When eventually discovered and arrested, he shouted: "People! Will you let your deliverer die?" as they carried him in chains to the Vatican.[60] After torture and a quick trial Porcari was executed on January 9, 1453.

Although writers at the time condemned the conspiracy, they also remained fascinated by Porcari's idealism and composed literary works about the republican hero.[61] Although the famed humanist and architect Leon Battista Alberti was an exiled Florentine, not a Roman, he was alienated and embittered by church corruption, as is reflected in a letter he wrote about the conspiracy.[62] In it he condemns Porcari, but in the effort to be objective, thorough, and dramatic, Alberti ends up producing a sympathetic portrait of the conspirator. In fact, Alberti's account has been viewed as a reliable source regarding Porcari's actual political ideas. Another humanist, Orazio Romano, composed a bizarre epic poem, the *Porcaria,* which he dedicated to Nicholas V.[63] It begins with a description of Porcari's body dangling from a rampart of the Castel Sant'Angelo and of the republican's sister wailing over the mangled corpse. Then the scene moves to the afterlife. Porcari comes in tears before Minos, who, as in Dante and Virgil, is a judge in the underworld. Minos asks Porcari to explain why he is there, and Porcari recites his banquet speech. Despite its contrived poetic form, Orazio's version of the banquet speech bears a resemblance to Porcari's earlier orations, which suggests that this epic poem contains sections of relatively accurate reportage.

In his banquet speech Porcari claimed to be a prophet, chosen by an omen and sent down from the stars to liberate Rome from papal tyranny.[64] In his *Florentine Histories,* Machiavelli also presented Porcari as a self-proclaimed prophet and averred that Porcari saw himself as the knight in Petrarch's poem, "whom all Italy honors, more thoughtful of others than of himself." Machiavelli called Porcari a "Roman citizen, and a noble by blood and learning but much more by the excellence of his spirit."[65] Alberti explicitly says that "Porcari was moved by love of country and not wealth. He cared more for the honor and happiness of the citizens than for any personal advantage."[66] Another contemporary, Stefano Infessura, also praises Porcari for his altruism, calling him "a man of honor, a friend of Rome's welfare and liberty. He dedicated his life to delivering Rome from bondage."[67] Many others, too, saw Stefano Porcari as a liberator of Rome, a hero who could revive the glory of the ancient republic.

Other sources were not as positive, however. In his dialogue on the conspiracy, Pietro Godi has his character Bernardino accuse Porcari of cowardice, with a slur on his manliness: "Stefano was not brave but eloquent; and eloquence rarely leads to bravery. His bravery turned into womanly fear. Indeed Stefano reduced himself to a little woman. If he had been brave, he and his accomplices should have ridden through the city shouting: 'Long live liberty and the people!'"[68] Godi criticizes Porcari for not being strong enough and in fact asserts that the conspiracy could have easily succeeded, had he not been a coward, for Nicholas had few guards and the people would have been attracted by the possibility of plunder. Observing the conspirator's mutilated corpse, a Roman in Orazio's poem similarly accused Porcari of cowardice: "When weapons required hands and it was time to do the deed, he preferred to hide and was captured."[69] In Orazio's poem Porcari's eternal punishment follows Dante's principle of *contropasso:* the punishment fits the crime. Minos says: "Since you so often spoke vain and empty words to heaven, your false tongue will be torn apart by savage snakes; and since you dared to violate the father, swift chariots will seize you with reins and tear your joints and limbs in different directions."[70] Porcari's eloquence deceived, therefore his tongue is torn out; he aimed to dismember the body politic and is therefore ripped apart himself, like Muhammad in Dante—poetic justice for a republican idealist.

The works written in response to Porcari's conspiracy advised the pope on how to deal with the criminals and how best to avoid future threats to his rule. The authors urged the pope to show clemency toward the conspirators' families.[71] Mercy, not harsh justice, will win over the Roman people. If you inflict the death penalty on all the guilty, their number will grow to become infinite. In the last hundred lines of one poem a humanist named Bripio advises the pope on how to avoid further threats to papal rule: Build more fortifications, and whenever you go into the church, take an escort of three hundred armed guards.[72] Giannozzo Manetti, in his life of Nicholas V, also stressed the need to erect impregnable fortifications: had Eugene IV and Nicholas V had them, no one would have dared to conspire against them.[73] But Bripio introduces another daring suggestion; one fortress, he says, is stronger than any other: *civis amor,* the citizen's love. No fortresses can stand for long without that love. Therefore, he advises, be generous to the poor, honor the Romans, and employ humanists.[74] Bripio's emphasis on *civis amor* is reminiscent of one of Porcari's speeches in which he told the Florentines to nurture "civic love [*civile amore*] toward their republic, for danger and ruin come to a city when its citizens abandon the public good for private passions, domestic luxuries, ambition, and avarice."[75] This same civic ethos is now being urged on the pope, but in a very different way; Nicholas has become the common good, and he needs to cultivate the people's love. Bripio's formula for a stable papacy is simple—bread and circuses to the Roman people and largesse to humanists like himself.

These calls on Nicholas to be merciful had little effect. On the pope's orders, nine conspirators were hanged in one day, and several others were hunted down and executed. Some contemporaries called him cruel. According to one report, the pope afterward regretted his harshness and said that under the influence of wine he had forgotten to pardon some of them. Another contemporary, however, praised Nicholas's restraint and kindness in not punishing more conspirators. To justify the executions, the Church immediately published Porcari's confession, elicited under torture. After the conspiracy Nicholas employed armed guards, built additional fortifications, and became more reclusive and suspicious toward the Romans. Platina writes: "Until that point, Nicholas had helped the Romans with every kind of service and generosity. He was more accessible than any pope had been before him. After that he became more guarded toward everyone, especially the Romans."[76] In January 1453 Nicholas had a statue of the archangel Michael placed at the top of the Castel Sant'Angelo, perhaps while

Porcari's body was still hanging from a lower rampart. The statue recalled an ancient miracle, but with Michael's sword held high over Rome it also emphasized the pope's dominance over Porcari and any other threats to papal power.[77] Nicholas, it would seem, turned to force, fortifications, and armies, rather than to love of the people, in self-protection.

The not especially learned Pope Paul II had probably never read the *Porcaria,* Alberti's letter, Bripio's poem, or other humanist writings on the subject. He nevertheless followed their advice to a large extent. Paul, who was against the death penalty, was more merciful in general than Nicholas V and refused to execute even those who had plotted to kill the pope, as we have seen, although he did have them tortured and imprisoned (as discussed in the epilogue). It is true that the humanists never confessed in the way that Porcari did. Paul also increased the number of papal guards, especially when Emperor Frederick III came to Rome in 1468 and during other festive times. His palace was an enormous fortresslike structure, situated in a neighborhood controlled by his allies the Colonna. He often chose to remain in his palace, instead of the customary residence of pontiffs at the Vatican, especially during times of danger, such as when the news of the conspiracy broke in 1468. Most of all, Paul tried to nurture *civis amor,* by sponsoring elaborate festivals, banquets, processions, and entertainments. The one recommendation Paul failed to follow was to cultivate the humanists—a strategic mistake that left him open to attack.

If Paul learned vital lessons about effective rule from the Porcari conspiracy, the humanists were inspired by Porcari in the opposite way. Porcari's eloquent speeches were considered models of the Italian language, and they were copied numerous times in fifteenth-century manuscripts. Enchantment with the classical works of Roman republicanism by Cicero, Livy, and Sallust and obsessive reading of those authors had led Porcari to lay actual plans to reinstate the republic. Leonardo Bruni and other Florentine humanists admired Sallust for his

Tomb of Paul II, by Mino da Fiesole, Museo Petriano, Saint Peter's Basilica, Vatican State. © Alinari / Art Resource, New York. Inscription: "A constant defender of Church liberty and majesty, zealous preserver of peace . . . corrected the people's errors like a most indulgent parent [and] suppressed raging armed heretics."

condemnation of monarchy and his conviction that competition for government office and the ideal of liberty were the reasons for Rome's success.[78] Sallust was the first to connect Rome's rise to power with the city's liberation from the tyranny of the kings and preservation of liberty. Sallust famously said that kings are more suspicious of good men than of bad, and that rulers always fear the virtue of others. Once the kings had been overthrown and liberty won, he said, the Roman state grew incredibly fast.

The humanists of the Roman Academy were also fond of these classical authors of republicanism. Pomponio Leto wrote an extensive commentary on Sallust's works.[79] Another humanist, Marcantonio Altieri, says that Pomponio and Platina taught him about the famous republican heroes of ancient Rome. When he was a young student, Altieri dedicated a poem to Pomponio about the founder of the Roman Republic, Romulus. Altieri praises his mentor for rediscovering Latin poetry and the triumphant Rome of antiquity, before going on to lament the state of modern Rome.[80] In another work, Altieri reports a conversation that he had with Pomponio and Platina at the funeral of Altieri's uncle in 1472. Pomponio and Platina admonished the nephew about "the sweetness of liberty" and about how "the free man enjoys happiness and glory wherever he may be in the world." The conversation then turned to the topic of papal Rome: "Pomponio went on to say that Rome was no longer a city, but that a more appropriate title for it would be the truest seminary of servants, or rather slaves. It is ruled in order to please God, for the benefit and convenience of those who hold power because of their good fortune."[81] These are the exact sentiments expressed in Porcari's banquet speech.

Pomponio was firmly republican in his view of Roman history. He praised Livy and other republican writers and saw the empire as decadent. The emperors, he wrote, "reduced everything to the will of one man and oppressed the people."[82] Altieri had studied Roman history with Pomponio and later in his dialogue offers a very Pomponian history of Rome. The papacy, says Altieri, just continued the dissolute dictatorship of the Roman emperors. He describes the ancient republic of Rome as based on a harmonious division of power among several magistracies. When the republic ended, a "dictatorship suffocated friendship, family, and patriotism." The Romans "lost their liberty and citizenship." Turning to the Rome of his own day, Altieri announces: "Miserable and sad, we have lost our soul and body in pain. Neither nobility nor age nor patriotism nor honorable habits suffice to survive; but because of this misfortune we are forced by our most vile and miserable living conditions to yoke ourselves to the cowardly, uncouth government by animals." After this bleak portrayal of clerical Rome, Altieri turns to the subject of tyranny and the justification for tyrannicide. The killer of a tyrant, he says, achieves eternal fame.[83] The logical conclusion of Altieri's conception of Roman history is crystal clear: if the popes have enslaved the Romans and reduced them to living like animals, the popes are tyrants, and, therefore, their murder is completely justified. Altieri was fond of Stefano Porcari and directly cites one of Porcari's Florentine speeches.[84] The humanists of the Roman Academy, with their love of republican liberty, would have felt similarly inspired by Stefano Porcari's words and actions.

Pius II and the Roman Insurrection of 1460

Before 1468 the most recent antipapal rebellion in Rome had nothing to do with republicanism and little to do with humanists. In 1460 a gang of young men, taking advantage of Pope Pius II's absence at the Council of Mantua, seized control of Rome and set about terrorizing the Roman nobility. The leaders were two brothers named Tiburzio and Valeriano. Their father and eldest brother had been executed for their participation in Porcari's plot, and Porcari himself was their maternal uncle. Despite these connections, the brothers seem to have had few of the classical ideals that inspired Porcari. Tiburzio set himself up as king, and the rebels caused no end of misery to the Romans. The members of the gang robbed, pillaged, stole, and raped. The policing magistrates were outnumbered by the growing number of youths attracted to the mayhem. The governor was even forced to abandon his palace and take refuge in the Vatican. The rule of law collapsed completely, and matters deteriorated yet further. Wives were violated and girls drowned if they resisted. One gang member, named Innamorato, dragged a bride away in the middle of her wedding. When the magistrates finally acted to arrest Innamorato, the gang took up arms and kidnapped the relative of a senator. The people had had enough and demanded that the governor do something. The rebels retreated and took refuge in the Pantheon. Fearful neighbors supplied them with food.

Our best source for the rebellion is Pius II. He presents the conspirators as a group of worthless, violent bandits. His bias becomes clear, however, at such moments as the following. The rebels were not attacked in the Pantheon, he says, because "the magistrates did not dare risk setting citizen to fight against citizen, for fear that if the people were armed, the city would throw off the yoke of the clergy and assert its independence."[85] This passage implies that the rebels had popular support and that the Romans may have even preferred rule by the conspirators to that of the pope.

Instead of besieging the Pantheon, the magistrates negotiated the return of the senator's kidnapped relative. The rebels soon abandoned their hideout and continued to molest the Romans. The gang took possession of a cardinal's palace, held all-night banquets, and planned further robberies. Tiburzio became even more dictatorial: "When anyone asked what Tiburzio was doing, the answer would come, 'The master is doing' this or that." Assuring Tiburzio that the pope's wrath against him would know no bounds, Roman nobles pleaded with him to leave the city. The "master" indeed decided to decamp for the more secure outlying towns controlled by the Savelli family, which was often at odds with the pope. Tiburzio swaggered to the gates of Rome and saluted the numerous citizens who had come "to watch him as though he were the captain of a mighty host." By this time Rome was in shambles.[86]

Gianantonio Campano visited the city during this period of upheaval. He came to inspect the ruins of ancient Rome and, evidently not realizing that the pope was absent, to obtain his blessing. The state in which Campano found the Eternal City disgusted him, and he lamented the ruination of Rome. In contrast to Altieri and Porcari, however, Campano concluded that the only "dignity" left in Rome rested "in the virtuous priests." He said:

> The people of Rome, with their disgusting looks, jumbled speech, indiscipline, and boorish demeanor, are more similar to barbarians than to Romans. It is no wonder people from all over the world flood into Rome as if it were a slave farm. Very few citizens retain any of the ancient nobility. They have discarded glory, military honor, empire, and morality as old and foreign and fallen head over heels into luxury, effeminacy, poverty, insolence, and unbridled lust. Priests have made Rome Roman, and they did this not with the bravery of Romulus but with the holiness of Numa Pompilius. But not everyone can be a priest. The rest are a mob of servants, cooks, tailors, pimps, dandies, and good-for-nothings. These inhabit the homes of the Gracchi, the Scipios, and the Caesars. They sully and defile the statues of these famous men with filth, the refuse of food and drink, and every kind of dirt.[87]

In praising the Church, Campano refers to the king of Rome, Numa, who used the power of pagan religion to lend authority to his rule. Numa claimed that a nymph guided all his decisions.[88] In praising the beneficial role of religion, Campano does not distinguish between pagan and Christian. For him the Church was the only remnant of ancient virtue, and Rome would have been lost without the pope.

Only after the rebels attacked the Church directly did Pius decide to return to Rome. Gang members had broken into a convent, raped the nuns, and stolen the church silver. This was too much. It was time for the pope to restore order. He would return, he said, within twenty days: "When the news reached Rome, there was as much rejoicing as if a great victory had been reported, as if it were then that the city itself had first been established and built. A solemn procession wound through the streets, bonfires were lit, and prayers were offered at all the shrines for the pope's safe and swift return."[89]

The danger to papal Rome had not abated. It became clear that the gang was planning much more than its members' immediate sensual gratification. A Roman citizen named Luca Tozzoli, on being arrested, revealed a much larger conspiracy against the pope. Tiburzio was in league with the Colonna family, the prince of Taranto, Count Everso, Jacopo Savelli, and the French ruler Jean d'Anjou: "There was no doubt Rome would be captured, for the pope was away, and the conspirators would admit the enemy. Tiburzio, Jean d'Anjou, and the prince of Taranto had gone to Jacopo Piccinino and promised to betray the city." They planned to murder the pope's nephew and plunder the cardinals' palaces and considered that it would be easy to carry out the scheme, "for they had free access to the city night and day, where they had on their side no fewer than five hundred daring young hotheads, the sons of leading citizens."[90] Even if the rebels of 1460 may have had no such plans, others took advantage of the situation and hoped to establish some sort of alternative government to the papacy.

The pivotal role of Jacopo Piccinino is particularly telling. Like his father before him, he was one of the most sought-after mercenary captains of his time. Tiburzio, in a confession made under torture, said that in exchange for military aid, he offered Piccinino the city of Rome: "I promise you Rome, the mother of cities, the capital of the world. I am a Roman citizen of no mean birth. All the youth of Rome follow me; five hundred bold and energetic young men have sworn allegiance to me; the citizens are ashamed and sick of the papal power. If you give me your word that you will lead an army into Roman territory at once, I will go on ahead, and when I have encouraged the conspirators, who desire nothing so much as a revolution, I will open the gates to you."[91] Tiburzio then tried to further entice the mercenary captain with a description of the plunder to be had. But Piccinino had set his sights on a prize more alluring than plunder. The pact with Tiburzio would have given Piccinino what he had long been craving: his own city-state, and what was more, great Rome itself.

In the words of the famous nineteenth-century historian Jacob Burckhardt, "[Jacopo] Piccinino filled the imagination of the whole country. It was a burning question of the day, if he would succeed in founding a princely house."[92] A contemporary said that Piccinino's "spirit was troubled on a daily basis by an immoderate lust for power." He was the younger son of the more accomplished condottiere Niccolò Piccinino, who had also been involved in a rebellion against the popes. According to Machiavelli, Jacopo "had less virtue and worse fortune than his father."[93] Jacopo not only learned essential skills from his father but also inherited from him the legendary mercenary company of the famous Braccio da Montone, which he commanded in practically all the wars of mid-fifteenth-century Italy.

In 1452–53 Piccinino had fought for Venice against Francesco Sforza and Milan. The Roman poet Porcellio lived with Piccinino, observed him in action, and wrote a lengthy account of the campaign.[94] The poet also received safe-conduct from Sforza and observed the enemy camp firsthand.[95] To add classical pretension, Porcellio casts Piccinino in his commentaries in the role of Scipio Africanus, and Francesco Sforza as Hannibal. But Porcellio insisted that he had been an eyewitness to the events he reports. "I stick so close to Piccinino," he wrote, "that hardly anything could happen that might escape me at his side."[96] In his dedication, he begged the king of Naples: "Accept this little gift, which I wrote not at home and at leisure but in military camps and in the midst of battle, at the greatest risk to my life."[97] Porcellio calls Piccinino the "first son of Mars." He assures us, "Victory follows Piccinino wherever he goes." When wounded in the thigh by an arrow, Piccinino tells no one, lest it dishearten the soldiers, and pulls out the arrow alone in his tent. His great constancy is most worthy of a Roman emperor. The fear of Piccinino's name alone captures the enemy, and many desert and join his forces. To his soldiers, Piccinino declares: "Other commanders seek wealth; I place honor and glory before all things."[98] Porcellio's Piccinino is headstrong. He is portrayed as a brave and honest warrior who relies on his own virtue and the goodwill of Mars to win battles. Porcellio's protagonist nobly battles Francesco Sforza, often presented as avoiding pitched battles and winning thanks to traps and subterfuge instead.

Other contemporaries, however, emphasized Piccinino's brutality, excessive plundering, and addiction to rape.[99] A bellicose image of Piccinino can also be found in the commentaries of Pius II, who presents himself as the ultimate peace lover, and Piccinino as a staunch advocate of war. After the campaign against Milan, which ended in stalemate, as often happened in Italian wars, Piccinino tried to seize Siena and make himself its ruler in 1455. Pius writes that even soldiers in the pay of the mercenary captain's adversaries protected Piccinino, gave him food, and supplied information, for, Pius writes: "The Italian mercenaries had realized that if Piccinino were overpowered and captured, they would have to go back to tilling their fields, for peace would reign everywhere. Piccinino alone could provide occasion for war, and so they worshipped him almost like a god."[100] The rebellion against the pope was one of the endless wars that wore down the people as it enriched mercenaries.

The 1460 insurrection in Rome took place in the middle of the long war of succession over the throne of Naples. Alfonso of Aragon died in 1458 and left the kingdom to his son Ferrante. Nevertheless, the French ruler Jean d'Anjou arrived in Italy to assert his claim. Pius II and Francesco Sforza backed Ferrante, who had the stronger position. Piccinino joined Jean d'Anjou. At the first encounter, Ferrante suffered a serious defeat at Sarno in July 1460. After Sarno, Piccinino marched into battle against Alessandro Sforza and fought what contemporaries called the most ferocious battle in memory.[101] Piccinino fought bravely and won. He then made a lightning march northward, plundered Lazio, and threatened Rome. That was the point at which Tiburzio met with Piccinino.

Pius, who was returning from the council of Mantua, had to

shorten his trip because of the upheaval that Tiburzio had caused in Rome. In Viterbo ambassadors from Rome informed the pope of the situation and begged him to hasten his return. Pius praised their loyalty, while emphasizing that papal rule was superior to all other forms of government, especially in economic terms:

> You are truly wise and upright men, faithful servants of your master—though your servitude is in fact sovereignty. For what state is more free than Rome? You pay no duties; you have no tax burdens; you hold honorable offices in the city; you name your own prices for the wine and grain you sell; your houses earn you high rents. And who is your master? A count, perhaps, or a marquis, a duke, a king, an emperor? Greater than all these is he whom you obey, the Bishop of Rome, the successor of Peter, the Vicar of Christ, whose representative he is on earth. You are indeed wise, men of Rome, to obey, honor, and revere this lord of yours. For it is he who gives you fame and riches, who brings you the wealth of the world; and the Roman Curia, which you maintain, itself maintains you and brings you gold from every corner of the earth. . . . We rejoice that a joyful city awaits us. . . . No people is dearer to us than the Romans.[102]

The emphasis here on the practical and financial advantages that will accrue to the people from papal rule is startling.[103] Serve the pope, and you will get rich!

Piccinino was rapidly closing in on Rome. He had a great deal of help from his allies. "The youth of Rome had taken up arms and were eager for revolution." The pope's allies from Milan and elsewhere had not yet arrived. "Piccinino had already overrun some territory and towns; the people of Rieti, Tivoli, and several towns of the Campagna were siding with him; and there was no doubt he would soon be master of Rome." The situation seemed hopeless. It was too dangerous for the pope to enter Rome. The cardinals begged him to stay in Viterbo: "The pope would be trapped in Rome; the Romans . . . would conspire against him to betray the city to Piccinino. Where could the pope turn in such a crisis? There would be no escape by land, nor by sea, which was under blockade by the French fleet. The pope would have to take refuge in Castel Sant'Angelo and in the end he would have to surrender there—a fate far worse than death itself." The cardinals recalled the rebellions against Eugene IV and Nicholas V. "The Romans, they said, could never endure fortune good or bad: in hard times they broke into open rebellion and were overbearing when things were going well. The pope would not be safe among them unless surrounded by armed guards."[104] The cardinals' distrust of the Romans recalls the advice given to Nicholas V about fortifications and armed guards as the best security. The plea also leads nicely into some rousing papal propaganda.

Pius disagrees with the cardinals and insists on returning to the Eternal City at once:

> Unless we enter Rome before Piccinino, our kingdom is lost, and we doubt whether Rome could be regained in our lifetime. Pope Eugene lost it and wandered for nine years lodging with others. What glory is left to the pope if Rome is lost? His letters seem to have no weight unless they are dated from St. Peter's at Rome. You say Piccinino holds the countryside. . . . But if we take into account every danger which may conceivably arise and fret over it, what in heaven's name will we have the courage to do? The roof could fall in and crush us here and now. . . . We may be trapped in the city, as you say; we may be captured; we may be killed. We do not deny it. But what more honorable place is there for a bishop of Rome to die in than Rome? What tomb more fitting than the Vatican? . . . To meet death for the patrimony of St. Peter is a glorious thing; to flee from it is shameful.[105]

Pius was determined to enter Rome. Piccinino may have had a hold on the Roman countryside, but it was worth taking a chance to regain the Eternal City. The next day, Pius proceeded toward Rome amid great fanfare. Young men who had been accomplices of Tiburzio and revolutionaries vied for the chance to bear his litter into Rome. The pope was warned not to allow them near him, but he let them approach anyway. Pius entered the city "like a triumphant hero. . . . All along the way he saw houses decorated, the squares covered in carpets, and the streets everywhere strewn with branches and flowers."[106] Porcellio, who seven years before had lionized Jacopo Piccinino, composed a poem on Pius' entry: "togaed Rome greeted its pope, the author of peace and founder of tranquility."[107] The golden age had returned.

The pope's presence immediately brought order to Rome. The authorities, emboldened, set traps and began arresting the conspirators. One of them, Bonanno, escaped half-naked through a back window, after noisy soldiers surrounded the house of a whore he was frequenting. He was, however, later captured in the Colosseum. Tiburzio, thinking that his brother Valeriano had been captured with Bonanno, led fourteen other conspirators back to Rome, to "change the government of the city and free the captives." He asked his allies to send troops "to help start a revolution in the city." With the pope's allies advancing on Rome, no troops could be spared, but Tiburzio entered Rome nonetheless. "Everyone they met they urged to take up arms, saying: 'The time has come to liberate the city from the foul yoke of priests. Allies with large armies are near and will help the Romans who assert their liberty. So rouse yourselves, Romans, and dare to do something for freedom! Wish not to be worse than your ancestors, for whom death was preferable to slavery!'" Another source reveals that some Romans answered, "There is no longer time," a response implying that Tiburzio might have counted on popular support had he moved sooner.[108] When they failed to gain popular support, the conspirators seized a young Sienese as a hostage and frog-marched him into the center of the city. Alarmed, and fearing that the armed rebels would succeed in toppling papal rule, a mob of Romans awoke the pope from his midday nap and begged him to save them from the great danger. The pope reassured them: "Calm down! There is no danger. I know the hearts of the citizens. They want the pope to be their lord, not thieves. Tiburzio is captured unless he takes flight or hides. He has made his own trap and fallen into the net. This day will be the conspirators' doom." At these words, the citizens rallied, took up arms, and attacked the fourteen conspirators. The pope's favorite, Alessandro Piccolomini, led the papal guard. At its approach, the rebels fled in all directions—but within the city walls they could not get far. They had to find hiding places until nightfall. "They hid in a dense valley of high reeds, brambles, and grass. Alessandro saw the direction they fled, sent out dogs, and had his foot soldiers search through the hidden places. They found Tiburzio's crossbow, which he had thrown down in exhaustion, and this meant he was not far. They searched and eventually found him. Others were found not far off hiding their heads in the grass like pheasants and were dragged out by their feet." The rebellion was over. Piccinino was apprehended by the pope's allies, Federico da Montefeltro and Alessandro Sforza, who had chased him down the peninsula. A worse fate, however, awaited the conspirators: "They were dragged through the city with hands tied behind their backs. The Romans scorned them and derisively called Tiburzio their lord, king, tribune of the Roman people, champion of ancient liberty, and founder of peace. Answering nothing, his eyes cast down to the ground, Tiburzio passed by in silence."[109] Under torture, Tiburzio confessed everything: how he wished to avenge the death of his father and uncle and how he had made alliances with the pope's enemies and offered to give Rome to Piccinino. Then he shared the same fate as his father and uncle: like Porcari, Tiburzio was hanged, along with Bonanno and six others. The remaining conspirators were sent into exile.

Although Rome and the pope were safe again, fighting continued over the throne of Naples. Jean d'Anjou fought on with the help of Piccinino until 1463, when the French ruler suffered a devastating defeat and returned to France. Ferrante was now the uncontested king of Naples. Near the end of the war, Piccinino was surrounded and outnumbered by the soldiers of Alessandro Sforza and other mercenary captains. Without surrendering, he met with his enemies and talked his way out of a bloody and hopeless confrontation. First, he said that they could not take him by assault, since he held the higher ground. According to Pius' account, Piccinino then boldly declared:

Suppose it were possible to defeat and imprison Piccinino. Whom would you defeat and imprison? Am I not the one who supports you? I give you wealth, luxury, and power. Because of me you have been called to battle, you who would otherwise be sitting idle at home. . . . I have made you glorious. Do you therefore persecute me, the source of your welfare? If I am captured or die in battle, what profit is left to you? Do you answer to yourselves or others? When I am dead, Italy will be at peace, [and] peace is only useful to merchants and priests. You will fatten the priests, if they are not fat enough. . . . What is richer than the Roman curia? . . . Why do priests have such great wealth and power? It is right for those who bear arms to rule kingdoms. Let priests administer the sacraments. If you trust me, we will easily obtain the riches of the Roman pontiff, the cardinals, and the merchants. [So] don't yearn to win; prolong the war, for when it ends so does a soldier's profit. Wise men do not rush to end their own advantage.

The soldiers listened and agreed: "Peace," they said, "brings death to us; we live in war. Let him who provides us the means of life live." Pius again paints Piccinino as an unabashed warmonger but also conveys a probably accurate sense of the soldier's hatred for corrupt papal government.[110]

Piccinino's attack on the clergy recalls Porcari's banquet speech. Like Porcari, the mercenary wanted to rid Rome of papal rule. Unlike Porcari, he had an army. Unfortunately for him, so did the pope, and the pope's army kept Piccinino from reaching the walls of Rome. We can only imagine what might have happened had Piccinino reached Rome before Pius and his protectors. Would the Eternal City have joined the republicans in overthrowing church power?

In the enemy camp, his words had the desired effect, and Piccinino escaped to fight again. The war ended, and he reconciled with Ferrante, or so Piccinino thought. He was still a force to be reckoned with when Paul became pope in 1464. Paul criticized the mercenary captain for inspiring men to "spurn the authority of the Church."[111] Still without land to call his own, Piccinino married Drusiana Sforza, the duke of Milan's daughter, in 1465. Francesco Sforza, however, did not trust his son-in-law. A few months later, after an elaborate nuptial banquet in Naples, King Ferrante, with Sforza's consent, had Piccinino jailed and then strangled to death. Echoing Sallust, Machiavelli ascribed the cause of that treachery to Sforza's envy and fear of Piccinino's popularity: "So much," he writes, "did our Italian princes fear in others the virtue that was not in themselves."[112] Like other historians, Machiavelli could not help respecting the defiantly ambitious mercenary captain.

The insurrection of 1460 thus collapsed in defeat. The young rebels did not garner enough popular support to resist the papal forces. They might have succeeded, however, had their accomplice, the legendary mercenary captain Jacopo Piccinino, made it to Rome in time. In 1468 Paul II was fully aware of how such alliances could endanger papal rule and his life. Although the humanists supposedly responsible for the plot of 1468 may have posed little threat in themselves, Paul could not discount their connections with powerful outsiders, such as the king of Naples or the Ottoman sultan. It is also possible to read the events of 1460 as a vivid example of what can happen when the pope is absent from Rome. Paul paid heed: he rarely left the Eternal City.

Earlier rebellions and violence against papal rule were still very fresh in everyone's mind in 1468. The idea that there was a plot against his life resonated deeply with Paul himself: in his lifetime the authority of three different popes had been challenged. Not only did Paul live through the upheavals of 1434, 1453, and 1460, but he had experienced the serious threat of rebellion early in life. Paul had been only seventeen at the time he entered church service and went to stay with his uncle Eugene IV in 1436, while the exiled pope was leading the

Church from Florence. Paul's older brother was fighting against the rebels alongside Bishop Vitelleschi. Stefano Porcari's failed conspiracy showed the threat that idealism could pose to the papacy. The literature of pagan antiquity could inspire rebellion. Both Eugene's and Nicholas's brutal suppression of rebels might have also instructed Paul in the expediency of mercy, for the insurrection of 1460 was a direct result of the summary punishment Nicholas had meted out in 1453. Tiburzio and Valeriano, Porcari's nephews and Angelo di Maso's sons, admitted that one of their motives had been to avenge their relatives.

The figure of Luca Tozzoli directly connects the upheaval of 1460 to the conspiracy of 1468. Tozzoli was a lawyer, a Roman citizen who had been arrested and interrogated in 1460. Under duress, he revealed the secret alliance that the rebels had made with the mercenary Jacopo Piccinino. Tozzoli was a known associate of the Orsini, who had opposed Paul's election and were the sworn enemies of this pope's supporters the Colonna. When the alarm was first raised in 1468, Paul moved from the Vatican, near where the Orsini family lived, to Palazzo Venezia, which he had purposely built in a neighborhood controlled by the Colonna.[113] By this point Luca Tozzoli was living in exile under the protection of King Ferrante of Naples and serving on his council.

Relations between Paul and Ferrante had historically been strained at best. Border disputes between the king of Naples and the popes went back at least as far as the struggle between Ferrante's father, Alfonso of Aragon, and Pope Eugene IV, which had formed the immediate context for Lorenzo Valla's attack on papal temporal power and the Donation of Constantine in 1440. Despite Pius II's support for the succession of Ferrante to the throne of Naples, the king continued to encroach on papal lands. In the summer of 1468, in fact, after months of tension, Neapolitan troops attacked the stronghold of Tolfa and forcibly took control of the town of Sora in Lazio. Ferrante then continued his march north and threatened to lay siege to the city of Rome. He had the support of Paul's Roman enemies, the Orsini. Ferrante's advance on Rome terrified the pope so much that he hid his jewels in the Castel Sant'Angelo and made plans to flee. Although the king was persuaded to retreat, relations between Naples and Rome continued to deteriorate in the fall, when Ferrante concluded a secret alliance with Roberto Malatesta and defended Malatesta's claim to Rimini against Paul.[114] Although open warfare did not break out until months after the 1468 conspiracy was uncovered, the simmering conflict between the two powers gave the pope reason enough to think that Ferrante had played a part in the conspiracy, especially given his connection with Tozzoli.

Suspicion naturally fell on Tozzoli in 1468. The "philosopher" who first informed Paul of the threat said that he had observed Tozzoli amassing an army of bandits and other exiles just outside the city. According to other reports, Tozzoli's army consisted of four hundred to five hundred brigands. Tozzoli was also rumored to have corrupted the guards of the Castel Sant'Angelo with a bribe of a thousand ducats, so that when the mayhem started, the stronghold would fall to the rebels with little resistance. After killing the pope, sacking the church, and deposing the priests, Tozzoli reportedly planned to introduce a new state, over which he would rule.[115] Paul offered a reward of five hundred ducats for the capture of Tozzoli, but only three hundred for Callimachus. Tozzoli, it turned out, had never left Naples. He had in fact sent a thousand ducats to Rome not to bribe papal guards, but to serve as a dowry for his daughter, who planned to marry a doctor.[116] Tozzoli was innocent this time, but the rumors circulating about him demonstrate that the earlier rebellions were very much on the minds of Romans and of Pope Paul in particular—hardly surprising, given the violent turmoil that had nearly destroyed the papacy so many times in the half century preceding 1468.

CHAPTER FOUR

A Pagan Renaissance

Sodomy and the Classical Tradition

They not only loved the language and literature of the ancients but also habitually took their beliefs about morals, good and evil, and God himself not from Christian philosophers, as is right, but from those ancient pagans.

—AGOSTINO PATRIZI, PAPAL MASTER OF CEREMONIES

POMPONIO HAD left Rome for Venice with the intent of boarding a ship bound for the East. Since he was broke, however, the offer from a nobleman to stay on awhile in Venice and teach his sons seemed attractive. The sons, too, were attractive. They proved to be diligent, dedicated, and gifted students. Pomponio's admiration for the boys matched the esteem in which they held their charismatic teacher. It was a difficult spot for anyone who admired male physical beauty as much as did Pomponio, who had already scandalized the Romans with his homoerotic longings. This time the Venetian authorities became involved. Pomponio had incautiously penned erotic love poems to the boys, comparing one of them to Jupiter's young lover Ganymede, who was abducted to Mount Olympus to become the cupbearer to the gods; but the Venetian boy surpassed Ganymede in beauty:

> I wish those golden early centuries had borne you,
> For you could have aroused the gods with your beauty.
> A stranger would never have turned into a winged lover
> Nor would a Trojan boy have shone from the sky.[1]

Had he seen the Venetian, Jupiter would never have taken Ganymede to Mount Olympus. Love for the boy also inspired Pomponio to compose a rather risqué encomium: "Happy is he to whom the stars have given a tender ass; the ass seduces Cupid. Riches and honors are showered on the ass; and kind fate favors a magnificent ass."[2] Sodomy was a capital offense in Venice, yet plotting to murder the pope was evidently a still more serious offense. The Council of Ten was preparing to prosecute the case, when the situation in Rome claimed everyone's attention. The council postponed the sodomy prosecution and, as requested, extradited Pomponio to Rome to answer charges of conspiracy.

In Rome officials immediately identified the conspiracy as heresy. Heresy encompassed many kinds of sins and vices; it was a sin against church doctrine and God's law. Christians who espoused pagan ideas and morals were heretics. Suicide and sodomy were forms of heresy, for they were abuses of God's gifts. That is the reason convicted sodomites suffered the same fate as heretics, who promoted theological opinions that were at variance with church doctrine. Both sodomites and heretics were burned at the stake. A charge of heresy did not supersede a charge of treason. Indeed, to many minds it was clear that sodomy and heresy were closely linked and that together they might have motivated the humanists to murder the pope. Clearly, their obsessive reading and imitation of ancient pagan literature had not only excited in them an unnatural lust toward one another; it had further incited the humanists to engage in arrogant mockery of the papacy and the Church. The plot was sheer lunacy, brought on by this dabbling in classical literature. Epicurus and lust had replaced Jesus and charity in the hearts of these reprobates. Paul was convinced that paganism had played a central part in the conspiracy. In direct response to the episode, the pope publicly condemned pagan classical literature and culture.

Paul's View of Classical Antiquity

Pope Nicholas V had given the Eternal City a complete renovation to rival the splendor of ancient Rome (see Chapter 3). The same Renaissance ideals had guided Paul's predecessor, Pope Pius II, who was an accomplished classical scholar and something of a sensualist. He loved the Roman poet Virgil so much that he took the name Aeneas, after the Trojan hero in Virgil's *Aeneid*. In his youth, Pius had written erotic poetry, an obscene comedy, and a novella about two lovers, in which he offered a sympathetic treatment of sexual desire. In a letter to his father Aeneas had also justified his own dalliance with a Tuscan maid. While staying at an inn, he wrote, he had been bewitched by a pretty girl. The future pontiff reflected on Moses, Aristotle, and all the great men who had fallen under the spell of women. Overcome by desire, during the night he sneaked into her room. Rather than expressing shame afterward at having given in to his lust, he saw it as a natural attribute of youth. Aeneas even rejoices in the letter at the birth of the son born of this brief affair.[3] At the time, Aeneas was thirty-eight: in the Renaissance he would have been considered old. After becoming pope, Pius claimed to have mended his ways. He nevertheless retained an admiration for the literature and eloquent language of pagan antiquity and even wrote his best-selling *Commentaries,* about his life and times, in classical Latin. He also employed numerous humanist scholars at the Vatican, including Platina.

Pope Paul's first act, as we have seen, was to fire most of these humanists. As is clear from the imagery featured at the fetes he sponsored, however, Paul was not completely adverse to classical culture. Not only did he collect antiquities, particularly statues and medals, but he commissioned more classically inspired medals than any other pope of the fifteenth century. Humanist scholars tried to win his patronage by dedicating to him their translations of classical texts and commentaries on the church fathers, but in vain. Although the first printing presses in Rome were set up during his rule, it is unclear how much familiarity Paul had with the new technology. Unlike cardinals' palaces, Paul's immense Palazzo Venezia had no library, but it did boast grandiose halls hung with tapestries and lined with exquisite cases displaying his precious jewels and gold and silver plates. Paul did restore some ancient monuments, but most if not all were early churches. In fact, Platina blames Paul for demolishing the fragment of the majestic ancient building called the Septizonium.[4] Before 1468 Paul seems to have been tolerant toward academies in Rome dedicated to the study of antiquity. Platina and other humanists, for example, were not deterred from meeting to share classical knowledge and debate ancient literature in eloquent Latin at the house of Cardinal Bessarion.[5] Paul provided assistance to the elderly and indigent humanist Flavio Biondo, but such patronage was an exception during Paul's reign. As we have seen, Platina and other humanists lost their means of livelihood when Paul drastically reduced the number of papal secretaries in 1464. Before departing for Venice, Pomponio Leto claimed that he had worked for a year without pay and as a consequence was "reduced to desperation, on account of his extreme poverty, privation, and misery."[6] Paul was, in fact, so suspicious of learned writing that he was not even convinced of the importance of his own official biographies.[7]

Contemporary reports highlight Paul's animosity toward humanists and the literature of pagan antiquity.[8] Paul felt threatened on a personal level by humanist learning, according to Platina: "Paul wanted to appear sharp and learned in everything; he likewise wanted to appear witty; he ridiculed and despised almost everyone."[9] Platina's ironic attitude had been still more explicit in a phrase deleted from the final version of this assessment; originally it read: "Paul wanted to appear sharp and learned, although in talent and skill he fell short of the mark." As further proof of Paul's arrogance and ignorance, Platina reports that the pope became enraged after misunderstanding a pun that Pomponio had made in Latin. At the beginning of the final version of his life of Paul, Platina writes that Paul's childhood teacher "used to praise Paul's diligence in [studying letters]"; but in the original the historian had added, "although Paul's mind was unskilled."[10] Platina presents Paul as a struggling student and an embarrassed adult angered by his inability to keep up with the witty banter of the humanists.

Surprisingly for a Renaissance pope, Paul avoided using Latin and preferred the vernacular even for official business.[11] This preference perhaps reflects Paul's Venetian origins, for Venice had a stronger vernacular tradition than did other Italian cities. In the face of Paul's evident lack of interest in the humanities, humanists mounted an impassioned defense of the value of literature. One contemporary who criticized the pope warned about the dangers of offending the writers of history: "The things he did gave Paul a bad reputation, and many ill words were thrown at him in conversation and writing. By this example he learned . . . that literary men are never injured with impunity . . . for the learned are to be feared more than armed soldiers, a pen more than swords, eloquence more than an army. You can sometimes resist the latter, but never the former; the latter inflict honorable, temporary, and curable wounds, but the former disgraceful, permanent, and incurable ones; the latter rob one of wealth, land, and cities; the former dignity, fame, and eternal life."[12] From his prison cell, Platina wrote a letter to Paul in which he defended the role of humanists and stressed the dire consequences that may befall leaders who deny the importance of writers: if poets and orators are needed to memorialize great men—Christ is known through the Evangelists, and Achilles through Homer's verse—then how will the pope be remembered?[13] Literature, Platina argued, records and popularizes the deeds of even its greatest critics. But Paul had already chosen how he would be remembered by posterity: not so much through the words in the two biographies of himself that he commissioned but in the coins, titles, statues, festivities, banquets, and churches.[14] All these acts and images would recall imperial triumphal Rome, not a civic-minded republic of letters.

Paul was clearly critical of the classical ideals the humanists had adopted. At the equivalent of a press conference concerning the conspiracy, the pope "damned humanist studies" and expressed his intention to make it "illegal to study pagan literature, for it is full of heresy and immorality." Paul continued with a revealing discourse about the nature of sin and the need to maintain a certain holy ignorance: "Before boys have reached the age of ten and gone to school, they know a thousand immodesties; think of the thousand other vices they will learn when they read Juvenal, Terence, Plautus, and Ovid. Juvenal is a teacher of vice, just like preachers whom we have reprimanded for teaching lascivious behavior that a man never knew before, when they say 'these are the ways in which you sin.'"[15] Whereas Socrates famously taught that to know virtue is to be virtuous, Paul argued that knowing about sin leads to sinning. The pope's example of bad preachers recalls Poggio Bracciolini's invective against friars in his *Dialogue against Hypocrites* (1447). One preacher, Poggio says, was so explicit in his diatribe against female lust that husbands rushed home to try with their wives the sex acts they had just learned about in the homily.[16] By describing sin, Poggio argues, bad preachers end up teaching sin. Knowledge is dangerous. This precept is in tune with the medieval Christian condemnation of curiosity, and of Augustine's related temptation, "lust of the eyes." Censorship is necessary to protect morality and prevent heresy.

Paul certainly had good reason for calling the Roman satirist Juvenal a teacher of vice. Juvenal was mocking immoral behavior in his Satires, but even more than the bad preachers condemned by Poggio, Juvenal revels in describing, often in obscene terms, the acts that he condemns. Most university classics courses on Juvenal today in fact skip over the infamous Second Satire, in which the poet railed against effeminate men and homosexuality; the Sixth Satire, the attack on marriage, in which sleeping with a boy is recommended as an alternative to the troubles of living with a woman; or the vivid, grotesque image of sodomy in Satire Nine, in which a servant complains about having to penetrate his master so deeply that he can tell what the master ate for dinner. Such obscene imagery makes it clear that Paul was not being unduly reactionary in deeming Juvenal inappropriate reading for schoolchildren. Before becoming Pope Pius II, by contrast, Aeneas Piccolomini, in his treatise *The Education of Boys* (1450), had praised Juvenal as a model for teaching Latin eloquence to boys. Although the author admits that Juvenal "said many things with excessive license," Piccolomini calls him "a poet of high genius" who "in some satires shows himself so religious that he might seem second to none of the teachers of our faith."[17] Piccolomini thus presents Juvenal, far from being a teacher of vice, as a proto-Christian theologian. Unlike Pope Paul, Pius had taken the time to study and accept the good in pagan learning. Juvenal's satires, which were especially popular in Renaissance Rome, were a favorite subject of study for members of the Roman Academy. The Vatican Library, in fact, possesses a manuscript, in a humanist's hand, containing Juvenal's Satires and a detailed commentary. It is dated as having been completed on February 23, 1468, during carnival.[18] Could one of the conspirators have finished his commentary on the very day he was arrested?! Juvenal was obviously mocking sodomy as immoral, obscene, and even monstrous, yet according to Pope Paul, the humanists used Juvenal as a manual.

Paul had been forewarned about the dangers of pagan literature thirteen years before the conspiracy, when he was a cardinal. In 1455 the bishop of Verona, Ermolao Barbaro, had dedicated a work condemning classical literature to Barbo, the future Pope Paul. In *Orations against Poets,* Barbaro asserted that pagan poetry and theater were detrimental to morality. He praised Plato for forbidding "innocent youths to read and hear about Jupiter's debaucheries" and repeated the story found in a work by the ancient Roman playwright Terence about the pornographic effects of these myths. A youth looking at a painting of Jupiter in the form of a golden shower raping Danae, becomes so "excited toward evil that he not only corrupts a virgin but corrupts her entire household."[19] Augustine also quoted this passage in two places.[20]

Pope Sixtus IV and Platina in the Vatican Library, painting by Melozzo da Forli, Ospedale di San Spirito, Rome. © Scala / Art Resource, New York.

Whereas Saint Augustine follows Terence in emphasizing the hubris of the youth, who in imitating Jupiter sees himself as a god, Barbaro stresses to a greater extent the dangers of lust. Reading ancient literature is akin to looking at pornography, in that it incites lustful acts.

In direct response to the conspiracy, in March 1468 Paul, citing the danger of heresy, officially forbade schoolteachers to teach the pagan poets.[21] The connection is explicitly drawn in a little-known contemporary source: "Paul II, after reading the poems of some poets, decreed that no one should promote pagan literature in the future, for poetry corrupts young minds. . . . Among all peoples [pagan literature] has been greatly reviled, because pagan poets introduce civil unrest [and] the poisonous discord of conspiracy."[22] Paul considered mere acquaintance with the works of pagan antiquity dangerous. He reportedly declared: "No one can hope to call himself erudite without detracting from religion."[23] Reading pagan authors, he felt sure, necessarily made a person irreligious and immoral and incited rebellion.

Renaissance Pagans

The head of the Roman Academy, Pomponio Leto, in addition to editing and teaching the works of ancient Latin authors, including Sallust and Virgil, wrote a guide to the ruins of Rome, transcribed ancient inscriptions, and collected ancient statues. Pomponio had been a student of Lorenzo Valla (1407–1457) and succeeded him as professor of rhetoric at the University of Rome.[24] Valla himself had been attacked for being dangerously pagan. As a young man, Valla had argued in his controversial dialogue *On Pleasure* (1431) that the Christian message had been blurred by the ascetic ideals of Stoicism and that true Christianity was on the contrary close to Epicureanism in its affirmation of nature and the body.[25] Epicurus, who taught that pleasure was the highest good and the purpose of life, was reviled in the Middle Ages as a teacher of vice. Renewed access to ancient sources in fifteenth-century Italy, however, had led to a reevaluation of Epicurus' teachings.[26] But whereas other scholars had tried to make Epicurus palatable to a Christian audience by asserting that the ancient philosopher's doctrine of pleasure referred only to intellectual pleasure, Valla insisted that Epicurus alluded also to sensual pleasure. It was perhaps no coincidence that in the conspiracy of 1468 Pomponio and the humanists of the Roman Academy were accused of being Epicureans addicted to sensuality and sodomitic lust.

According to his biographer, Pomponio Leto was "at first a despiser of religion, but as he grew older he began to take an interest in it."[27]

Nobody loved antiquity more than Pomponio, who abhorred his own age. "Most of all he venerated the genius of the city of Rome."[28] Later, in defending himself against charges of heretical paganism, Pomponio insisted that he was still a practicing Christian. Church officials were also angry over Pomponio's barbed remarks about corrupt priests. He admitted to having satirized the priesthood but ascribed his criticism to the fact that he had not received any of his promised salary from the pope for a year.[29] At the time, many good Christians complained about misbehaving priests. Corruption in the Church had become so widespread that the immoral cleric was a stock literary figure. In the fourteenth century Dante had placed his contemporary popes in hell and Boccaccio stressed the contradictions between ideal and reality in his many tales of degenerate priests and friars.[30] In the fifteenth century, anticlerical sentiment became even more pronounced.[31] Unflattering images of the clergy were so common as not to cause offense; but in Paul's Rome, Pomponio's bitter remarks were read as the troubling indication of a hidden agenda.

Pomponio understandably became even more resentful after his arrest in 1468: "He was a little more aggressive toward the clergy and more outspoken in criticizing the pomp and luxury of the great prelates. But his carping was so gentle that thanks and applause rather than hatred came of it. Several prelates and high-ranking clerics befriended him and assisted him financially."[32] Pomponio later took pains to affirm his Christianity and to offer his praise for Pope Paul.[33] In his funeral oration for Pomponio, the humanist Ferno defended his teacher from the charge of paganism: "Unreliable men, gossiping chatterboxes, accuse the best poets and humanists of paganism and treachery. Death attests to how his life was most holy. [Pomponio] demanded to confess his mistakes not only to bystanders . . . but to his Savior himself. He religiously prepared himself for a most religious death, or rather eternal life."[34] Like his friend Pomponio, Platina was accused of showing a heretical devotion to pagan antiquity. In a letter from prison to Cardinal Ammannati-Piccolomini, a former patron, Platina wrote: "Once they cleared the charge of conspiracy, they accused me of impiety. But this disgraceful charge, I think, has not stood, for I can prove that since the age of eighteen I have never missed confession or Holy Communion. As far as possible, I have always attended holy services on feast days. As much as human weakness allowed, I observed God's commandments, and never distorted the articles of the faith. Whoever does this and lives a virtuous life of diligent learning and hard work should not be tortured with physical torments and disgrace."[35] Platina was trying to persuade the cardinal to intercede with the pope and obtain his freedom, so it is not surprising that he would protest his innocence and insist on his devotion to Christianity. Platina remained tainted by the charge of paganism, however. In 1477 the bishop of Ventimiglia wrote an invective against Platina: "Some say that you are more pagan than Christian and that you follow the pagan practices more than ours; some say that you call Hercules your god, others Mercury, Jupiter, Apollo, Venus, or Diana; that you habitually swear by these gods and goddesses, especially when you are with men of similar superstitions."[36] Almost ten years after the humanists' arrest, rumors still abounded concerning Platina's pagan ways.

As proof of the humanists' heretical beliefs, the interrogators brought up the pagan names that the academicians had adopted. Paul questioned Pomponio: "Why did you call the humanists by pagan Roman names?"[37] Although Pomponio in Platina's account responds that the names served as an inducement to practice the ancient virtue, Paul's official biographer Canensius interprets them as a rejection of Christianity: "Scorning our religion, they think it most vile to be named after a saint, and instead of their holy baptismal names they use pagan ones."[38] Whether or not they were practicing pagans, academy humanists did carry their love of antiquity to extremes. The writings of academy members contain numerous references to pagan gods.

On his transcription of the works of the Roman love poet Propertius, one academy humanist wrote an epigraph to the work containing a votive offering to Apollo; and Pomponio dedicated a work on the regions of ancient Rome to "most ancient Jupiter."[39]

Other contemporary sources point to the heretical pagan beliefs of the Roman humanists. The papal master of ceremonies, Agostino Patrizi, wrote: "They not only loved the language and literature of the ancients but also habitually took their beliefs about morals, good and evil, and God himself not from Christian philosophers, as is right, but from those ancient pagans. For them it was not enough to speak ill of the pope, all the orthodox bishops, and the entire clergy, but they attacked our religion, and spoke about it as if it were a matter of the imagination and fable."[40] The Milanese ambassador went further in his report on the conspiracy: "The humanists denied God's existence and thought that the soul died with the body. They supposed that Moses was a great deceiver of people and that Christ was a false prophet. Instead of Christian names, they used academic and Epicurean ones. . . . They seduced young men . . . and boasted of their wicked life and heresy."[41] The seemingly harmless adoption of classical names had become a sign of outright atheism.

The charge of paganism took on a more philosophical dimension when some observers asserted that the humanists' heretical ideas about the immortality of the soul were in keeping with those of Plato: "They wonder why not Aristotle but Plato is condemned, who came closest of all to Christianity, if we believe Augustine."[42] Theologians had debated since antiquity about whether Plato's ideas about the body and the soul were compatible with Christianity. In the fifteenth century, as humanists studied these texts with renewed rigor, additional questions arose about sexual morality in Plato's works. During his interrogation for the conspiracy of 1468 Platina defended Plato's view of the soul and added: "Cicero called Plato a god among philosophers."[43] Platina, who had studied Plato under John Argyropoulos in

Florence from 1457 to 1461, was also a friend of one of the foremost Platonists of the day, Cardinal Bessarion in Rome, a friendship that must have made him even more suspect in the pope's eyes.[44]

Bessarion, who was such a powerful cardinal that many thought he would be pope, to a great degree lost favor under Paul II. After all, it was Bessarion who had tried to force the new pope to recognize the validity of a document limiting the pope's powers that had been signed by all the cardinals, including the pope, before the election. Matters then worsened for the cardinal: his intellectual rival George of Trebizond, who at one point had served as tutor to Paul, came into favor with the new pope. Since at least 1458 George and Bessarion had been enmeshed in a furious row over which was superior, Aristotle or Plato. After meeting the flamboyant Greek Pletho, Bessarion's teacher and a promoter of the pagan revival, George became convinced that a Platonist conspiracy was afoot. It would corrupt the West and become uncontainable if Bessarion were to become pope, as he almost did at the conclave of 1458.[45] Among other things, George attacked Platonism as a hedonistic doctrine. Referring to specific passages in Plato's works, he called the philosopher an "enemy of nature, a destroyer of morality, an adherent to boys' buttocks."[46]

In several places, in fact, Plato seems to condone homosexuality and pederasty. In *Charmides,* Socrates gawks at beautiful boys in a gymnasium, delights in catching a glimpse of Charmides' genitals, and is "overcome by a sort of wild-beast appetite" at the sight. In *Phaedrus,* Socrates openly flirts with a young man and, after hearing him give a speech about lovers, describes the effect as "ravishing." The most explicit images of pederasty, though, are found in Plato's *Symposium,* where men at an all-male drinking party debate the meaning of love. Here, Alcibiades relates how he tried to seduce Socrates, among other things by sleeping next to him naked; Phaedrus praises love between men as the source of bravery in war; and the whole search for philosophical truth seems to start with the erotic attraction to boys. In

Plato's time the higher form of love, the meeting of two intellects, was only really possible between men, because women were not educated. Although Plato later condemns homosexuality as "against nature," his frank descriptions of erotic attraction and his praise for the love between men and boys were stumbling blocks for Christians.

In order to defend Plato from the charge of advocating unnatural love, Bessarion followed the Neoplatonic tradition of reading homosexual love in Plato as a metaphysical eros. In Plato's *Symposium,* Socrates repeats what he learned from a wise woman named Diotima, that physical beauty and sexual love are only the first rung on the ladder that eventually leads to a higher form of love. Augustine, Proclus, and pseudo-Dionysius expanded on this concept and distinguished two kinds of love: the earthly form of love, built on shameless, selfish lust, and the divine form that originates with God and leads to virtue, truth, and generosity. According to Bessarion, George misinterpreted Plato's praise of divine love as an argument for lust. He confused the two loves. Bessarion and his friend Marsilio Ficino, whose commentary on the *Symposium* was already becoming famous, reintroduced the doctrine of platonic love to the West.[47] An elevated, purified Platonism purged of any sexual impropriety became the fashion in intellectual circles all over Europe and has survived to this day in the use of "platonic" as an adjective meaning "nonsexual." Under Paul II, however, the once-powerful Cardinal Bessarion had fallen from favor, and Platonism seemed destined to expire, as an immoral heresy.

The new pope's favorite, George of Trebizond, now publicly attacked as heretical Cardinal Bessarion's theories about the Eucharist. Then George convinced the pope to fund a trip to Constantinople, where the unstable humanist hoped to convert the Turkish sultan and gain an important ally against the threat of Platonism.[48] George made the voyage in 1465 but returned empty-handed, having failed to gain an audience with Mehmet II. In his efforts to pay court to the Ottoman sultan, however, George overstepped boundaries. He had a prophetic vision of the Turk's inevitable conquest of Europe. Bessarion discovered and disclosed letters in which George described Mehmet as "the king of the whole world and of the very heavens."[49] George was imprisoned for four months. His disgrace, however, did not allay Paul's fears about Platonism. Soon after George's arrest, Fernando of Córdoba, a member of Bessarion's circle, composed a treatise in praise of Plato, which the pope ordered a censor to investigate for "anything that might detract from the faith and corrupt pious ears, or any poison therein that might lead to ruin."[50]

Plato and the pagan classics clearly had the power to corrupt morals and lead Christians astray. Humanists in Bessarion's circle were in fact accused of sexual promiscuity. One, Niccolò Perotti, was rumored to have had intercourse with his own nephew.[51] Perotti was also a member of the Roman Academy, and in the 1470s he and Pomponio together wrote a commentary on the Roman poet Martial.[52] The works of Martial, Juvenal, and other poets of pagan antiquity are repeatedly mentioned in the sources as corrupting influences and factors contributing to the conspiracy.

Sodom and the Dangers of Literature

Official records for the conspiracy trial are missing, but both Pomponio and Platina wrote eloquent defenses, which are extant, of their own morals and actions. Against the charge of sodomy, Pomponio claimed that his affection for one of his two students was purely intellectual: "I praised the Venetian boy for his beauty, nobility, and dedication to me. . . . He followed in my footsteps, clung to me, loved, esteemed, and respected me, and often tried to delay my departure. . . . He never left my side unless given permission. His mind was pure and virtuous, full of modesty, judgment, and honor. . . . Who would not praise and embrace such great virtues of the mind? . . . I justifiably praised the boys in two letters for their gifts of nature, meaning

their beauty; their virtue, meaning their love of letters; and their diligence."[53] All these traits, Pomponio continues, perfectly conform to
those the ancient educator Quintilian mentions in his precepts on the
ideal teacher-student relationship.[54] Quintilian (35–100 CE) stressed
that a teacher should play the nurturing and kind role of the parent
toward his charges.[55] Pomponio writes unabashedly of daily intimacy
but casts this as a love of beauty, virtue, and shared study.

Pomponio then turned to the question of his praise of the boy's
body, by referring to Socrates, the ancient poets, and historians, who
all praised the physical beauty of young men as a sign of their virtue.
Socrates "wanted man to excel in both beauty and morals." Pomponio
continued: "Why else was there a law in antiquity that forbade an ugly
man from entering the priesthood? Throughout history, many peoples
have chosen kings on the basis of their physical beauty. I could find
endless examples in books, but I think the example of Socrates alone is
enough to defend me."[56] Pomponio tries to sidestep the accusation of
sodomy by claiming that his interest was simply chaste admiration for
male beauty.

From his prison cell in the Castel Sant'Angelo, Pomponio wrote a
letter in self-defense to his former employer, the father of one of the
boys, Giovanni Tron: "I have decided to inform you of my innocence.
My habits are well known to you, and I completely entrust myself
to your care." Tron and Pomponio's other Venetian patron, Antonio
Moroceno, were evidently not convinced that the humanist had done
anything wrong, for Pomponio thanks them for writing letters on his
behalf. Further on in the letter, Pomponio tells his patron to give
his regards to another member of the Roman Academy in Venice,
Palladius Rutilius. He then somewhat cryptically says: "Please tell him
to be a more faithful informer next time, as he was perhaps deceived, I
believe, by the charms of a Judas Iscariot. It is not fitting for a man
who makes his living from literature to be deceitful. I am referring to
the frivolous matter of Greek lust."[57] It appears from this that it was

Pomponio's friend Rutilius who denounced him to the Venetian authorities. Pomponio never denied writing the homoerotic poetry; instead he presented his passion either as innocent platonic admiration of boyish beauty or as a harmless infatuation. Pomponio's homosexual preferences are nevertheless undeniable. In a later, perhaps damning criticism of Pomponio's sexual morals, his contemporary biographer, Sabellicus, said that Pomponio "loved Roman youth to the point of scandal."[58] Pomponio must have been notorious for his homoerotic passion if even Sabellicus, a friend and student whose biography celebrates the life of his mentor, described Pomponio's behavior as excessive and shocking.

In Renaissance Europe, sodomy was legally defined as any form of nonreproductive sex, which also included heterosexual mutual masturbation and anal intercourse.[59] Although priests reprimanded married couples for practicing anal intercourse as a form of birth control and condemned masturbation, most of their ire was directed against same-sex male sodomy. In Renaissance cities, public brothels were opened and prostitution condoned in an effort to make women more available to men who were too young to marry but needed an outlet. In Florence the Dominican preacher Girolamo Savonarola (1442–1498) criticized parents for encouraging their sons to engage in same-sex unions in order to avoid the shame of unwed pregnant daughters. Sodomy was considered so great a threat to civic stability that Venice, Florence, and other Italian cities set up special judiciary offices to entrap and prosecute sodomites. In Florence alone, seventeen thousand males were accused and three thousand convicted of homosexual acts between 1432 and 1502. If the archival numbers are correct, this could mean that by the end of the century two of every three Florentine males had been accused of sodomy at some point in their lives.[60]

Prosecutions for sodomy in Venice had risen significantly in the 1460s. The Decemviri, the council of ten wise men, who investigated accusations of sodomy, were in fact busier than they had ever been before.[61] Pomponio concluded his defense against the charge of sodomy with an argument from authority: "If the Decemviri of Venice, the defenders of propriety and masters of morals, had seen this wicked behavior in me, they would never have sent me here but would have condemned me there according to practice. For in the most holy Venetian state this crime is detestable and abominable."[62] That same year, in fact, a man suspected of sodomy in Venice was punished with twenty-five lashes.[63] The members of the Council of Ten concluded their letter on Pomponio's transfer with a stark request: "If His Holiness finds the defendant innocent and not worthy of death, may he deign to send him back to our authority so that he may be purged of this filthy vice."[64] Perhaps being extradited to Rome saved Pomponio from a sodomy conviction in Venice. The humanist would never return to the La Serenissima. As far as we know, the Roman authorities did not specifically charge Pomponio with sodomy, but the charge of pagan immorality and heresy implies sexual deviance.

Pomponio's defense of his intimate relations with beautiful boys is part of the broader homoerotic and pederastic culture at the Roman Academy.[65] In his report on the conspiracy, the Milanese ambassador said that the humanists "committed carnal acts with males and females, and a thousand other wicked deeds." He reported that Callimachus was the ringleader and that at his house they "found obscene epigrams, poems, and sonnets addressed to boys, which demonstrate the lewd behavior of the humanists."[66] As with many of the charges leveled against the humanists, the accusation of sodomy was never substantiated.

Callimachus' extant epigrams undoubtedly account for most of the obscene poetry.[67] They are modeled on the epigrams of the first-century Latin poet Martial. Like Juvenal, Martial was attacked as a teacher of vice, because his collection of witty poems includes numerous particularly obscene descriptions of pederastic desire and sodomy.

In his treatise *The Education of Boys* (1459), Aeneas Piccolomini (the future Pius II), who, as we have seen, had praised Juvenal as a model of Latinity for young boys, called Martial "pernicious" and said that the poet was "so thick with thorns that you may not pick his roses without being pricked."[68] But Renaissance intellectuals must have loved Martial's poems, for they repeatedly copied out his writings by hand in elegant script. In fact, over 110 fifteenth-century Italian manuscripts of Martial's work survive. He was a popular author among humanists but especially among members of the Roman Academy. Numerous Martial manuscripts in the Vatican Library contain Pomponio Leto's annotations or those of his students, including Lucio Fazini and Settimuleio Campano, who suffered the same fate as their teacher in the dungeon of the Castel Sant'Angelo. In imitation of Martial, these humanists wrote epigrams, often about other humanists.[69] Callimachus penned the most unabashedly homoerotic epigrams concerning members of the Roman Academy. The authorities went after him in 1468, but having been forewarned by Cardinal Bessarion, Callimachus evaded the pontifical guard, escaped Rome, and eventually settled in Poland, where he enjoyed great success at the court of Casimir IV.

In one epigram addressed to Platina, who was to host a dinner party, Callimachus declares his love for the young humanist Lepido, beside which all other pleasures pale: "What is this madness of yours to empty your pockets preparing extravagant banquets, poet to poet? Jupiter despises banquets of ambrosia and nectar, if Ganymede does not adorn them. Corydon is not content if you take Alexis away from him. Do you think that a meal without Lepido could be pleasing? I would have preferred that you offer me chestnuts and little mountain mushrooms and whatever vegetable honors a rustic table, provided that snow-white Lepido join us and that he be locked tight, tight to my side."[70] Antonio Lepido was an actual person attached to the Roman Academy, a student of Pomponio Leto.[71] Corydon and Alexis are two male shepherds who pine for each other in Virgil's *Eclogues*. This reference, along with the one to Jupiter's beloved cupbearer, the beautiful boy Ganymede, emphasizes the homoerotic nature of Callimachus' longing for Lepido. In another epigram, Callimachus similarly praises the vintage wine and the exotic and expensive delicacies to be served at a banquet but concludes: "What use is a dinner bought at great expense, since you can be more splendid than food alone? Give me a poor man's morsels and dry cups; if you add Lepido, all will be precious."[72] In yet another, Callimachus deifies Lepido by placing him astride a horse among the stars.[73] These epigrams and others paint a picture of the cultured dinner party atmosphere of Roman humanism in the 1460s. Platina himself wrote a popular cookbook, in which he mentions a number of the academy humanists who attended the dinner parties.[74] As with the symposia of ancient Athens, these all-male dinner parties were the occasion for learned discourse and flirtation.

The young humanist Lucio Fazini was another object of homoerotic infatuation. Callimachus takes eighteen lines replete with classical references to describe the beautiful body of the young man. He has a "face brighter than Venus' and the hair of Phoebus Apollo . . . [more striking] than the stone polished by Phidias or the paintings of Apelles." *Lucido,* Callimachus concludes, is a most fitting name for a beauty of that order, for it means "luminous." Martial used a similar construction with a long list of comparisons to describe the fragrance of a boy's kisses.[75] Callimachus wrote an entire poem about a growth of stubble on Lucio's chin: "A scattering of the snowy elegance of stubble now flickers on little Lucio's face. It is not a rough and rigid beard, such as usually grows on the chins of hungry Cynics and Stoics, but the down of young virility, which draws female interest, whereas his face was pleasing only to males before. Wear this down with two little kisses and the slightest touch of the tongue." [76] Martial similarly praises the soft "down" on the chin of a youth: "Your down is so fragile, so soft, that a breath or sunshine or a light breeze might take it away. It is like the wool that comes on Cretan quinces, which shine after being polished by the fingers of a virgin. Whenever I manfully press upon you five kisses, I become downy from your lips, Dindymus."[77] Martial also talks about how boys with facial hair are less attractive to men and laments the cut of the barber's blade on the first growth. The ancient poet explains in one poem that Ganymede will lose his job as cupbearer for Jupiter because the "early down" on Ganymede's chin signifies that the boy has become a man: "But if the barber's cut has given you a man's face, who will mix my nectar in your place?"[78] Callimachus uses the same word as Martial—*lanugo*, meaning "soft down"—for the boy's first growth of beard. The humanist knew Martial's poetry intimately and imitated ancient homoerotic sentiments and images in his own love poetry.

Callimachus' poem about Lucio was addressed not to him but to another young humanist in the circle, Settimuleio Campano. In prison Platina exchanged letters with Lucio, who was also tortured and incarcerated, and called him the "most innocent of all."[79] The warden of the Castel Sant'Angelo said that because of his youth Lucio was best able to endure the torture and adversity.[80] Paolo Marsi, a friend who was absent from Rome during the trouble, lamented the youth's fate in a Martialesque elegy: "O unworthy wickedness! Neither beauty nor youth have protected the gifts of your mind. Who permitted himself? What impious man could bind your snow-white hands with rope?"[81] Even the young man's torture inspired homoerotic fantasy.

Callimachus also imitates the ancients in using sodomy as an insult in some of his poems. Whereas the poems about Lepido and Lucio are affectionate and build on the pagan culture of boy-love, other epigrams are clearly satirical about that sexuality. Callimachus, for example, advises an elderly man to be passive: "Although the reverence of a wrinkled brow with white hair is esteemed . . . Quintilius should prefer to be effeminate, so that he might always be ready for the prostitutes and the boys."[82] In antiquity and the Renaissance, the older, active

Fifteenth-century torture chamber in the Castel Sant'Angelo (author photo). "The cries of the tortured humanists resounded so loudly that you would have taken the Castel Sant'Angelo for Phalaris' bull" (Platina, 1468).

partner in homosexual relations was seen as virile and masculine. He was a real man imparting his power to the younger recipient.[83] Boys were still not men and not yet completely distinct from females. The sexual act between an adult male and a passive youth was considered a sin and a crime in Italian cities. But laws were much stricter and the penalties dire when an adult male allowed himself to be sodomized by a youth. This role reversal broke social boundaries and upset acceptable gender relations. Callimachus' epigram could be seen as shocking in that he advises an elderly man ("wrinkled brow and white hair") to be *mollem* ("soft" or "effeminate"), in order to attract boys. Callimachus is following his ancient models in using effeminacy or a man's enjoyment at being the passive partner in homosexual relations as an insult.[84]

Callimachus presents another satirical image of sodomy in the following epigram: "Because Archephylax once . . . said [to his wife]: 'Imagine you are a boy bride,' you always allow him to sodomize you, Iolla, and always to enjoy his wife as Ganymede."[85] This could be read as an insult against both the husband, who prefers sex with boys, and the wife, who must pretend to be a boy and be sodomized. As with pederasty and homosexual intercourse, heterosexual sodomy, though harder to police, was illegal and considered morally reprehensible in the Renaissance.[86] Like Archephylax, the ancient poets showed a preference for boys over women. After praising the attributes of five boys, Martial writes that he prefers them to the richest dowry. In another poem, a husband chastises his jealous wife, saying that he prefers Chian figs to *marisca* figs. Chian figs were evidently big and juicy, whereas the *marisca* were tough, dry, and tasteless.[87] Callimachus, again, had ample models in the ancients for his poetry. Even if some of his poems are clearly satirical, they still reveal the rich variety of pagan homosexual culture and its reception in fifteenth-century Christendom. And as Pope Paul suggested with his image of the bad preacher, detailed criticism of sin and homosexuality could have the opposite effect and educate the curious in the habits of vice.

In addition to the works of Juvenal and Martial, the humanists found models for obscene Latin verse in the *Great Priapea,* an ancient collection of poems about the god Priapus and his garden. The collection is full of obscene images: Priapus threatens to sodomize any thieves he finds in his garden and offers advice to boys about their sexual preferences. An earlier humanist, Antonio Beccadelli, had imitated the Priapic poems in his notorious collection of obscene verse, the *Hermaphroditus* (1435). The *Great Priapea* first appeared in print in 1469.[88] Its publication in Rome might be seen as strong evidence of increased tolerance on the part of the censors and the pope after the conspiracy, but it seems unlikely that Paul had any idea what the *Great Priapea* was, or that he exercised any control over the fledgling printing business.[89] The *Great Priapea* was popular largely because it was incorrectly believed to be the work of the most famous Roman poet, Virgil. Callimachus in fact defends his obscene poetry at the beginning of his book by citing the example of Virgil.

Callimachus knew that his epigrams would shock, and his explicitly erotic and homosexual verse was probably the main object of the pope's censure. Seemingly in answer to the pope's condemnation, Callimachus wrote: "You see my little poems as universally unrefined or lewd. If you think them unfit to be read to boys and chaste girls, let no boy or girl read them."[90] The intent of classically inspired literature of this kind is not to offer an education in ancient virtues—rather, it is an adults-only form of intellectual intercourse.

In defending himself, Pomponio understandably tried to distance himself from Callimachus: "As soon as I recognized his derangement and dishonesty I immediately became his enemy and began to hate not the man but his perverted habits, so abhorrent to me. I have always loved frugality, thrift, and sobriety; he devoted himself to Bacchanalian revels, drunkenness, and every kind of intemperance."[91] Pomponio leaves open the question of Callimachus' participation in the conspiracy. Platina, however, at least in his version of the interrogation, defended Callimachus against the charge of conspiracy by presenting him as an incompetent buffoon. Callimachus could not have thought up such a plan, he writes, "because he lacked judgment, eloquence, valor, troops, clients, arms, and eyes. For he was somewhat blind, sleepier than P. Lentulus, and on account of his weight slower than L. Crassus. Furthermore, he was not even a Roman citizen, who could hope to liberate his homeland, nor a bishop who could take over the papacy after Paul was killed. What could Callimachus do? What would he dare? Was he practiced in eloquence or valor? Had he chosen and enrolled men to undertake such a difficult task?"[92] By describing

Callimachus as a fool, Platina distances himself from his erstwhile companion, without accusing him of any crime. Nevertheless, in a bitter letter from prison to Cardinal Bessarion, Platina refers to Callimachus' fantasies, which might have included murdering the pope: "After drinking and eating, Callimachus would ramble on however he wished, shamelessly distributing kingdoms and riches [to anyone he pleased]. We, who sinned only through imprudence, by not revealing the dreams of an idiot, have been tortured and are held in this most miserable prison."[93] In a happier time, before the conspiracy, Platina had offered a more endearing portrait in his cookbook of their "nearly blind" friend Callimachus: "While he is eagerly preparing these [eggs], [he] makes us laugh, as he clings spellbound to the pan."[94] Although Pomponio refers to Callimachus' "perverted habits" and "intemperance," implying that he was guilty of sodomy, neither he nor Platina explicitly refers to Callimachus' homosexuality or pederasty. In fact, Callimachus' homoerotic poetry is limited to his youthful days in Rome, preconspiracy. Once he is safely exiled to Poland his poetry turns heterosexual; his love for the woman Fannia takes center stage, in marked contrast to the polysexual openness expressed in his earlier poems, in which men have sex with boys, women, and in one poem a cow. Callimachus' metamorphosis could be read as a cautious reaction to the violent events of 1468.

Callimachus' penchant might have been the most outré and the evidence for it the most inescapable, but other humanists of the academy also engaged in homoerotic exchanges. The humanist Lucillus, Platina reports, "was dragged to the city as if guilty of a capital offense. . . . A letter he wrote to Campano was intercepted in which he decried the love affairs of a certain Heliogabalus; but the meaning was so concealed that no one except someone involved could understand the matter."[95] The emperor Heliogabalus (204–222 CE) scandalized the Romans by openly holding homosexual orgies. Straightforward criticism of Heliogabalus could not have been problematic, so Lucillus' secret letter must have betrayed homoerotic leanings that were discovered despite the attempt at discretion.

Unlike Pomponio and Callimachus, Platina does not seem to have been explicitly accused of indulging in homoeroticism. He was, however, charged with sexual promiscuity. In 1477, eleven years after the conspiracy, Bishop Battista de' Giudici wrote an invective against him because Platina had seduced a "most vile" girl in the bishop's household.[96] As if in response to accusations of sexual license, Platina wrote in the first version of his life of Paul: "They dragged to jail not those whom they suspected of conspiracy but those whom they either hated on account of some quarrel or wished to separate from their consorts' embraces to satisfy their own lust."[97] Here, he suggests that it was the papal officials, not the humanists, who were guilty of promiscuity.

Platina promoted himself as an expert on love. His treatise *On Love* was first written in 1465 but was later revised twice, each time with a different dedicatee. In this work Platina attempts to cure a lovesick friend by attacking sexual love. He praises friendship among men and advocates marriage mainly for purposes of procreation. As a young man, he says, he burned with lust but found relief in philosophy. Platina ends with a diatribe against the female sex.[98] In response to this work, however, Giannantonio Campano wrote a poem in which he termed Platina's moralizing about sexual love hypocritical: "My friend Platina rants against 'alluring' loves. Do you know why? He doesn't like respectable women."[99] Instead, Campano continues: "Platina loses himself for an entire night in oral sex with Thais, the Athenian courtesan. Ursa, the she-bear, also jumps into his bed. A fool for girls, he lies about his loves . . . but, Platina, should I praise your mind or condemn your behavior? You write well but love badly."[100] The criticism pegs Platina as decidedly heterosexual. These are accusations not of homosexuality but of general promiscuity and bad taste. Many of Callimachus' homoerotic epigrams, however, were addressed to Platina, who was therefore aware of the homosexual activities of his friends and perhaps even participated.

Although homosexuality did not for the most part exist as an identity in the modern sense, a strong homoerotic culture had survived from antiquity, and Pomponio, Callimachus, and other humanists of the Roman Academy revived it as an ideal. Callimachus was one of the few to express openly (and foolishly) a still officially forbidden form of sexual desire, but it is clear from the humanist epigrams that homoerotic culture and activity were not only acceptable but quite prevalent. Earlier humanists had imitated the obscene literary forms of the ancients, but Callimachus emphasized the homoerotic and added a much more dangerous element. His poems were explicit avowals of sexual infatuation on the part of a specific man, a member of the Roman Academy, to an actual youth, another member of the same group. It is hardly surprising that sodomy was practiced in the holy city of Rome, an overcrowded, highly trafficked pilgrimage destination of celibate young clerics. In the pope's eyes the paganism of the humanists, who imitated the homoeroticism found in classical literature not only in their poems but also in their bedrooms, and their immoral behavior in fearlessly expressing and defending their pederastic desires, proved that they were heretics dissolute enough to contemplate murdering the most Holy Father and allying themselves with the Turkish infidel.

CHAPTER FIVE

Consorting with the Enemy

Mehmet II and the Ottoman Threat

The hair of his just-grown youthful beard was entwined like gold wire; his hero's moustache was like fresh basil over a rosebud, his lips were pistachios.

—SEYYID LOKMAN, OTTOMAN COURT POET, DESCRIBING MEHMET II

*T*HE GREAT SULTAN loved all the cucumbers in his garden, but he became attached to one in particular. He visited it every day and ordered that no one was to touch it. But one day it was gone. When no one could tell him what had happened, the sultan became enraged and decided to investigate for himself by eviscerating his gardeners; fortunately, the entrails of the first one disclosed the remains of the cucumber.[1] The Grand Turk was renowned for his cruelty. He massacred his enemies after subjecting them to extended bouts of torture. Sometimes he would leave them impaled or order them to be skinned alive and hanged by the feet to suffer a slow, painful death; at other times he would have them sawed slowly in half. When Christian slaves tried to escape during sea battles, he would nail their hands and feet to rowboats, which were then lit on fire and set adrift. The sultan allowed his worst enemies to be devoured by wild beasts right before his eyes.[2] These were the stories that circulated in Christian Europe. Mehmet II himself cultivated this image of horrifying cruelty to terrify and unnerve his enemies. Given his infamy, how could the humanists of the Roman Academy have ever considered conspiring with the Grand Turk to kill the pope and betray Rome, the seat of Western Christendom?

Monster and Ally

Western Europeans had been terrified of the prospect of an Ottoman invasion since at least 1453, when Constantinople, the Jewel of the East, fell at the hands of Mehmet II. The twenty-one-year-old Turkish sultan ever after was called Fatih, the Conqueror. Only seven thousand soldiers had guarded fourteen miles of walls around Constantinople against an advancing Ottoman army of eighty thousand. After a heavy pounding by the largest cannon in history, the ancient walls of the city still stood. The Byzantine Greeks held out for fifty-three days, until the Janissaries discovered a hidden door and hordes of them flooded in. Janissaries were crack troops known for their savagery and readiness to sacrifice their lives. The defenses quickly fell apart, and the great gates lay open to the invading army, which had been promised three days of plunder. The soldiers killed so many people that torrential rivers of blood poured down to the Bosporus. Churches were sacked, altars defiled, and nuns raped. After only a half day of this mayhem, the slaughter was too much even for Mehmet, who ordered an early end to the violence.[3]

Notwithstanding the particular horrors of the sacking of Constantinople, some Christian thinkers tried to justify the slaughter on the basis of ancient history and classical literature. The apologists regarded the Turks as the descendants of the ancient Trojans, who were redressing ancient wrongs by fighting the Greeks.[4] Mehmet II himself, as his semiofficial chronicler Critoboulos reports, saw the Turkish conquest of Greece as justifiable revenge for the sacking of ancient Troy.[5] In another account the sultan is said to have raped a Greek virgin in the Church of Santa Sophia, in order to avenge Ajax's rape of Cassandra in the temple of Athena after the fall of Troy (*Aeneid*, 2.403ff.). Giovan Mario Filelfo similarly blamed the Greeks in an epic poem on the deeds of Mehmet II, the *Amyris* (1471–1476).[6] The crusading pope Pius II did not believe in any of this. He insisted that the Ottoman

Sultan Mehmet II, "the Conqueror," painting by Gentile Bellini, National Gallery, London. © Erich Lessing / Art Resource, New York. "You will conquer Rome, which is the blind part of Israel, and will reunite all the people of God. You will rule, as Scripture states, from one end of the world to the other" (George of Trebizond).

Turks were descended from Scythian barbarians.[7] They were, he said, a "most squalid and ignominious race, involved in every kind of rape and sexual perversion." In his short poem, "Against Mehmet, the Wicked King of the Turks," Pius furthermore alleges that the only achievement and glory of Muslims is their abstinence from wine. For Pius, Mehmet was the personification of evil. He had "a terrifying face and dark black eyes; he ordered murders with a dreadful voice, cruel words, and wicked nods. He demanded the slaughter now of this one, now of that, and he washed his hands in Christian blood. He befouls and pollutes everything."[8] Pius draws a racially charged caricature of a villain, a violent scourge.

Pius II had spent most of his papacy holding out for a Crusade against the Ottoman Turks. In fact, he died in 1464 on the shores of the Adriatic, after two weeks of waiting for the Venetian ships to gather for a new Crusade. The doge himself eventually did set sail with a dozen galleys, but three days later the pope was dead. Everyone went home, and no Crusade took place. Paul II vowed to continue the crusading effort to win back Constantinople and stop the Ottoman advance. As an enthusiastic young cardinal, he had accompanied Pius to the departure point for his would-be Crusade. Paul sent Crusade funds soon after his election, to Matthias Corvinus, the king of Hungary, which was considered the first defense of Europe. Paul then tried to convince the Italian powers to provide assistance, but political rivalries made it almost impossible.[9] Italian city-states did not as consistently oppose the Turk as the papacy would have liked. In fact, at different times the king of Naples, the lords of Rimini, Milan, and Mantua, and Lorenzo de' Medici of Florence all formed alliances with the sultan against other Christian rulers of the Italian peninsula. During the French invasion of Italy by Charles VIII in 1494, even the pope, Alexander VI, held secret negotiations with the sultan and warned him of the French king's planned eastern campaign.[10]

In Venice itself, which had suffered most from the loss of its lucrative eastern colonies and markets to Ottoman incursions, certain powerful patricians advocated making peace with the Turk. A Milanese ambassador said that in addition to making peace, some Venetians wanted to give Mehmet an unencumbered path to Rome, in order to punish the priests. Although the republic supplied the essential fleet for a Christian Crusade against the Turks, Venice was in constant conflict with Rome over patriarchal appointments and the taxation of church property. After the Venetian government exacted a particularly onerous tax on church holdings owing to a recent Ottoman incursion, Cardinal Gonzaga and others in Rome questioned Venice's allegiance and suggested that the Serene Republic might actually have made a pact with the Turk in order to extort money from Rome.[11] A few days before the disastrous battle of Agnadello in 1509, when all the Italian powers and France and Spain joined forces to destroy Venice, the Serene Republic did actually ask the Turks for military support.[12] In 1468, however, Venice was in the middle of a devastating sixteen-year war with the Turks, with no prospect of an acceptable truce to save her eastern colonies.

Benedetto Dei, Ottoman Spy

To the envy of other Italian powers, Venice had grown rich and powerful from her colonies in the East, and Venetian merchants continued to prosper under the Ottomans as they had under the Byzantines— that is, until 1463, when a war started that was to last sixteen years. Given the power of the Venetian naval and merchant empire, war with the expanding Ottoman state was inevitable. Venice's rivalry with Florence, however, hastened the onset of hostilities. Florence and its port of Pisa had a strong commercial presence in the East, but Venice had been there longer and had far more extensive colonies and contacts. To gain the advantage over the hated Venetians, always lording it over the other Italian states, Florentine merchants were ready to do anything. Their chance came in 1460.

In that year at the Council of Mantua, Pope Pius II urged the Italian powers to unite and launch a Crusade against the Ottomans. Not long after Sultan Mehmet II learned, to his dismay, of the council and the probability that he would face a united Christian front, Florentine merchant galleys, laden with textiles and oil, sailed into the Golden Horn:

> Overjoyed by their arrival, the Grand Turk boarded one of the vessels, summoned their captains and the consul, and asked them to tell him the truth about what was going on in Italy. The Florentines told him everything, and in return he gave them and all Florentines full access to his lands. He said that they could carry arms night and day, and that they would be honored as the best friends he had. He gave them a church and allowed them to live as they pleased with crosses and all the ceremonies of their faith. The Florentines told the Grand Turk to fortify [various Greek cities], because the Venetians were planning to do battle in the Morea. They told him that Florence was an enemy of Venice and an ally of the duke of Milan, who was also an enemy of Venice. They told him not to worry about an attack from Italy, for they had influence with the pope, King Ferrante, and the duke of Milan; and they showed him how he could become lord of the Morea and all the Venetian holdings in the East.[13]

The spies sent by the sultan to investigate the Florentine reports confirmed the information, and Florentine merchants soon benefited from the promised privileges. Florence had become an informal ally of the Grand Turk.

Matters went downhill from there for the Venetians. A Florentine merchant and spy, Benedetto Dei, intercepted correspondence between Venice and its merchants in the East that contained explicit information about Venetian plans for a large-scale attack by land and sea against the sultan.[14] Mehmet took the letters to the Florentine consul, and asked and obtained his advice. When the Venetians realized what was going on, they protested to the Florentines—but it was too late. The sultan unleashed his wrath on the Venetian merchants. He had them arrested, tortured, and imprisoned, their merchandise confiscated, and their ports in Istanbul closed. Benedetto Dei took particular satisfaction in the torture of the hated Venetians.[15] In Florence Benedetto had been a member of the silk and wool guilds, but he was much more than a merchant. He worked as a kind of double agent supplying important information about Venice to the Turks, always with the aim of furthering Florentine interests.[16] During the antipapal rebellion of 1434, Benedetto had been a guest of the Medici bank in Rome. He held prominent military commands and traveled extensively on the Italian peninsula. In 1458 he left Florence and after wandering from Tunisia to Timbuktu, settled in Constantinople, where he worked for a Venetian cloth merchant for almost two years, perhaps to obtain inside information.

Benedetto regularly corresponded with the de facto ruler of Florence, Lorenzo de' Medici, and as far as possible promoted Florentine interests in the Ottoman Empire. Benedetto worked his way into the sultan's inner circle. It is unclear whether Lorenzo and the Florentine government explicitly charged him with carrying out some mission there, for the relevant documents are missing (perhaps because they were purged from the Florentine archives).[17] Be that as it may, from the day he proved himself by intercepting the letters and revealing Venice's plan of attack until his return to Italy in 1467, Benedetto had the ear of the sultan. He conversed with Mehmet, traveled with him, and accompanied him on military campaigns against the Christians. At one point earlier, a Venetian in Cyprus had tried to enlist him in a plot to poison the sultan, but Benedetto declined. Having always detested the Venetians and their arrogance, he rejoiced to see the Turks at war with them. It was because of the people of Venice that Mehmet had been able to take Constantinople in the first place: in 1453 "they could have easily defended the city, but they did not want to spend the money." Instead, "they were waging a war with the king of Naples to become lords of all Italy." Benedetto's hatred of Venice, as we have seen, went to such lengths that he boasted in an open letter to the Venetian government that the Florentines had showed the sultan the way to "become lord of the Morea and all the Venetian holdings in the East."[18] Venice, alone of the Italian powers, did battle against the Turks. Although Pius II had called on others to join the Crusade, none took up the invitation: Venice was powerful, and they saw much to be gained by the Venetians and the Ottomans' destroying each other. This was the argument that the Florentine ambassador made to Pius in 1463:

> Would you wage war against the Turks, so as to force Italy to be subject to the Venetians? You are helping them by aligning your arms with theirs against the Turks, and you do not see into what abyss you are hurling Italy. These are the dangers your wisdom must confront, not those lesser ones that we fear from the Turks. Let them fight it out between them. They are well matched in strength. I propose a more advantageous plan in telling you that not only the Turks who are threatening the lives of Christians, but the Venetians too, must be repulsed. You are wise enough, I think, not to despise or belittle the advice of the Florentines.[19]

The pope was shocked at the betrayal of the Florentines. Would they rather be enslaved to the Turks than subservient to the Venetians? The Turks, he said, were far more powerful than the Venetians, who would fail on their own. If Venice were destroyed, Italy would be lost. Only together could the Italian city-states defeat the Turk. Once defeated, the pope continued, the Ottoman lands would be evenly divided up among the crusading powers; Hungary would benefit the most, become powerful, and keep Venice in check. After the ambassador left to carry the pope's message to the Florentine Senate, Pius called the cardinals together and announced a new strategy. The only way he could convince others to lend their support to the cause, he reasoned, would be for him to lead the Crusade himself. Even after he had arrived in Ancona to await his armada, Pius received no support from Florence. The Florentines, he concluded, were "traders, and a sordid people who could not be persuaded to do anything noble."[20] With their rival out of favor and preoccupied with the war effort, however, Florentine merchants had a free hand in Constantinople.

The Florentine colony in Pera was a particular beneficiary of the Venetian problems with the Turks. In exchange for their new privileges and favors, Florentines provided the sultan with information about other Christian powers. Benedetto Dei wrote: "Whenever Florentine galleys entered the port in Istanbul they told the Grand Turk about Christian preparations against him and how he could defend himself against them. They promised that they would do all they could to dissolve the Christian league and ruin their plans. The hatred of the Venetians, and the hope of becoming sole masters of commerce in Ottoman lands, led them to such great wickedness. The Grand Turk therefore prepared for war against the Christians with the advice and planning of the Florentines." Elsewhere, Benedetto stated that Florentine spies "from 1460 to 1472 always shared intelligence with the Grand Turk."[21] The Florentines had thus gained the upper hand over other Italian merchant powers in the East, but at a price. After Mehmet conquered the Genoese colony of Lesbos and expelled its Gattilusi rulers in 1462, he invited his "kind friends" the Florentine merchants in Pera to help celebrate his victory. Three Florentine galleys, which happened to be in the harbor of Istanbul, joined the festivities. Mehmet's Grand Vizir had a new suit made and enjoyed great hospitality on the Florentines' tab. But other Italian "nations" in Istanbul were not so pleased: "The Venetians and Genoese were worried when they saw how much the Turk loved and trusted the Florentine nation and wished it well. The Grand Turk had begun to realize who the Florentines were, their power, their banks and mercantile houses."[22] When Ottoman forces took Bosnia in 1463, the sultan formally invited the Florentine consul and merchants of Pera to celebrate his victory and adorn the streets and houses with silk cloth and carpets.[23]

Bosnia lies just across the narrow Adriatic from Italy. From there it would not be hard for the Ottomans to harass and make inroads into Italy. It would have been a difficult victory had the Bosnian rulers not betrayed their country. First, the governor of the impregnable fortress of Bobovatz opened its doors to the Ottomans and gave up without a fight, only to be condemned to die by hanging from the castle's cliff—when he protested his fate, the sultan asked how he could trust a man who had already been a traitor. Then Tomashevich, the king of Bosnia, readily surrendered to save his own life. As part of the terms of his surrender, the king wrote letters to all his generals and commanders and ordered them to surrender. Over seventy obeyed, and Bosnia was taken with hardly any bloodshed. Next, Mehmet used a legal excuse to invalidate the terms of surrender promised by his lieutenant. Tomashevich was summoned before the sultan, possibly flayed alive, and then decapitated.[24] Benedetto Dei accompanied Mehmet on the Bosnian campaign and would have seen the sultan kill Tomashevich.

After his victory Mehmet looked across the Adriatic to Italy. He asked his Florentine friend about the cities of Italy: how they were governed, how rich and strong they were, what their relations were with one another, and which of them had seaports. Benedetto gave the sultan a detailed response and in conclusion asserted: "Considering their power on land and sea, the Italians would do much better than our ancestors. As you know from reading Leonardo Bruni's work on the first Punic War, which was translated for you, seven hundred thousand Asian and African soldiers invaded Italy, destroyed it, and left the Italians of central Italy for dead. But the Italians fought back and to this day have won great battles against Christians and non-Christians. Italy is stronger and more powerful today."[25] Benedetto's patriotic assertion is out of place, given that he had just given the sultan information necessary for a successful invasion. Leonardo Bruni was a humanist, chancellor of the Florentine republic, and best-selling author. The fact that Mehmet was given his history of the First Punic War and had it translated shows not only the Florentines' habit of exporting their culture for political gain but the sultan's great interest in ancient Roman history.

Mehmet delivered an ominous response to Benedetto about his plan to invade Italy:

> My Florentine friend, I understand what you have said about Italy, and if I believe correctly, as I have gathered information for many years, Italy could not today perform the wondrous deeds of her past, for the ancient Romans were so powerful because they alone ruled Italy. Today you are twenty states at war with one another. This I understand from the Venetian consul I have in prison, the Genoese, the Milanese, and the Florentines here. The four powers you mention battle among themselves, each taking the other's cities and lands. All these conflicts serve my plans. I am young, rich, and favored by fortune. I desire and intend to surpass by far Alexander, Cyrus, Hannibal, Scipio Africanus, Pyhrrus, and a thousand other rulers, for I am better prepared, better equipped, and richer than they were. Believe me, my Florentine, I will not lay down my arms before toppling the Venetians and destroying their empire in the Levant, because this is justly mine, just as I toppled the empire of Constantinople with blood, the sword, money, and time, and everything of the Venetians' that now belongs to me. Know for certain that I will show my power to the Venetians and anyone allied with them against me.[26]

The sultan says that he has been gathering information about Italy from the Italians in his realm for years. The secret of Mehmet's success lay in his ability to unite all the peoples in the lands he conquered and to induce them to be loyal to the Ottoman Empire. This had been a prerequisite for any empire, from that of Alexander of Macedon to the Roman Empire. Divided and constantly at war with one another, the

Italian powers would prove no match for the united war machine of the Ottoman Empire. Although schooled in Arabic, Persian, and Turkish and having little knowledge of European languages, Mehmet placed himself firmly within the European cultural tradition. Cyrus may have been the emperor of ancient Persia, but he was remembered because his life was recorded by Herodotus and Xenophon; Hannibal, though he came from Carthage in North Africa, achieved fame in the pages of the Roman historian Livy. Mehmet longed to surpass Alexander the Great in the reach of his empire.

After speaking his piece, the sultan turned and walked away. Benedetto, if we believe his account, could not resist, ran after him, and made a concluding patriotic declaration: "My Lord, may I remind you that Italy's coast is 1,750 miles long and full of well-fortified harbors and cities, fearless and ready for war. The Christian rulers of France, Spain, Germany, England, Portugal, Hungary, Scotland, and Cyprus are all powerful and related by marriage to Italian rulers. When you make war on Italy, all these Christians will move against you. If they have not helped the Venetians, it is because the four powers in Italy are enemies [of the city] and would like to see Venice toppled. But if you invaded Italy, believe me, they would all move against you."[27] Benedetto's patriotism may be explained by the fact that he composed his history after returning to Italy. Although he wrote for a Florentine audience, Benedetto nevertheless treads a thin line between being a traitor to Italy and being a patriot of Florence.

To celebrate his victory in Bosnia, Mehmet said that he personally wanted to enjoy banquets and festivities with the Florentines in his realm. Perhaps they had no choice, but the Florentines obeyed. They adorned their church with precious ornaments and set off fireworks from house to house. The sultan feasted at the house of two rich merchants, Carlo Martelli and Giovanni Capponi.[28] Bosnia was the last stop before Italy. The Florentine merchants of Constantinople had led the Turks to the threshold of their homeland. The sons of Florence could sincerely celebrate the humbling of Venice, but what would they do if Italy itself were to fall into Muslim hands?

The war with Venice dragged on. Florence continued to supply Mehmet with vital advice. In 1464 and again in 1466, Benedetto Dei and the Florentine consul showed the sultan more intercepted correspondence. Although written two years apart, the two letters carried the same message: Venice informed her merchants that with the help of the Venetian pope they were sending an armada to punish the Turks, attack the Florentines, and retake their possessions in the East. By November, the letter boasted, "Venetian priests [would] be saying Mass in Hagia Sofia." In 1464 the sultan sent eighty-three galleys to the Greek island of Lesbos to punish the Venetians. A battle ensued, and the Venetians lost. Benedetto gladly led the escort for the Venetian prisoners who had been captured and enslaved. In 1466, when Benedetto again intercepted Venetian correspondence, he went as Mehmet's personal ambassador to alert the Mamluks to the Venetian threat. Benedetto was not acting alone on these missions. He had the full backing of the Florentine consul in Constantinople, as is shown by the fact that Benedetto gave the Venetian letters he intercepted to the consul, who then sent them on to the sultan.

Benedetto names four other Florentines who advised the sultan and helped him in the Venetian war. One of them was Jacopo Tedaldi, who had escaped Constantinople in 1453 and who revealed the sultan's plan to attack Venice by means of a pontoon bridge from Marghera. Jacopo later returned to Constantinople in 1465 and became a close adviser of the sultan. In 1466 Mehmet showed the Venetian letters to these four Florentines, who assisted the sultan in the construction of a castle, and "he placed thirty large cannons on it as the Florentines had shown him."[29] But Benedetto (at least to his way of thinking) had a special relationship with the sultan. After Benedetto returned to Italy, his own correspondence fell into the hands of the Venetians in a well-played tit-for-tat. No vital information seems to have been lost, but in a letter to Lorenzo de' Medici Benedetto boasted that he would "return to the Grand Turk to avenge myself."[30] He openly talked to the de facto ruler of Florence about his personal relationship with Mehmet.

The events of the sixteen-year war between Venice and the Ottoman Empire reveal the complex relations and subterfuge that characterized Italian politics. No clear division existed between Christian and Muslim powers. In a world of interconnected economic and geographical interests, pragmatism trumped religion. Florence and other Italian powers readily and sometimes openly allied themselves with the infidels against fellow Christians. Venice's war with the Turks was also hardly ideological: the Ottomans were dismantling the eastern empire of the republic and the source of its wealth piece by piece. Spying and double-dealing marked not only the behavior of individual Florentines but the policy of Florence itself. Benedetto Dei and the Florentine consul in Constantinople used every means to win the sultan's favor and to gain an advantage for Florentine interests in the East, which would ultimately affect Florence's influence at home.

Ottoman Plans to Conquer Rome, and the Allure of Islam

A Persian astrologer read the sultan's horoscope before every military encounter. Portents and astrological signs promised him Italy, including Rome itself. They indicated that he had already "taken the daughter by force, Constantinople, now he could seize the mother [Rome]."[31] Rome, the seat of the papacy, was the ultimate prize to which Mehmet aspired. The Eternal City, according to an old Ottoman prophecy, was the "red apple," the "land of the infidels" that a "padishah of Turks," a sultan, was destined to conquer. All Christendom, especially the pope, lived in apprehension. A Hungarian ambassador had reported that the sultan's army was advancing to the battle cry of "Roma! Roma!"[32] In 1480 Mehmet closed in on his prize when he successfully landed an army, then sacked the southern Italian city of Otranto and occupied it for almost a year. Indeed, the sultan was obsessed with Rome.

Could the conspiracy of 1468 have been part of a much larger Ottoman plan to invade Italy and replace the pope in Rome? The sultan's immense wealth and power were legendary in Italy. Ottoman spies were everywhere. During the Venetian-Ottoman war Venice arrested at least thirteen men, mostly Italian, who on being tortured confessed to spying for the Ottomans and revealed the extent of Mehmet's vast espionage network in Italy.[33] They had run certain risks, but the sultan paid well. Were the humanists of the Roman Academy spies in league with the nefarious Turk?

All during 1467 and the beginning of 1468, Mehmet II waged war on Albania. He spent winters in the Balkan mountains. His cavalry controlled the countryside, if not the city of Croia, which held out during the summer campaign of 1467. Such proximity to Italy raised alarm. The Albanian hero Scanderbeg (1404–1468) fought ferociously to save his homeland. He had grown up as an Ottoman hostage in the court of Murad II, who had him instructed in the Muslim faith and gave him a title and a post in the army. But when he discovered that the Ottomans planned to invade his homeland, Scanderbeg escaped in 1443, abjured Islam, and united the Albanians against the Ottomans. Scanderbeg, having gained considerable financial backing from Italy, met with success. His native knowledge of the mountainous terrain and of guerrilla tactics kept the Ottomans at bay until his death in 1468. Venice and Naples had supplied him with troops and money for years, but the other Italian powers were wary of funding an ally of their enemy. Venice pleaded with the pope to send help to Scanderbeg: "We are writing to inform you about the grave news we have learned from Albania, where besides the horrible slaughter and cruelty he is daily inflicting on that province, destroying everything with fire and sword and savagely exterminating that people, the Turk himself with a most powerful army is intent on invading our lands and cities. He will first occupy the city of Durazzo, then secure for himself the road and crossing into Italy!"³⁴ Little came of its petition. Scanderbeg fought bravely, but the Ottomans were relentless. After his death on January 17, 1468, Albania crumbled.

Albania fell into Muslim hands just as the news of the conspiracy came out. On February 22, 1468, soon after Scanderbeg's death, Pope Paul II issued a bull in which, noting the "disastrous state of the times and the savage and enormous persistence of the Turks against the Christians," he pledged his financial and moral support for a Crusade.³⁵ At the same time the pope proclaimed peace among the Italian powers. Once they could stop bickering with one another, the Italians could unite against the sultan's forces. Negotiations had been under way throughout the previous year. Venice, Naples, Milan, and Florence had to work out the terms of peace within thirty days. Initially, the mercenary captain Bartolomeo Colleone was to be appointed general of the Christian troops, paid a hundred thousand florins, and sent to Albania to fight the Turks, but Milan and Naples refused to pay Colleone, for the mercenary had led the Venetian army in countless battles against Milan. With some revisions the peace was finally ratified on May 8. A feast day was proclaimed, and in Rome a solemn procession was to mark the occasion.³⁶ In a letter to the Florentines in praise of the peace, Paul wrote: "From the start of my pontificate, I have ardently striven for nothing other than to liberate Christendom from that most cruel beast and not only to restrain that most wicked enemy but to dash him to the ground."³⁷ The pope then followed the declaration of peace with the formal call for a Crusade. The peace of Italy was meant to reinforce the Peace of Lodi, which had been concluded in 1454 in response to the fall of Constantinople. Fourteen years later Italians had to be reminded who the real enemy was.

The ambassadorial accounts of the conspiracy to murder the pope report that the humanists were interested in Islam and suggest that they had formed or were planning to form an alliance with Mehmet II. The humanists, one ambassador reported, "said that Moses was a great deceiver of men with his teachings, Christ a seducer of peoples, and Mohammed, a man of great intellect."[38] The ambassador's assertion about the humanists' beliefs, however, is hardly evidence of conversion and indeed reads like a slur against the academicians. For one thing, the revelations of Moses and Jesus are cornerstones of the Koran. Most Christians viewed Islam not as a separate religion but as a heretical sect of Christianity. Dante had placed Muhammad and his disciple Ali among the sowers of discord in the eighth circle of Hell.[39] Centuries of violence between Christians and Muslims had created prejudice on both sides. In Christian Europe, the rhetoric demonizing Muslims began with the incessant calls for Crusades in the ninth century.[40] Nevertheless, Italian Christians regularly abjured their native faith and converted to Islam.[41] These renegades usually did so to escape poverty and the social inequality of Italy for a chance to rise to social and political prominence in the sultan's army or government, where merit was said to matter more than birth. A number of defectors from Christianity in fact held important positions. If such apostates were captured by Christians, however, special horrors awaited them. The suspected renegade Andreas of Chios, for example, being suspected of apostasy, was publicly tortured for ten days before he died on May 29, 1465.[42]

According to another ambassador, "these rebels [conspirators] sometimes said that they wanted to go find the 'Turk' and that one of them, who was in Venice, went to Venice because he wanted to go find the 'Turk.'"[43] After making these general statements about the humanists' desire to visit the Grand Turk, the ambassador singled out Pomponio Leto, the head of the Roman Academy. Pomponio had in fact more than once expressed interest in learning Arabic in order to study the sources of Islamic thought. Later in life, he wrote a laudatory life of the Prophet Muhammad as part of a history of the later Roman Empire. Among other accolades, Pomponio offers praise of Muhammad's "quick wit" and "affability and readiness" when the Prophet was a young man.[44] Pomponio left Rome for Venice in the summer of 1467. His professor's salary at the Sapienza, the University of Rome, had been suspended, and he had lived in poverty for over a year. It was this miserable existence, he said in his *Defense,* that drove him to say things against the Roman clergy that he later regretted. Pomponio admitted that after working in Venice he planned to go to Greece and Constantinople to study Greek and Arabic.[45] His desire to learn Arabic reflects the curiosity of a scholar rather than the zeal of a convert. Pomponio nevertheless had both an economic and an intellectual motive for allying himself with the Conqueror: he was desperate for patronage, and Mehmet would make a fine benefactor.

Sultan Mehmet II, Italian Culture, and Christianity

Crusading propaganda presented the Turks as being hostile to civilization and the world of letters.[46] This was far from true, however. The sultan, as was well known, was very interested in ancient history and the classical world, which the humanists also revered. He was said to speak at least five languages, including Turkish, Persian, Arabic, Greek, some Slavic language, and some Hebrew.[47] He had a Latin and a Greek tutor, who accompanied him during his preparations for the siege of Constantinople in 1453 and would read to him every day "the histories of Laertius, Herodotus, Livy, Quintus Curtius, the chronicles of the Popes, the Kings of France, and the Lombards."[48] Apart from their literary and narrative qualities, these works could have practical applications and revealed much about Mehmet's interests and his plans for conquest. The sultan modeled himself on the life of Alexander the Great, as told in Quintus Curtius' (ca. 41–54 CE) popular histories.[49]

Mehmet's enthusiasm for Italian art rivaled his interest in European history. In his youth, the sultan himself had produced figurative drawings of heads, animals, and stylized portraits, which betray the influence of European drawing techniques.[50] Mehmet's patronage of portraiture in particular was very un-Islamic, for most Islamic cultures prohibit the portrayal of people. After the war with Venice ended, the Venetian artist Gentile Bellini spent sixteen months in 1479–80 in the Topkapı Palace, where he painted portraits of the sultan and court officials, and decorated the walls of his Seraglio with erotic pictures.[51] Mehmet also had a passion for portrait medals and asked Italian rulers to send metalworkers to Istanbul. Ferrante, the king of Naples, sent Costanzo da Ferrara, and Venice sent Bartolommeo Bellano along with Bellini to the sultan. Mehmet's artistic eye is evident in his criticism of Bellano's work, which the Venetians tried to defend. An Italian art critic had already confirmed the sultan's opinion, however, when he judged the artist a "clumsy craftsman." By the end of his life Mehmet had established a fairly large workshop of Italian artists in Istanbul.[52] In addition to portraits, surprisingly enough, he appreciated artwork treating Christian themes. He was famed for employing skilled European craftsmen, including the metalworker from Transylvania who cast the massive cannon the sultan hoped would batter down the walls of Constantinople.[53]

It is possible that Mehmet's mother was Christian, for he also made efforts to learn about Christian theology and culture. He delighted in his collection of plundered Christian relics, which he used for barter with the rulers of Europe. Some even claimed that the sultan had secretly converted and had a special devotion for the relics. Although there is no reason to believe that Mehmet was in fact a Christian convert, surviving documents demonstrate that the sultan had a great interest in and even respect for the ideas and sacred objects of Christianity. He commissioned a painting of the Madonna from Gentile Bellini to adorn the palace collection, and reportedly flew into a rage when his librarian, Molla Lutfi, used the "stone from the nativity" (crêche) to reach a book from the top shelf. Gennadius, the Greek Orthodox patriarch, instructed Mehmet in Christian theology and even prepared a "profession of faith" for him. An early biographer called Mehmet "one of the most acute philosophers."[54] After conquering Trebizond in 1461, the sultan saved the Greek philosopher George Amiroutzes, made him a part of his household, and had frequent discussions with him about philosophy and theology. George afterward published a dialogue reproducing their conversations, which included topics such as the resurrection and the body-soul dichotomy.[55]

The rumors of Mehmet's covert Christianity led to various attempts to convert the sultan, such as the letter that Pope Pius II supposedly wrote in 1461 but never sent to Mehmet. In the letter the sultan is addressed as the "illustrious prince of the Turks" and told, "We [Christians] are hostile to your actions, not to you." Islam and Christianity, the letter says, share many points of faith, such as respect for Jesus and Mary. The document goes on, however, to argue for the superiority of Christianity: "Your religion promises rivers of milk, honey, and wine in the next world . . . plenty of wives and concubines, relations with virgins, angels to assist in these foul pursuits; in short, all that the flesh desires. This is the paradise of an ox or an ass, not of a man!" The letter also refers to the benefits the emperor Constantine gained from conversion. Pius probably did not write the letter. In one particularly problematic passage, the author discusses the sacrament of baptism: "A little thing can make you the greatest and most powerful and illustrious man of all who live today. . . . It is a little bit of water by which you may be baptized and brought to Christian rites and belief in the Gospel." The author seems to trivialize the holy sacrament of baptism and calls Mehmet "the greatest and most powerful" (albeit only if he converts). These are highly unlikely words from a pope who despised the Turks and was obsessed with crusading—in fact, Pius was announcing one at the same time the letter was written in 1461–62.[56] Whether or not Pius wrote the letter, its existence shows that the idea of converting the Turk was not out of the question.

A Greek refugee from the Ottoman advance, George of Trebizond, was an unlikely person to fall under the conqueror's spell. George was living in Rome and at one time was the tutor of Paul II before he became pope. While some interpreted the fall of Constantinople in 1453 as divine punishment for Christian sins, others, including George, saw it as a fulfillment of a prophecy. God, they reasoned, did nothing in vain. Mehmet's success and the rise of Islam corresponded to the reign of terror that prophetic scripture said would end when the last true Christian emperor vanquished the Turks. After that event, another period of upheaval would follow, with the arrival of the Antichrist and finally the end of the world. George interpreted the prophecy in a radically different way, one that dared to rewrite all the prophecies. What if the reign of terror could be shortened or avoided altogether? If Mehmet converted to Christianity, he could be the last true Christian emperor and bring peace and unity. In a treatise composed only a month after word of Constantinople's fall arrived, George exalted Mehmet the Conqueror as "king of all the earth and heaven," "king of kings," "supreme autocrat," and "the greatest emir." George asserted that Islam and Christianity could be reconciled, then presented elaborate arguments to prove the validity of the Trinity, Christ's incarnation, and the resurrection.[57] The two faiths could be reconciled—but only if Mehmet converted to Christianity!

In his 1457 *Comparison of Aristotle and Plato* George of Trebizond asserted that the Prophet Muhammad was a "second Plato," but "more sensible than the first one" because he corrected Plato's immoral teachings and "added practical rules of conduct." George continued: "Consequently, after the perverse philosophy of the first Plato enervated Byzantium from within, the devotees of the second more astute Plato conquered it from without."[58] Far from being hedonistic heretics, Muslims were intelligent and superior to the Orthodox Greeks, and should therefore be converted. God had sent Mehmet to destroy the Eastern Church and to unite all faiths in one Christian Church. Cardinal Bessarion, as discussed in Chapter 4, defended Plato against

George's attacks, but at that time there was little reaction to his views on Islam.

When Pietro Barbo became Pope Paul II in 1464, he showered favors on his old mentor, and George rose to prominence. Evidently without revealing the full extent of his ideas, George convinced the pope to send him to Constantinople to convert the sultan. He failed to gain an audience but on his return voyage wrote a work, which he dedicated to Mehmet, called *On the Eternal Glory of the Autocrat.* George asserts in the treatise: "In your victory, Mehmet, God transferred the kingdom to you in order to gather through you all the races into one faith and one church, and to exalt you as the autocrat of the whole world and king not merely of things perishable, but also of the very heavens." George moreover called Mehmet emperor of the Romans.[59] When the pope heard about the treatise, he assigned four cardinals to investigate its contents. George tried to explain his reference to the sultan as the ruler of the world as strategic flattery, but it was too late. By mid-October 1466 he was imprisoned in the Castel Sant'Angelo. Two letters, furthermore, were found in which George praised Mehmet in even more explicit terms. In November the Milanese ambassador reported that George "continues to praise the Turk, and to maintain that he will be the universal lord of the world."[60] After four months in prison George was released; his statements were found not treasonable, and the pope took pity on his former tutor.[61] Once released, George promptly wrote another treatise entitled *On the Divine Manuel, Shortly to Be King of the Whole World.* He refers to Mehmet as Manuel, a title used in the Old Testament to denote the chosen one: "Now you, Manuel, as a son of Ishmael and a descendant of Abraham, are the fulfillment of the prophecies. . . . You have come to unite all peoples, as David prophesied [Ps. 21:28]. . . . You will conquer Rome, which is the blind part of Israel, and will reunite all the people of God. You will rule, as Scripture states, from one end of the world to the other."[62] George was utterly convinced of his message. Prison and the sultan's refusal to see him had not changed a thing. The warden of the Castel Sant'Angelo, Rodrigo Sánchez de Arévalo, later tried to refute George's ideas in a book entitled, *On the Wicked Deeds and Misfortune of the Perfidious Turk*.[63] George was stubborn. He insisted that Mehmet was going to subdue Italy and conquer Rome: it was meant to be.

The sultan's interest in Italian culture has sometimes been seen as purely practical. Italian history provided useful information about a country Mehmet planned to invade. In this view, far from being a Renaissance man, the sultan had nothing in common with Italian princes except "his cruelty and the exploitation of those in his service."[64] This interpretation, however, is misleading. The "enlightened" Renaissance rulers of Italy, including Federico da Montefeltro and Sigismondo Malatesta, were primarily interested in classical literature for the same reasons that Mehmet was. They read ancient treatises on war, studied the famous battles, and sought to equal the deeds of Alexander the Great and Julius Caesar. The poets at their courts praised them above all for their military prowess. Ancient examples of famous men provided practical blueprints for achieving success in war and virtue in peace. Artists at Italian courts painted frescoes and designed weaponry, as incongruous as those combined endeavors may seem today. In any event, the sultan's interest in art and Christianity certainly went beyond the purely practical. On succeeding his father as sultan, Bayezid II promptly sold off Mehmet's prized relic collection and got rid of the painting of the Madonna that Mehmet had commissioned from Gentile Bellini.[65] The dialogues with George Amiroutzes also indicate that Mehmet took an interest in the finer points of theology. If the sultan was less interested in being a patron of literature, Italian humanists were not necessarily aware of this. Indeed, many tried to win his patronage. Mario Filelfo would not have composed his lengthy Latin epic poem on the deeds of Mehmet if he had not thought he might gain the sultan's patronage. Pomponio and the humanists of the

Roman Academy, poverty-stricken and desperate, might have similarly figured that they could secure a long-term patron in return for their role in the conspiracy.

The Turks and the Conspiracy of 1468

During the interrogation in 1468, Platina was asked under torture about the nature of his conversations with Sigismondo Malatesta when the latter was visiting Rome.[66] Although Sigismondo had recently been campaigning against the Turk, the mercenary captain and lord of Rimini had a reputation for treachery. Seven years earlier he had even tried to form an alliance with the sultan. Back in 1461 Sigismondo had been bested in a long territorial war with Pope Pius II. Even the tolerant humanist pope felt that Sigismondo's interest in pagan religion made him a heretic. Against papal interdict, he had carried the body of the scandalous pagan theologian Plethon from Greece to Italy and had deferentially placed it in a tomb on the side of his Malatesta Temple. Although it became a Christian church, the temple itself was full of zodiacal and pagan symbols. Its namesake was a notorious mercenary captain who had no problem switching sides to win a better price or a political advantage. Pope Pius' reasons for despising him so much were, however, purely political. Rimini was a part of the papal states and as such was supposed to pay an annual tribute to Rome. As lord of Rimini, Sigismondo was only the temporary protector of the pope's lands. Sigismondo, however, declaring himself sole ruler of Rimini, not only refused to pay the tribute but also took control of the surrounding cities and seemed intent on expanding even further. War was inevitable. As he had done before, the pope hired Federico da Montefeltro of Urbino and his mercenary army to reassert the papal interests.

Pius was so furious with Sigismondo that he performed a reverse canonization: "Sigismondo Malatesta has today been cursed. . . ."

Let him be enrolled as a citizen of hell. Sigismondo's crimes, unprecedented in our age, call for new and unprecedented procedure. No mortal heretofore has descended into hell with the ceremony of canonization. Sigismondo shall be the first to be deemed worthy of such honor. By order of the pope, he shall be enrolled in the company of hell as comrade of the devils and damned. Nor shall we wait for his death, if haply he may come to his senses, for he has left no hope of his conversion. While still living, he shall be condemned to Orcus, and perhaps while still living he shall be hurled into the flames."[67] Sigismondo's crimes, which were legion, included "robberies, arson, massacre, debauchery, adultery, incest, murders, sacrilege, betrayals, treason, and heresy."[68] Pius looked on him as the "prince of all wickedness."[69]

When the war was at its height, Sigismondo, desperate for allies, tried to form an alliance with the Ottoman sultan.[70] In addition to supplying him with essential geographical information for an invasion of Italy, Sigismondo sought to win Mehmet's support through his interest in Italian art. He sent the Riminese court artist Matteo de' Pasti to work at Mehmet's court.[71] The artist moreover carried with him two much more important gifts for the sultan, a treatise on the art of war and a detailed map of the coast of Italy. Mehmet himself had requested the map, which had obvious strategic importance. Roberto Valturio's manual on warfare was based on the ancient Roman treatise by Vegetius and as such would not have had much practical application to Renaissance warfare, but Mehmet believed that any historical or theoretical military information about Italy would be useful in planning the invasion. Valturio's treatise also contained colorful illustrations of siege engines, which would have appealed to and perhaps inspired the sultan, who was known for using elaborate and inventive mobile fortresses against walled cities and castles. In the dedication, Valturio calls Mehmet "the wondrous glory of the world's princes" and "most invincible." "In military matters," the Italian strategist continues, "you surpass not only all of our age but all the commanders and emperors of earlier times." Valturio compares the sultan to Alexander the Great in his love of art—just as Alexander had Apelles, Mehmet has Matteo de' Pasti."[72] The artist and the treatise, however, never reached Constantinople. The Venetians stopped Matteo on the island of Crete and discovered the map and the military treatise. They immediately understood what was going on, arrested the artist, and sent him to Venice to be tried for conspiring with the Turks. Matteo was found innocent and released. He was, after all, only a pawn in the operation. The episode started a rumor that Sigismondo had invited the sultan to Italy and offered to assist him in the invasion.

In the end, the sultan did not come, and Sigismondo lost the war with Pius II and the papacy. He paid tribute to Rome and was allowed to remain as lord of Rimini. Pope Paul, however, did not trust the mercenary general and insisted that Sigismondo remain in Rome under his hospitable but watchful eye. The lord of Rimini lived off and on in Rome from 1466 until his death in October 1468. When news broke about the conspiracy in 1468, Paul immediately suspected Sigismondo.[73] Could he in fact have been in league with the Ottomans? Platina insisted that when he and Sigismondo had met, they conversed about literature, arms, and the great minds of the past and present. A single meeting with the dark lord, however, was enough to support the suspicion of a larger conspiracy to kill the pope involving Sigismondo Malatesta and the sultan.

Platina was the least likely of the humanists implicated in the conspiracy to be in league with the Turks. Although he had lost his job when Paul reduced the number of abbreviators in 1464, Platina still enjoyed the patronage of Cardinal Gonzaga. He certainly had motives to join a conspiracy against the pope who had taken "his livelihood" away and transformed the papacy into an autocracy. Facilitating an Ottoman invasion of Italy would have been a different matter, though. In his dialogue *On the True and the False Good* (1464), Platina considered the sultan a "savage barbarian" and charged: "Every day [he] thinks up new kinds of tortures to satisfy his thirst for cruelty."[74] While in prison in 1468 Platina composed an *Oration against the Nefarious Turk,* in which he praised Paul's crusading zeal and insisted that the Conqueror had to be stopped at all costs. It was clearly in Platina's interest to praise Paul, but the oration is much more than an encomium. It is an argumentative piece meant to convince the pope of the necessity of a Crusade. The Turk, Platina wrote, had already overrun most of Greece, defiled churches, raped virgins, and destroyed everything in his path. Later, in his monumental *History of the Popes* (1475), Platina repeatedly refers to the Turks as a just punishment for church corruption and declares: "Believe me—and would that I were a false prophet—the Turk will come, a crueler enemy of Christianity than Diocletian and Maximian. He is already knocking at the gates of Italy! Lazy and half asleep, we await universal destruction, more concerned with our own private pleasure than with public utility."[75] Platina never said or did anything to justify the suspicion that he had any interest in Islam or any desire to help the Ottomans. He had nothing to gain from an alliance with the Turks. Callimachus, however, was another story.

The purported ringleader of the 1468 conspiracy, Callimachus, was a Tuscan by birth who had links to Florence. When he was warned of his impending arrest, Callimachus fled to southern Italy, where he enjoyed the protection of Ferrante of Aragon, the king of Naples. The pope had reason to suspect that Ferrante might have formed an alliance with Mehmet II. Soon after becoming pope in 1464, Paul had demanded large sums of money from the Italian powers for a Crusade against the Turks. While Venice, Florence, and Milan tried to negotiate papal concessions in exchange for the money, the king of Naples refused not only to contribute to the Crusade fund but also to pay his annual tribute to the pope. In his justification, Ferrante claimed that the sultan had offered him eighty thousand ducats to start a war in Italy. This was the exact amount that Paul wanted Ferrante to hand over for the Crusade. When further negotiations stalled, the king openly threatened to form an alliance with the Grand Turk. Paul did not budge but imperiously instructed the emissary: "Go tell your king that if he ever decides to ally with the Turk, we have made enough provisions to expel him from his kingdom and the Turk from Christendom."[76] Ferrante would later (1477–78) open the port of Naples to Ottoman ships for their offensive against Venice.[77] The king of Naples certainly used the possibility of an alliance with the Turks to browbeat other powers into granting political and economic concessions. He may also have considered such an alliance a way to gain a foothold in the lucrative eastern markets and obtain outside military support for security and expansion at home. As often happens today, political and economic advantages outweighed religious and cultural affinity.

In 1468 Ferrante helped Callimachus escape and despite the protests of the papal nuncios ensured his safe passage to Crete and Cyprus.[78] In the summer of 1469 Callimachus traveled to the island of Chios, which was a semi-independent colony of Genoa.[79] There, he became involved in a Florentine plot to deliver the island of Chios to the Turks. As an enormous Ottoman fleet of more than two hundred and fifty ships approached the island, however, the Chiots uncovered the plot when they intercepted damning letters that Callimachus had sent from the Florentine colony of Pera in Istanbul. The letters, directed to his accomplice Marc'Antonio Perusin, contained detailed instructions about the plot. Perusin was himself a former student of Pomponio Leto and a member of the Roman Academy. Callimachus had by this point arrived safely in Istanbul, where he would remain for several months. His accomplices were tortured and hanged.[80]

As a Tuscan, Callimachus could have been acting on behalf of Florence, much as Benedetto Dei did. Paul, of course, was Venetian, and Florence had a long-standing rivalry with the Serene Republic. His relations with his native city, however, were often less than amicable. Before he became pope, the Venetian Senate had seen Cardinal Barbo as an ally, but the cardinal made clear that his first allegiance was to the Church. In 1459 Pius II appointed Barbo to be bishop of Padua against the wishes of the Venetian Senate, which had reserved the place for a noble of higher rank. A heated battle ensued. Finally, over a year later, Barbo renounced his claim to the position and Pius chose a third candidate, to avert a total Venetian victory. After this, the Senate no longer regarded Barbo as an ally of Venice. In fact, Venetian ambassadors were given instructions not to speak with him at the Council of Mantua in 1460. In 1462 an envoy was similarly told to avoid him, for "[Cardinal Barbo had] always opposed our wishes."[81]

Relations improved, however, when Pietro Barbo was elected pope in 1464. There was great jubilation in Venice, and the Senate sent a large embassy to congratulate the new pope and swear the customary allegiance to him. Some worried that Paul's Venetian loyalties might damage the papacy. Cardinal Ammannati-Piccolomini immediately attacked Paul's first choice of a papal name, Mark II, as being an explicit avowal of allegiance to Venice. Indeed, although the new pope focused on the welfare of the Church as a whole, he started to show favor to his native city. After all, Venice was the strongest of the Italian powers. Because the republic was already at war with the Turks, it was the natural choice to lead a Crusade. When Paul declared the peace of Italy in 1468 and called for a Crusade, he put Bartolomeo Colleone, captain general of Venice, in charge of the Italian forces. Colleone had recently led a large army of Florentine exiles against Florence. Venice had supported the exiles, and the pope was also rumored to be favorable toward their effort.[82] In the same year, Venetian ambassadors acknowledged Paul as "our Venetian pope" before the sultan.[83] Even though they most likely did not have any direct involvement in the conspiracy, the people of Florence might well have welcomed a new pope, one less wholeheartedly supportive of Venetian interests.

The Chios plot also demonstrates that Callimachus was much more than the drunken, babbling fool that Pomponio and Platina present. His leadership role in it shows that he was politically savvy. With this in mind, it seems entirely possible and maybe even probable that Callimachus was in contact with Ottoman agents during his time in Rome. His anticlerical outbursts and threats against the pope might have developed into an organized conspiracy, had there been time.

All the direct and indirect evidence makes an Ottoman connection to the conspiracy highly likely. Nevertheless, it would be hard to argue that the humanists of the Roman Academy as an organized group had cemented an alliance with the sultan. Nothing but scorn for Turks is evident in Platina's writings, and we have no reason to believe that he would have converted to Islam or even contemplated killing the pope and helping the Muslim invasion of Italy. He had solid patrons in Rome, including Cardinals Gonzaga and Bessarion, and was financially solvent, as we have seen. Whether or not Sigismondo Malatesta was still in contact with the sultan, Platina would never have considered betraying his faith—he would of course go on to write a best-selling history of the popes! Pomponio's situation was more desperate, but if anything he was attracted to ancient Roman paganism, not Islam. His financial problems had been somewhat alleviated by the remuneration he received for his tutoring work in Venice. Callimachus is the only one of the three who would have trafficked with the Ottomans. Even his connection to them was probably through Florence, which was informally in league with the sultan. Still, the Chios plot and the fact that Callimachus escaped to Constantinople and resided there for months after the conspiracy suggest that at least one of the humanists did want to betray the pope to gain the sultan's favor.

When the humanists were arrested, the papal authorities genuinely feared that the conspirators were aligned with the Turks. As we have seen, this was not such an outlandish accusation: many Italians, rulers and private citizens, made alliances with the Turks against their own fellow Christians or even renounced their faith and converted to Islam, with the aim of rising to positions of importance as apostates in the Ottoman Empire. In a world where the determining factor in diplomacy was not religion or culture but political expediency, Mehmet —much like Pope Paul II, who so strongly opposed him—was feared, but he was also admired by Muslims and Christians as a powerful ruler and potential patron.

CHAPTER SIX

The Emperor's Tomb

I have not seen a better-protected or more appropriate fortress for papal dignity than this one. Although far different from the original intention of Hadrian, it is suitably positioned both for repelling external attacks and for compelling citizens to perform their duties. He wanted the structure to preserve his ashes and bones, not to become a prison and house of correction for the living. As their faces and unkempt beards show, these are prisoners, and among them is our Platina.

—Marcus in Platina's dialogue

THE CASTEL SANT'ANGELO had been the mausoleum of the Roman Emperor Hadrian (117–138 CE). It was a fitting place for the pope's dark and gloomy dungeon, in which unfortunate inmates were essentially entombed. The humanists were tortured there, then locked away for over a year in cold, damp cells to ponder how they might have offended the pontiff. The tearing of their ligaments and crunching of bones from the raising and dropping of the ropes in the torture chamber might have ended, but then another form of pain began. This was a long-term kind of suffering, caused by the physical and psychological hardships of premodern incarceration.

The Castel Sant'Angelo was the medieval Italian equivalent of the Bastille. To gain some idea about what the humanists had to endure while they languished there, it is helpful to have an overview of the history of the dungeon, and to consider the experience of a few of the many other inmates who underwent torture and incarceration in Hadrian's Mausoleum. In 1379 the Romans had tried to destroy this symbol of papal tyranny. French mercenaries had set up cannons and over the course of a year leveled all the surrounding buildings and killed countless Romans. The French antipope Clement VII (1378–1394) was trying to force his rule on the unwilling inhabitants, who had chosen to back an Italian pope, Urban VI (1378–1389). When Italian mercenaries prevailed over the French forces in the epic battle of Marino, Clement had to flee the city, and his mercenaries surrendered the fortress. Urban wanted to keep it for himself, but the Romans would not allow it. In a frenzy of destruction they rushed at the mausoleum and destroyed everything they could. All the marble they removed and used to pave roads or repair private homes. Only the foundation remained, but it was enough to enable subsequent popes to rebuild a papal stronghold on the ruins.[1] In the 1450s, when Pope Nicholas V moved his residence to the Vatican from the Lateran Palace, he used the imposing structure of the Castel Sant'Angelo as a base of power in the neighborhood and the city.

Porcellio: A Bad Poet Responds to Torture

After the rebellion of 1434 was suppressed, Eugene had the ringleaders hunted down and quartered. The severed limbs were hung up on the four principal gates of the city as a warning to all. More than two hundred accomplices were arrested and put on trial for high treason; they were all condemned to prison or the scaffold. As we have seen, one of those was the humanist Porcellio, who was tortured and thrown into the Castel Sant'Angelo. In numerous poems from prison Porcellio described his wretched living conditions, bewailed his sufferings, and pleaded for mercy:

> Phlegethon of Tartarus is my abode. I am oppressed beneath a black, sunless mound in a disgusting cave. Mice and feral cats wage bizarre battles here; beetles and a company of centipedes flee the place; unknown monsters and wild beasts feed on my banquet scraps and drink my rancid wine. In my wretched state, I have no fine linen coverlets; only the earth offers me a soft bed; I have a heavy, grimy beard, my hair hangs down my forehead in long strands, and six-legged fleas bore into

The Castel Sant'Angelo (author photo). Formerly Emperor Hadrian's Mausoleum, converted in the Middle Ages into a papal fortress and dungeon.

my legs and head. My eyes are utterly denied sweet sleep; anxiety presses my bones into the ground. . . . A composite stench emanates from this dark prison. My shinbones bear tough calluses from the chains; everything is the latest cause of my death.[2]

If they were not so heartrending, Porcellio's poems would seem laughable in their overblown classicism. Porcellio begged for mercy and a release from his torments. At one point he complains about his loose verse, saying "my Muse, summoned by my tears, has fled from them." He calls on his son Lorenzo to plead his cause: "Do not be ashamed: tell them that I am free of fault or crime. A large cell holds your father, though he has done no wrong; a large cell holds your father bound in chains." Porcellio next writes to Giovanni Mileto, the man who accompanied Eugene on his chaotic escape from Rome. The poet falls into despair: "Why was I born so unfortunate in my native city? . . . What is the reason for my sadness? Why am I so distraught, I who usually praise distinguished men to the skies? Why am I bound in chains in a dark prison? Tell me what I did, why I bear these fetters, why the earth is my bed, when I have committed no crime, and I alone am trustworthy, without deceit? If I confessed to wickedness, if I am guilty, take my body, and apply torture to this blighted body. But may a three-forked thunderbolt rend my heart rather than that my descendants should read that I was dishonorable."[3] Here, Porcellio alludes to his role as a flattering courtier as if it were a guarantee of his virtue. He appealed to anyone he could for his freedom. His only weapon was the poems in which he described his miserable state, in the hope of eliciting pity. "Go swift winds," he writes, "carry my poems, tell them that I am blameless but bound by vile chains."

These supplications in verse finally paid off, and Porcellio was released from prison. His sentence was commuted to exile. Far from his family and from Rome, though, he remained unhappy, and doleful poems again began to flow from his pen: "Poverty and gnawing worry for my family still the multitude of things whereof my genius should sing. The rage and savage wrath of God have exiled me, and they terrorize an innocent man; for many years already I've been torn from the embrace of my wife; I am old now, and she is aged too."[4] Again, Porcellio offers his services as a court humanist and panegyrist and simultaneously laments his personal travails. Pope Eugene, nevertheless, did not relent. Porcellio's torture, imprisonment, and exile demonstrate that even an inept humanist courtier could be taken seriously and seen as a threat to papal power. Pope Eugene IV reportedly reformed the prisons in Rome, but in 1468 the humanists still suffered under the same conditions that Porcellio deplores in his plaintive poems.

Fifteenth-century prison cell in the Castel Sant'Angelo (author photo). "Six-legged fleas bore into my legs and head. . . . A composite stench emanates from this dark prison" (Porcellio, 1434).

Benvenuto Cellini

One of the most detailed accounts of conditions in the Castel Sant'Angelo during the Renaissance derives from the boastful autobiography of the artist Benvenuto Cellini. The irony of the situation is that only a few years before his incarceration, Benvenuto had heroically defended the fortress. During the sack of Rome in 1527, when Pope Clement VII (1523–1534)—not the same Clement as the earlier antipope of that name—lived for a month within its walls, Benvenuto set up a cannon on the roof of the Castel Sant'Angelo, and in his own words not a day passed without his killing one or more of the enemy or "performing some extraordinary feat." On one occasion, he boasted, he had killed thirty men with only one cannonball. Another time he demonstrated his marksmanship by killing the Prince of Orange as he rode past on a donkey. The pope blessed Benvenuto and forgave him the sin of homicide. The artist was also pardoned for the murders he had committed before entering the pope's service.

As the weeks passed, prospects looked bleak. Supplies of food and fresh water in the castle were dwindling, and the enemy's ranks were swelling. A wall running from Saint Peter's to the castle enclosed a covered walkway. Pope Clement VII had run down the passageway with a couple of bishops, who held up his gown and tried to block shots fired at the windows along the way. He survived for one month inside the castle, while mercenaries mercilessly plundered the treasure of the city, raped nuns, and tortured Romans. In an act of desperation, Pope Clement determined to have the jewels removed from his golden tiara and from other precious objects. He asked Benvenuto to sew them into the lining of the pope's clothes and later to melt down the gold, which weighed two hundred pounds. His confidant, who was an accomplished goldsmith, did as he was bidden. Soon thereafter, the pope surrendered, and a peaceful settlement was reached.[5]

A few years later, in 1539, Benvenuto was back in the Castel Sant'Angelo, this time as an inmate. There was a new pope, Paul III (1534–1549), whose son Pier Luigi did not care for Benvenuto. The goldsmith was accused of stealing some of those very jewels that he had so expertly sewn into the pope's garments during the sack of Rome. The warden of the fortress also hailed from Florence, and initially Benvenuto charmed him, to the point that the warden granted his prisoner the run of the castle, and the freedom to exercise his goldsmith's craft. Once he had the necessary materials, Benvenuto worked contentedly away. It soon became clear, however, that the warden was mentally unbalanced. He was manic, and he talked nonstop. Once he thought he was dead and ordered the guards to bury him. Another time he thought he was an oil jar. Then he became a frog and hopped around on all fours. On yet another occasion, imagining that he was a bat, the warden stood on the balcony emitting shrill screams and flapping his arms in an effort to fly. Finally, having become obsessively convinced that Benvenuto was trying to escape from the dungeon, he took away most of his privileges and confined him to his cell.

Matters were bound to deteriorate, Benvenuto felt, and he resolved to make his escape (thereby establishing real grounds for the warden's delusional apprehension). Guards checked his cell daily, but Benvenuto devised a way out. He slowly pried the nails from the hinges on his door and filled the holes with rust-colored dirt. In the meantime, he requested swaths of fabric for his work and wove a rope out of them. When all was ready, in the middle of the night he pulled the last nails out and shoved open the door to his cell. Once outside, he headed for the latrines, where he knew he could just manage to squeeze through a small window that looked out onto the tile roof. He attached the rope and lowered himself down. With two other walls remaining to scale, though, Benvenuto was running out of fabric rope. Fortunately, he found a pole ready to hand, which he used to climb the last battlement. On his descent on the other side, however, he fell and knocked himself out. When he came to, his leg was broken, his hands bleeding, and his head pounding, and the sun was beating down on him. Benvenuto had to crawl the rest of the way to freedom, by way of the little gate that led out into the city. He had escaped—only to encounter a pack of dogs on the other side of the wall. He slashed one with a makeshift knife and, somewhat mangled, continued his crawl. At that point a servant of Cardinal Cornaro, one of Benvenuto's patrons, recognized the poor artist and led him back to his master's house. The cardinal, once he had called a surgeon, entreated the pope to release the hapless goldsmith.[6]

The pope did acquiesce, but Benvenuto's troubles were far from over. Pope Paul, at the insistence of his son, soon had Benvenuto returned to the Castel Sant'Angelo, where he was to enjoy a pleasant room with access to a garden and sufficient food. All this, the pope claimed, was to help the artist recuperate from his broken leg. Benvenuto was suspicious. For fear of being poisoned, he refused to eat the food the pope had provided. In the middle of the night the guards came to transport the artist to an underground cell reserved for prisoners who had been condemned to death. Never one to be humble, Benvenuto proclaimed his innocence and compared himself to Christ, in that they had both been condemned to an unjust death. [7]

The warden, on seeing the artist returned to his care, gloated: "You see that I have recaptured you!" Benvenuto couldn't help pointing out that he had nevertheless escaped, as he had boasted he would. The warden, enraged, ordered him to be thrown into the darkest, dankest cell at the bottom of the Castel Sant'Angelo. At those depths, Benvenuto Cellini had to contend with swampy water, poisonous snakes, and giant spiders. His mattress of coarse hemp soon became soaked "like a sponge." His leg was still broken, and he could barely move from the mattress. When he had to relieve himself, he was forced to crawl to a corner of the cell to avoid befouling his mattress. A small opening let in sunlight for only an hour and a half each day. He used this scant daylight to read an Italian Bible. All that was left to him for the rest of the day was to meditate on his sad life and take temporary solace in sleep.

Benvenuto slipped into a depression so deep that he decided to end it all. Having nothing sharp in the cell with which to cut his wrists, he contrived to place a heavy piece of wood on a high ledge in such a way that it would fall and smash his skull. He reached up to topple the weight, but at that moment something pushed him with such force, he claimed, that he flew across the room. There, in terror, he "lay half dead." The next morning the guards came in to check on him. Convinced that he was dead, they sent for a priest to perform the last rites. Benvenuto believed that his life had been preserved thanks to divine intervention: his guardian angel had saved him. The following night he received verification when "a marvelous being in the form of a most lovely youth" appeared to him in a dream and chastised him for attempting suicide. On awakening, Benvenuto knew that he had to record the miracle in writing, yet he had no writing materials. He crawled to the door of his cell and with a convert's zeal gnawed a splinter off the door to serve as a pen, made a paste of crumbling brick in lieu of ink, and composed a short dialogue on the pages of his Bible. In it his soul urges his body to trust in God and not lose hope. From that point on, his faith in God restored, Benvenuto spent his time in joyful prayer. "There flowed into my soul so powerful a delight . . . that I took no further thought of the anguish I had suffered."

The physical hardships, however, did not abate. Benvenuto's nails grew so long that they curled, causing him great pain when they snagged on his clothes. His teeth abscessed; he pulled each one out "as though it were a weapon from a scabbard." But prayer and writing eased his mind. Benvenuto found a piece of charcoal and on the wall sketched a picture of God the father surrounded by his angels and Christ triumphant. The prisoner was convinced that angels had mended his broken leg; it was stronger than before. More than anything, though, Benvenuto longed to see the sun. He pleaded with God and vowed to make a pilgrimage to the Holy Land if his wish were granted. All of a sudden he felt himself transported to a large room. A "young man whose beard was just growing in, with a face of indescribable beauty," appeared and beckoned him to follow. He saw thousands of people walking through a great hall. The divine being led him through a small door and down a narrow street, where it allowed him to behold the bright splendor of the sun. Benvenuto begged the spirit to let him approach it; giant stairs appeared. Slowly he ascended. It hurt his eyes to look but he forced himself to contemplate the burning golden sphere of the sun. A feeling of ecstasy overcame him. The middle of the sun swelled up, and "suddenly a Christ upon the cross formed out of the same substance as the sun." The center of the sun became swollen again and "suddenly transformed itself into the shape of a most beautiful Madonna," with a child in her arms and a beautiful angel on either side. When the vision ended, Benvenuto was convinced that the divine figure was Saint Peter, intervening on his behalf. After experiencing the vision, the captive felt that nothing on earth could hurt him.

Distracted by this restoration of faith, Benvenuto gobbled down his morning meal, barely noticing the extra crunch and perhaps thinking that the salad had not been thoroughly washed. After the meal he noticed something sparkling on a stray leaf. On looking more closely, he determined that it must be fragments of crushed diamond. Diamond is the hardest rock in the world. When it is ground up, the dust becomes an ideal murder weapon. The tiny jagged particles, when sprinkled on food, tear up the lining of the stomach and bowels, so that the victim gradually dies a bloody and excruciatingly painful death. This was the manner in which the enemies of Benvenuto had poisoned him, and a painful death lay in store. All seemed lost; he pleaded for God to send him a merciful death. Yet one last test remained. He attempted to crush the particles, and to his relief they crumbled. The perpetrators' greed had saved him. The jeweler, Benvenuto believed, must have kept the diamond he received and instead ground up a much cheaper stone to supply the deadly condiment, in hopes that it would yield the same result. From then on, Benvenuto insisted that his food be tasted by a guard in his presence.

Once a week Pope Paul III overindulged in wine. He routinely drank to excess and then vomited. Benvenuto's patron the Cardinal of Ferrara, who had been invited to a private dinner with the pope, knew of his habit. The two ate well, and the cardinal plied his host with glass after glass of wine. As the laughter and conversation grew louder, the pope became tipsy, then visibly drunk. The cardinal seized the chance to ask the pontiff for the release of Benvenuto Cellini. The pope laughed, then suddenly stood up to vomit, swayed back and forth, and told the cardinal he could liberate the artist right then and there. The cardinal, who, one imagines, must have been somewhat more abstemious, immediately sent his servants to retrieve Benvenuto and escort him to the palace. At last the artist was free. He would, however, never be the same again.

Benvenuto believed that God was on his side. God, who had forgiven him for the murders that he had committed, knew that he was innocent and had been unjustly imprisoned. He enjoyed this divine favor for the rest of his life. In fact, Benvenuto tells us, ever after his miraculous vision in prison, a glorious halo could be seen resting on his head. He pointed it out to friends, who admired it. The best times to view the halo were during the first two hours after sunrise and at twilight. It was also more visible in Paris than in Italian cities, which tend to be foggier.[8]

Benvenuto Cellini turned his experience in the Castel Sant'Angelo into a story of personal triumph. As a heroic defender of the castle keep, he had saved one pope, only to be imprisoned in the same castle by the next. He managed to do what no other inmate had ever done and none would manage to do in the future: he escaped. The humanists accused of conspiracy in 1468 experienced the papal dungeon much differently. They had no miraculous visions or dramatic religious revelations to save them from the depths of despair. They did, however, have the sympathy of a learned warden who wrote them letters of consolation.

Platina's First Imprisonment (October 1464 to February 1465)

Few popes had had such a staunch defender and champion of the papacy as Paul II had in Rodrigo Sánchez de Arévalo. The Spanish bishop and warden of the Castel Sant'Angelo wrote treatises against heretics who attacked the wealth of the papacy and against reformers who argued for the superior authority of church councils over the pope. As we saw in Chapter 5, Rodrigo composed *On the Wicked Deeds and Misfortune of the Perfidious Turk* in response to George of Trebizond's praise for Sultan Mehmet II. Only the pope, the loyal warden argued, could bestow imperial dignity and had the power to depose kings. Although most of the warden's writings were aimed at a learned audience, Rodrigo also wrote a best-selling self-help book to assist young men in choosing the vocation best suited to their particular talents and dispositions. This career advice treatise was one of the first books printed in Rome, and between 1468 and 1683 thirty editions appeared in four languages.[9] As warden of the papal dungeon, Rodrigo showed the same generosity with his advice in dealing with the lost souls in his care.

Platina, during his first imprisonment in the Castel Sant'Angelo, in the winter of 1465, became quite close to Rodrigo. Indeed, Platina was sufficiently grateful to the kind warden to make Rodrigo the principal interlocutor in the dialogue *On the True and the False Good.* Although Platina complained about the harsh conditions in prison and the wailing of other prisoners, he was at least allowed to have writing materials and in fact was able to write the first draft of that dialogue during his stay. (He later revised it and presented it to Pope Sixtus IV in 1471.[10]) That first imprisonment caused Pope Paul II to regard Platina with all the more suspicion in 1468 (see Chapter 2).

The dialogue was one of the most popular literary genres during the Renaissance.[11] Plato, Cicero, and Tacitus, among other ancient writers, wrote dialogues that served as models for the humanists' efforts. The form could reproduce actual conversations and convey an easy atmosphere of discussion and debate. Dialogue also had the advantage of protecting the unorthodox views of an author, because he could always put the views expressed into the mouth of one of the other interlocutors. Lorenzo Valla and Erasmus both relied on this defense when critics questioned the orthodoxy of their works.[12] The dialogue Platina wrote in prison is supposed to reflect conversations that he had with the warden and visitors who tried to console the humanist. The first of the three parts is a discussion between Rodrigo and Platina on the highest good and philosophical truth. Platina tries to reconcile pagan philosophy, especially Stoicism and Epicureanism, with Christianity. In the preface Platina assures the pope that Christianity is the only true philosophy but then argues for the utility of pagan philosophy:

> If we examine and imitate the life and teachings of Christ, there is no need to look to Numa Pompilius' religion, Scipio's piety and modesty, Cato's courage, . . . the wisdom of Socrates, and the clemency of Caesar. Nevertheless, lest anything be lacking for a good and holy life, we should retrieve ancient philosophy and use it as a remedy, as far as possible, to cure the ills of our minds. If philosophers have debated in a variety of ways the principal good and ill, then much that is pertinent to us can be gained from their writings. There is no reason to fear that in reading and studying them we might slip into error, because the doctors of our religion have already separated the good from the bad, like the wheat from the chaff, in the sieve of wisdom.

Platina's argument in the preface is somewhat flawed, however, for if Augustine, Jerome, and the other doctors of the Church had already found all that was good in the ancients, one could surely read just the church fathers and not the pagans. The work loosely reflects the influence of Boethius' *Consolation of Philosophy* (525 CE) and poses the question, Can ancient philosophy provide therapy and consolation in the desperate circumstances of incarceration? The context sets the scene. The kind warden tries to console Platina, who is miserable in prison. Rodrigo upbraids the humanist for not bearing his misfortune with greater dignity: "Think about how many men have suffered greater disasters than you have in life. . . . How many kings and princes today are enslaved in chains and endure the most extreme conditions in prison? The Turk, who in our own time puts Christians to the sword and flame, has thrown many worthy men into fetters. I am not going to mention the new kinds of tortures and punishments which that savage barbarian thinks up every day to satisfy his thirst for cruelty. How many men are held right here in Italy in more squalid and fetid dungeons than yours? I will not speak about the harshness, strictness, and cruelty of their guards. The place where you are so well housed does not at all resemble a dungeon." Platina rejects Rodrigo's first attempt at consolation: "All these examples of men who have suffered as much as I, or more, provide little consolation and in fact do the opposite. For bitterness is banished not through bitterness, but through sweetness." This line of argument foreshadows the Aristotelian ethical teaching in the dialogue, which states that vices need to be corrected by their opposite virtues. Rodrigo now changes tack slightly and tries to console Platina with the idea that literature and the exemplary lives of ancient heroes inspire imitation and promote virtue. Alexander the Great read Homer on campaigns and used the example of Achilles to exhort his men in battle. Cato inspires a strong sense of moral duty, and Scipio Africanus modesty. Rather than feel sorry for himself, Platina should be encouraged by the heroes of the past: "When we were boys in school I remember how our spirits burned for glory on our hearing how one bore the death of his sons with constancy, another bravely put himself in harm's way for the republic's sake, and another for the sake of honor patiently endured incarceration, chains, and torture. Nor should secular literature be preferred over sacred texts, since nothing better can be found for a good and holy life. The same holds for study as for eating: just as we are delighted by a variety of foods, so although the most refined nourishment about life and God comes from reading sacred texts, I would not refuse a second course of pagan literature to refresh my spirits."[13] A smorgasbord of pagan and Christian learning should offer all the consolation necessary for a wise man in distress. The food metaphor was particularly apt, given that Platina had published a cookbook and was known for his enjoyment of food.

Platina answers Rodrigo with fulsome praise for his persuasive argument. The shrewd warden detects the sarcasm and presses him for a more thoughtful response. But Platina interrupts the discourse with complaints and requests: "I am unable to listen attentively to your advice, for the screaming of the other prisoners and the excruciating pain from these chains are very distracting. Please order the prisoners to keep quiet and give me some hope that I'll be freed of these chains soon." Rodrigo retorts: "You are too soft and delicate, Platina, to be undone by such troubles! But I see that you need that medicine which good doctors use for more serious illnesses."[14] The prescription is philosophical virtue.

Just as medicine, Rodrigo says, heals by countering the illness with its opposite, so do virtues combat their corresponding vices—for example, trust should be applied against fraud, courage against cowardice, honor against shame, and wisdom against ignorance. Rodrigo explains the Aristotelian habits of virtue, whereby the soul and body learn virtue by repeated practice: "A mind thus instructed bravely overcomes the weapons of ignorance and all vices . . . for virtue alone and of itself, according to the Stoics, suffices for a happy life. When one has gained virtue, he lacks nothing for the highest happiness." Platina then offers a section of Aristotle's *Nicomachean Ethics* that was a favorite of the humanists: "Wealth is necessary to practicing the virtues of magnificence and generosity." Rodrigo concedes but makes an important distinction: "I agree with them, if you look at civil happiness. But we were talking about the perfect wise man, whose entire happiness rests in contemplation."[15] Rodrigo's ideal wise man is a contemplative detached from society.

Platina emphasizes a very different conception of wisdom, one that is rooted in real life: "What? Will this wise man not eat, and will he lack clothes and shelter from cold and heat?" Rodrigo answers that the wise man is content with little. He is, then, Platina says, "no different from a beggar." The discussion continues along these lines until

Platina observes that he finds it hard to "study and think, when [he is] overwhelmed by poverty." Rodrigo's response is a direct borrowing from ancient Stoic and Epicurean philosophy:

> This is the sign of a sick mind and a virtue that has not been purged enough with the antidote. You lack for nothing if you use the gifts nature has given you. Nature made you naked, and God put a soul and mind into your little body so that you could procure everything for virtue. Coming into the light, you were first content with milk, then bread. This life we enjoy is short and like a dream, and we must die in the end and return what was given us. We must not fear what cannot be avoided; so it is foolish to fear death or old age. It is not death but the thought of death that we fear. Pain is easily dismissed, if we learn to die well. Philosophers die well. All philosophy, as Cicero says, is a meditation on death. If you look at the beginning, middle, and end of life, why would you despise poverty and seek wealth? To buy your way into the afterlife? He is no pauper whose needs are few and who is content with little.[16]

For ancient Stoics and Epicureans poverty was meaningless, because the wise man needs little. Nature supplies everything. Epictetus, Seneca, and other Stoics stressed that our life is not our own, and that death is merely the returning of something borrowed. Once we accept this idea, death is nothing. Philosophy teaches us how to die well.

Platina shifts the topic and complains about the hardship that troubles him most in prison: the loss of his freedom, which he defines as the power to come and go as he wishes. On the contrary, Rodrigo says, that is servitude: "Do people not go to commit rapes, robberies, and other crimes? Would that the human race were bound in chains and shackles!" Rodrigo then goes on to say: "Human nature is inclined toward evil, and it chooses to do good only with divine help. We should therefore be forcibly deterred from evil by means of punishments, for otherwise we would all be worse off in freedom. True freedom is holy and upright living—helping others and hurting no one. Whoever acts in this way cannot be called a slave or a prisoner, even if he is held in the gloomiest prison and in heavy chains."[17] This is a fundamental difference between ancient Stoicism, according to which virtue is attained by taking nature as one's guide, and Christianity, according to which man and nature are both flawed by the fall, and true virtue can be achieved only through God's grace. Man is corrupt and unless restrained will naturally do evil. Nevertheless, Rodrigo advocates a positive version of liberty: freedom is not lack of restraint but the ability to act in society and politics.[18]

Platina finds his argument in Rodrigo's social definition of liberty. He complains of loneliness and of missing his friends: "I enjoyed their company: we talked about pleasing and useful things, especially on subjects that each of us had read, heard, or gleaned for the common good, in order to find the truth." Friendship is not just a pleasure, it is a social duty: "The older and more accomplished should respect and love their equals and advise and assist their inferiors in whatever ways they can, which cannot be undertaken except by a free man."[19] The wise humanist finds truth and virtue not in solitary contemplation but in society.

The theme of liberty and social action continues in Book 2, where a different interlocutor, the Greek refugee and scholar Theodore Gaza, tries to console the humanist. Platina laments that his parents encouraged him to study the liberal arts. He says that it is harder for the learned to bear mental and physical pain than for the ignorant: "Farmers and workers are not ambitious. They care little about the future but make use of whatever is at hand. They have healthy bodies from hunting and physical work. But we scholars have willingly brought miseries and disasters upon ourselves. We have been so weakened by leisure and sleep that every fifth day we have to take medications for melancholy and other imbalances. We often work with cataracts, stomach and back pain, and gout, all ailments of too much leisure, for the body is not able to rid itself of extra fluids through physical exercise. We are thus unable to offer any help to our cities and families."[20] The scholar's life is already miserable; captivity and the loss of freedom make it intolerable. Platina's concluding sentence here sums up the greatest privation imposed on a humanist in prison: the inability to fulfill the goal of life: the attainment of knowledge, which is social and useful.

Theodore Gaza returns to the Stoic idea that to be content, the wise man requires only virtue and the life of the mind: "The freedom of the mind living honorably and virtuously is enough for a courageous and brave man. A man with such a mind could live honorably even in Phalaris' bull." Platina responds by quoting Cicero to the effect that "virtue consists in action." This is the crux of Aristotelian and humanist ethics; virtue is not a static, abstract property like honor but consists of acting honorably—not contemplating but doing. For Platina the question is, "How can someone held in chains and in prison live virtuously?" Virtue is a social duty: "The virtuous man must be public and free, so that he can assist the oppressed, teach the ignorant, chastise delinquents, lead the lost, nurture children, advise friends, and contribute to the city. He does so by accepting public office, by taking up arms against enemies, by vigilantly observing and encouraging virtue, and by banishing fear and cowardice. These things cannot be done except by a free and noble man."[21] This is the wise man of civic humanism. We are far from the contemplative hermit saint of Christianity and the politically disillusioned Stoic who turns to philosophy as a refuge. Ancient Stoicism was remarkably versatile, in that it promoted both the contemplative and the active life. Cicero was a Stoic both as a famous politician and as a reclusive philosopher. Italian civic humanists took as their role model Cicero the orator-statesman and committed republican activist.

In *The Republic,* Plato presents us with a wise man who, having escaped his chains and the world of shadows in a dark cave, discovers the true nature of things in the brilliance of the sun. Rather than remain in the world above, however, to bask in truth, the man sees it as his duty to return to the world of shadows and enlighten others who are still trapped there. The physical reality of the Castel Sant'Angelo embodied this famous metaphor. Friendship was an essential part of ancient philosophy. Epicureans would gather in a garden, Stoics on a porch, to converse and share experiences. Such a community bond lay at the heart of Roman humanism. In their later prison writings, Platina and Pomponio lament most of all the loss of community, of their friends who used to read and converse together.

Platina again advances the idea that an intellectual cannot practice virtue while shut up in a cell but must engage in political action. Pointing to the examples of ancient Rome, Athens, and Carthage, Theodore asserts that political states can never last, owing to the inevitability of corruption, ambition, and greed. Platina answers: "In your opinion, then, no one should ever accept political office or enter government service. If this were to happen, everything would be in shambles because of negligence and indifference." In this connection Theodore proceeds to criticize Plato, in a pragmatic way: "Those free of sin should work in government, as in religious life, and if possible those trained in all disciplines and especially civic virtue, for if this were to happen, as Plato says, we would have prosperous republics. If you can show me a state with citizens like this and show yourself to be the kind of citizen that a well-constituted state needs, I will not prevent you from proceeding." Platina points out that Theodore's ideal is unattainable and ultimately pessimistic: "With this severity of yours, Theodore, you would reduce to desperation the brave men who are moderately trained in politics. For as they say, we are not born civil servants, but the disposition grows little by little. Just as a strong and mighty oak is cut down not by one blow but by many, so the disposition toward civil government is gained not by one studious act but by several." Theodore responds by reiterating his point that civil servants and politicians need to be properly trained before "taking up the reins of government, so that one may not learn what is to the detriment of many." The topic of the conversation then shifts to ecclesiastical office, and both agree that "greater wisdom and learning is needed in those pursuing churchly as opposed to civil honors."[22]

The third and final book of Platina's dialogue introduces Marco Barbo, Paul II's nephew, as the humanist's interlocutor. Barbo, who had been a bishop in 1464, had become a cardinal. In that capacity, he presided over the 1468 legal proceedings. This book differs from the previous two in that Marco speaks much more than Platina and the subject is Christian theology. In the preface, Platina asserts that "Alexander the Great would not have achieved such success had he not had historians and poets to record his deeds for eternity." He goes on to say that Alexander had great respect for the philosopher Diogenes because Aristotle had taught him "to live and contemplate the divine life on earth." After this somewhat misleading preface, the character Marco explains wherein the error of the pagan philosophers lay. The Cynics and Epicureans mistakenly saw nature and pleasure as the highest good. The Stoics came closest to the truth, in seeing virtue as the highest good. These are not the same, however, Marco says, for virtue is the action that leads to the highest good, which is true happiness, and that can be found only in God.[23]

This last book seems to contradict the high praise bestowed on pagan philosophy and civic virtue in the two previous books. Platina is here reasserting his Christian orthodoxy, offering a sudden, guilty condemnation of his earlier argument: "I confess that out of ignorance and error up to now I have been foolishly desiring the image of a false good. I thank God for sending me you, who with your wisdom and learning have not only comforted me in my affliction but also brought me back from grave error to the straight and narrow."[24] Platina's sincerity in making the point is questionable. The disavowal the humanist proffers in the third book is rhetorically necessary to protect him from the charge of paganism.

Were philosophy and theology able to console Platina during his first imprisonment? In and of itself, it would seem not. But as a true humanist believer in the power of literature, Platina repeatedly praises the eloquence and logic of his interlocutors as distractions from his galling chains and depressing incarceration: "My pain finds no greater surcease than when I observe and hear you advise and teach. I am wonderfully refreshed by the sight of you. . . . For just as those in the underworld forgot their punishment when Orpheus was allowed to intercede to save Eurydice with his Cytherian lyre, so were my pain and misfortune granted abeyance when I heard your elegant and learned speech."[25] For Platina, the words themselves were the distraction—the true source of comfort—not the truth of the statements about virtue or God. Even when a man is in despair, form does what content cannot.

Platina's dialogue is a powerful statement of the peculiarly humanist conception of wisdom, virtue, and liberty. This is a work of fiction but one based, he says, on actual exchanges with the warden and other friends. Many of the same themes recur in the prison letters Platina and Rodrigo exchanged during his later and lengthier stay in the Castel Sant'Angelo in 1468. Platina later collected and no doubt revised these letters. Because of the application of torture during his second imprisonment, the harsher conditions and longer period of incarceration, and the extreme nature of the charge, the 1468 letters reveal a much greater sense of desperation than did the polished philosophical dialogue about his earlier imprisonment.

CHAPTER SEVEN

Humanism Imprisoned

Imprisoned in the Castel Sant'Angelo, the humanists were left to philosophize and to suffer until they might come to their senses and understand what they had denied, that the world is ruled by divine providence, not by chance, and that God guides everything he creates.

—AGOSTINO PATRIZI, PAPAL MASTER OF CEREMONIES, 1468

ACCORDING to his official biographer, Pope Paul II was so just and merciful that he always imposed light penalties on criminals, that his face became convulsed if ever the courts meted out capital punishment, and that whenever he heard the bell signaling an impending execution, his heart would suddenly start to race.[1] Indeed, the ringleaders of earlier antipapal conspiracies had all been executed. Callimachus, if he had not escaped first, would surely have tested the limits of the pope's clemency. Although the captured always tend to blame those who escape, as Platina and Pomponio did Callimachus, in this case abundant evidence also points to Callimachus' greater culpability. The arrested humanists were spared execution, but although they had not been convicted, they had to suffer torture and imprisonment, which Platina later called "a fate worse than death."

Platina was repeatedly tortured on the strappado. His dislocated arm would never heal properly from the trauma. In prison he also had to wear heavy shackles on his legs. His leg too would never be the same; each step later recalled a painful memory.[2] When the trial did not seem to turn up enough evidence for a conviction, Platina was hopeful that he and the others would soon be released. Two days after his incarceration began, the pope sent a doctor to tend to Platina's wounds. He encouraged the humanist but said that he would not be released anytime soon. The doctor explained that an early release, the pope feared, might signal that the humanists were innocent and had been unjustly tortured.[3] Freedom would have to wait. A few months later Platina admitted that the pope's initial reaction had been justified: "I would not deny that the pope's grievance is just and that the investigation of so great a matter was justified. But now that the matter has been revealed and understood he should free us from such great misery."[4] They would spend the entire year in the dungeon.

A Plea for Mercy

Platina's first response to imprisonment was to write three letters to Paul II, in which he protested his innocence and begged for mercy. In the first letter, Platina offers several excuses—too many. If he had offered only one excuse and laid off the flattery, bragging, and veiled criticisms of the pope, his letter might have rung true. He proclaims his innocence: it was Callimachus who was responsible, not I. Then he downplays the seriousness of the crime: I am guilty, yes, but of being careless, not malicious. He points to his poverty as the cause of his failure: harsh circumstances embittered him toward God and the Church. The pope, having deprived the humanist of his position at the Vatican, was in fact directly responsible for Platina's poverty. The rest of the letter is a self-congratulatory justification of his life. Platina was a dedicated scholar who had sacrificed everything and suffered poverty because he refused to accept money for his teaching. His students are the ones who suffer from his imprisonment, for Platina can no longer comfort and guide them. He even compares himself to the Apostles, before admitting that he is perhaps going too far. Platina is a martyr to humanism. He includes in his argument for the importance of literature both a promise and a veiled threat. Writers are necessary to preserve the memory of great men. If Paul releases the humanists and frees them from poverty, they will sing his praises.[5] Otherwise, Platina implies, the pope will sink into oblivion or live on in infamy. After Paul's death, Platina carried out this threat by writing his vicious biography of the pope.

The next letter is a direct appeal to the pope's vanity and love of pomp. It takes place during Easter celebrations. Platina begins with absurd exaggeration: "Your arrival at Saint Peter's basilica, most blessed father, brought tears to our eyes, and groans, for we were not permitted to accompany Your Holiness and greet you with applause, as we used to do. Oh, wretches, oh, unfortunates, we who on account of the stupidity of a monster were not permitted to enjoy the sweetest and most holy sight of you! I confess that we have suffered great discomforts in this calamity, but nothing greater than this, that alone, sad, weeping, and filling the air with groans and howls, we were deprived of such great happiness and public joy, when the entire college of cardinals and high priests, all the courtiers, and the Roman people accompanied you." Platina's flattery is comically excessive. In the rest of the letter Platina tries to capitalize on the fact that Easter was a traditional time for pardons. He tells the pope that he should practice mercy, like Christ and the ancient popes. The poor man has stooped to begging. In this letter the supposed praise is barely veiled criticism of the pope's unyielding harshness. In a later letter, to the pope's nephew Cardinal Marco Barbo, who was in charge of the formal investigation, Platina, again making use of disingenuous flattery as a way of criticizing the pope, begged the cardinal to intervene on his behalf, saying, "The intercession will be easier, for you have to persuade not the Pharaoh, the king of Judaea, or the emperor Nero, but Pope Paul, who is held to be the most clement of all people in our time."[6] The juxtaposition of Nero and Paul—even with the negative—is hardly flattering.

Platina's final letter to the pope returns to the theme of clemency. He promises to change his ways in return for mercy and suggests adopting a nonretributory form of justice: "I would not deny that

Fifteenth-century prison corridor in the Castel Sant'Angelo (author photo). "I was taken back to my cell in such great pain that I wanted to die, my limbs broken, shattered, and cut" (Platina, 1468).

criminals should be punished, but I would say it is better to save them, if they can be returned to sanity. Our minds would be curable, most blessed Father, if they should be anointed a little with the oil of your clemency." Platina argues for a specifically Christian theory of penal justice. Punishment should be not punitive but reforming: criminals can be cured. In essence, this was one of the fundamental tenets of Christian society. When sinners wronged the community by committing murder or adultery, they were separated through exile or prison. Once they had confessed and demonstrated contrition and a sincere desire to reform, however, they were allowed back into the community. The letter continues with an evocative portrayal of the perennially inebriated Callimachus, who "savagely attacks kings and redistributes kingdoms at will." Platina promises never to consort with men like him again. In exchange for mercy, the writer promises total obedience and says: "I would abandon poetry and rhetoric and dedicate myself completely to the sacred page, in which, as if in a rich and fertile meadow, I will gather the healthiest flowers for soul and body." In offering to renounce pagan literature, he both reiterates his innocence and offers to reform. In a later letter to Cardinal Barbo, Platina also tries to strike a deal: "Before God, I promise you that if I escape this great misfortune because of your efforts and the pope's clemency, I will make a point of living a more honorable life in my actions and studies, and I will switch from poetry to sacred letters, for this is pleasing to our most holy lord."[7] Needless to say, Platina never became a biblical scholar or theologian but rather continued to produce secular works.

In the letter to Paul, Platina refers to the dissimilar nature of secular studies to justify the liberal attitude of the humanists: "Forgive those who erred with me and enjoyed the academic license and freedom that are usually more extensive in nonreligious studies." His assertion is a subtle critique of papal censorship and an argument for academic freedom. In a letter to Cardinal Bessarion, Platina pursued the subject further by blaming the pope for misunderstanding the art of academic debate and the very nature of humanism, which used dialogue to explore different ideas, some of them heretical: "Our characters are indeed curable, and if we have erred in some way through our academic license, which is usually more liberal in university studies on account of our debating, let us constantly correct this, so that His Diligence may rejoice in having found the sheep that the Lord thought were lost."[8] Although claiming to desire his own reform, Platina satirizes those who equate the beliefs of authors with those of the characters in their dialogues and the points of view explored in their works.

After the direct approach failed, Platina wrote to patrons and church officials and begged them to intervene on his behalf. These letters extolling clemency are full of feigned adulation. Platina starts to break down, however, in the letter to his patron Cardinal Gonzaga. A different, more emotional, and desperate humanist appears. "I am tormented by physical sufferings, my spirit is in anguish, and there is no limit to my tears and wailing. I would certainly commit suicide and cut off this disastrous life with a knife or through some other violent act if the clemency of our most holy lord and your patronage, your kind nature, did not provide some comfort. . . . Unless I am released and go immediately to the baths, I will lose my right arm. Every day it weakens. O wretch that I am! If I become a weak invalid, I will have no desire to live. I prefer to die than to lose my right hand. Will you allow my right arm to wither and shrivel up, this right arm that has honored and exalted your homeland and commended it to posterity?"[9] (He had written three works in praise of the Gonzaga family and Mantua.) Platina attempts to elicit pity and an immediate response with his graphic threat to commit suicide. Although his right shoulder never healed completely from the torture, Platina was able to write, and he composed many works during and after his imprisonment. Cardinal Gonzaga eventually did secure Platina's release, but not until the humanist had languished in prison for more than a year. In the meantime, however, Platina made contact with other prisoners. Unable to converse with them, he made use of one of the few advantages imprisonment could not take away: his eloquence. The Latin letters of consolation he wrote were charitable in intention, yes, but they also kept him busy. Writing letters brought welcome distraction from the pain and from the loneliness of his prison cell.

Many years before, a large ceramic cylinder had rolled over on four-year-old Jacopo Tolomei and trapped him inside. It was dark and little air remained. Panic set in. Accidents like this one claimed the lives of many children in Renaissance Italy. Falls down steep stairwells or from high windows contributed to the elevated rates of child mortality just as inevitably as did sickness, disease, and malnutrition.[10] Jacopo would surely have suffocated, if an older child playing nearby had not by good fortune heard the boy's screams and pushed the cylinder off him. Years later, Jacopo looked back on the terrifying event as having presaged the seven years he would spend in the dark, stale depths of the papal prison. Jacopo Tolomei had been the governor of Spoleto and, oddly enough, warden of the Castel Sant'Angelo. He had benefited from the patronage of Pope Pius II but had run afoul of Paul II. Tolomei was imprisoned from 1464 to 1471 on a charge of corruption.[11] After attempting to escape, he was moved from a high chamber of the dungeon to a dark cell in the dank basement. He shared his cell with Campano and exchanged Italian poems with Pomponio. In fact, Jacopo claims that Pomponio "comforted all the prisoners and urged us toward a painful end with poison."[12] Whether or not Pomponio was serious in this encouragement, suicide is a theme that recurs often in Jacopo's prison poetry:

> If I were not afraid of the sin,
> I would with my own hand do as Cato did,
> Instead of living in this subterranean tomb.[13]

That Jacopo was seriously considering suicide is clear from a long poem he wrote on the subject:

Happy are they who, seeing themselves brought to extremity, fearlessly
deprive themselves of this vile life.

But our law clearly shows the eternal punishment that has caused many
a one to stay his hand.

The beacons that were Paul, Jerome, and Augustine pointed out eternal
grace and disgrace.

Had Mithridates known about this law, he would not have been so quick
to resort to poison.

If Cato, whose fame endures to this day, had not chosen immortality, his
chest would have remained unscathed. . . .

But each was devoted to honor alone and resorted to his chosen form of
relief to flee a wretched state.

Today my life is such a burden that were it not for these bitter restrictions,
I would free my soul from the onslaught and expunge my questionable
life.[14]

Desperation informs these bleak lines. Jacopo wavers between decrying the sin of suicide and admiring the bravery and immortal fame of those who commit it. If it had not been for his fear of a Christian hell, Jacopo would have ended his misery. He nevertheless remained sufficiently collected to frame his thoughts in Italian verse studded with classical examples.

Platina answered Jacopo's plea for help in the following letter:

Reason and time make the unbearable easier. If a wound is not mortal, it will hurt more when fresh than when it has begun to heal with medication and form a scar. I do not deny that we are moved more by the example of the living than of the dead. Your endurance and strength of mind have helped me more than have all those in history who have suffered with fortitude. But we should not reject history. . . . Do not accuse most brave Cato of impatience, for he was considered the most patient of all in suffering travails, thirst, and hunger for the benefit and growth of the Roman Republic. But once he saw that Caesar had taken control, he preferred to die bravely, following the Stoics, than to be killed for the republic and to look on the face of the victor. For it is the mark of a slave, not a brave man, to bear the yoke of a tyrant patiently. The same reasoning led the others you mention in your letter to think it more honorable to die than to serve barbarians and tyrants. I am very happy, for I learned from you that our companion [Campano] is bearing this disaster well, and I rejoice, for he helps us to endure and his virtue will save him in life and make him great after death.[15]

Although he repeats the examples from antiquity that Jacopo called to mind, the argument Platina offers against suicide is rather weak. Jacopo could have responded that if Cato and the other ancients were justified in refusing to live in bondage under a tyrant, we should follow their example.

Jacopo's cellmate, Settimuleio Campano, was only nineteen years old when he was arrested with the other humanists on suspicion of conspiracy. He was tortured and imprisoned for a year. In prison, Campano suffered from terrible nightmares. The warden, Rodrigo, tried to console him by pedantically explaining the principal causes of dreams. Some are caused by vivid impressions on the senses, some are sent by the devil to deceive men, and others, such as the ones interpreted by the biblical patriarch Joseph, are sent by God to instruct men. To alleviate Campano's anxiety, Rodrigo lent him three of his own works, including a Latin treatise *On Wardens and Prison Guards,* which must have been a real page-turner. To judge by Campano's laudatory remarks, the reading materials appear to have helped him psychologically, but his physical health deteriorated, and with it his mental stability. He suffered such violent fevers and acute stomach pains that he was unable to eat or find relief in reading. He felt he was at death's door.[16] Soon after his release, in fact, Campano died, at the age of twenty-one.[17] In prison, Campano was mostly held in isolation from the other prisoners. This isolation was especially hard for him. He began to regret his life. He bitterly exclaims in an epigram: "Study ruins, kills, and imprisons those who practice it; how much better it would have been had we cultivated the field with a plough, so that the love of vain letters might have perished entirely in us." In another poem Campano emphasizes the social character of humanism and wishes that he could chirp away his loneliness like a caged bird: "In misery, from this cage I watch my dear comrade, whom I saw before in the city as a free man. Here, we are not permitted to give voice to the slightest feeling; something which no one denies you, O talkative magpie. Since we share the same fate and are both imprisoned in a cage, why am I not given the same tongue as you?"[18] All their learning seemed futile in the grim reality of prison life. Conversation was the heart of humanism; without the ability to exchange views, the humanists' community could not exist.

Even Campano, who was driven to an early death, wrote letters to console others in prison. Here he expresses to Platina of the solace to be found in writing, now that society is denied:

> If I seem hapless to others, I do not to myself, for writing softens this most bitter misfortune. It is no small consolation to refresh a downcast and ruined spirit with shared conversation. But since that was taken from us, we must share in writing what we are prohibited to in speech. . . . We are less miserable than those who lack intelligence and cannot confront the attacks of fortune with the aid of the mind. The [uneducated] have nothing besides their tears; but countless examples in the literature and arts in which we were brought up offer us consolation. If we look to ancient history . . . we fortify ourselves with so many shields and such great bravery that we conquer all misery and squalor. Antiquity always esteemed those who were born for both fates. Everyone knows how to enjoy delights and peace; they merit no praise. But those who bear disasters and storms are thought to be worthy of immortality. . . . Nothing in this life is fixed, firm, or solid; all is uncertain and fleeting. Nothing bad can happen to the wise, for they foresee it and, as if prepared for battle, harden their spirit against any attack. Like a good sailor, you often said that a storm would overtake us. We suffer because we knew by signs most certain that we were going to suffer. We must bear patiently what cannot be avoided and must be borne. It is pointless to lament and be distraught when you gain nothing by lamenting. Arise, therefore, most constant Platina; consider who you are and what a great chorus of youth waits for you to slake its enormous thirst for literature at your fountain.

Even though incarcerated and mortally ill, Campano cites no Christian or biblical examples.[19] The consolation he offers is pagan and secular. It draws on Stoic philosophy, with its emphasis on fate and the wisdom of letting go of what is beyond one's control. Campano emphasizes the palliative and salutary nature of conversation. When actual dialogue is denied, the educated can turn to the ancients. He recalls that Platina had warned them that their activities could be dangerous. At last he appeals to Platina's instincts as a teacher. These are strong words for a twenty-year-old. Platina was forty-seven.

Consolation and the Failure of Humanism

The humanists arrested in 1468 never attempted to escape their confinement. Their warden, unlike the vindictive madman of Benvenuto Cellini's experience, offered them a gift of inestimable worth: consolation. Rodrigo Sánchez de Arévalo acted as mediator between the humanists and the pope and offered solace in the numerous letters that he exchanged with Platina, Pomponio, and the other ill-fated intellectuals. This prison correspondence dramatically illustrates the hardships, pain, and loneliness of incarceration. Although their devotion to pagan learning was a part of what got them into trouble, the literature and culture that the humanists loved took on a much greater importance in prison. Incarceration proved the supreme test of their classical learning.

Six letters from Rodrigo to Platina survive, but there must have been more, for in his first letter Platina thanks the warden for the consolation he affords: "Who could bear fevers, back pain, fatigue, headaches, poverty, hunger, thirst, chains, tortures, and mental ailments, unless there were some hope of better fortune? Your Platina has been abandoned amid such great ills, for no one except you cares about his life. If you had not consoled me with your learned letters, I would have

ended my life." In his response, Rodrigo draws on both pagan philosophy and Christian theology:

> I would grieve for you, if I knew you were grieving. But all those painful
> afflictions, even if they are a punishment to other men, are to a wise and
> brave man like yourself opportunities to exercise virtue. Most learned
> Platina, therefore raise your spirits and say with the wise man: I am not
> so mad as to desire sickness; but if I must be sick, I will not bear it like a
> woman. It is not desirable to suffer torture, but suffer it bravely. If you
> bear these pains and physical torments well, they will turn into joy. God
> has afflicted you with prison and physical ailments so that you might
> avoid eternal punishment in death. The wise man is not troubled by
> physical pain, as he relies on the strength of his mind.[20]

Tears and lamentation are for the weak—Platina should bear his suffering like a man. Rodrigo develops the Stoic idea that tragedy and
pain are opportunities to practice virtue and strengthen the mind. For
example, the loss of a loved one teaches the importance of detach-
ment; that all is fleeting except reason and virtue. Physical pain helps
fortify the sufferer's resolve. Rodrigo also advances the biblical notion
that tragedy and pain are punishments for sin, or trials whose proper
completion can lead to divine favor. In the Bible, Job is made to suffer
but is then redeemed. The Christian martyrs offered their pain up to
God and saw salvation in torment. "Cheer up, then, Platina, for nothing is more felicitous for you than to suffer adversity. The wise man
has no virtue in prosperity. That man is truly wise who is not worn
down by ruinous pain nor shaken in his resolve but bears all adversity
with joy. That is the mark of a wise man." Platina should rejoice in his
suffering, for it gives him an opportunity to prove himself.[21]

Rodrigo ends his lengthy letter with somewhat contradictory advice. First, he praises Platina: "You show yourself to be especially wise
in that you do not hide your pain and sadness. For when we share our
pain with friends, the pain diminishes, since, as Martial writes: 'He

truly suffers who suffers alone.' For the sympathy of friends alleviates the sufferer's burden, as his friends take on the weight of misfortune and help make it lighter. This is especially the case because they know that they are loved by their friends. Do not lament, therefore, but rejoice." To this explanation of the benefits of talk therapy, he appends some contradictory advice: "Do not make your misfortunes more painful and burden yourself with complaints. For if you give no thought to it, pain is light. By thinking it is light, you will make it light."[22] Even Rodrigo seems not quite sure what advice to offer to these men in their suffering.

Platina's immediate response is to praise Rodrigo and plead for his intervention with the pope. Then the prisoner presents his life story as a catalogue of woe:

> It is no vice for me to expose with tears and wailing the cruel fortune raging against me. From a tender age I dedicated myself to the study of literature and wore out my body and mind with worry and late nights to such an extent that I never knew pleasure. For virtue, I froze, sweated, and bore thirst and hunger. In leisure and shade I wore out my body, which was strong enough and could have been made stronger with exercise. But as I grew older, I realized that the darts of ill fortune were aimed at me. Worry and anxiety tormented my body and mind, and often I desired death. I frequently wonder why this savage beast has been raging against me for so long. I see no other reason than that I was born under an unlucky star or an evil fate. This wild beast has surrounded me with every danger. It has subjected me to the tongues of envious detractors, the dangers of sea and land, poverty and misfortune, derision and contempt.
>
> Although I helped many people before with my service and erudition, no one has been moved by my troubles or offered up even the smallest coin, let alone blood. I beat my chest, pull my hair out, and strike my eyes. I will not bear these afflictions any longer. I am afraid, as my woes are growing continually and there is no hope of better fortune, that I will deal more severely with myself and not withstand the blows of savage fate. I am worn out, my limbs weakened, bones dislodged, spirit bro-

ken, senses pounded, and no reason remains for which I should wish to persist in living. You say that virtue is the best antidote in sickness. But medicine cures a sick body only if some part of it remains intact. By immortal God, what is there left of me to offer any hope of salvation?

I live life in prison with an aching body and a sick mind. Not without tears and wailing do I recall the readings, free conversations with friends, agreeable routines, and pleasant walks of which, as of dearest sunlight, I have been deprived. I pass over how many troubles befall my friends who used to rely on me for advice. I used to fill my days with reading, teaching, and helping in whatever matters I could. Misfortune has disturbed this leisure of mine and brought me to such a point that I would gladly exchange my life for death.[23]

Here, humanism is failing as a way of life, in that it seems possible only in pleasant conditions, removed from painful reality. Yet Platina also laments the way scholarship undermined his physical and mental health before he was imprisoned. Depression has made him the harshest critic of his life decisions. He wants credit, however, for all that he suffered "for virtue." Besides the physical pain he has endured as a result of torture, his loneliness constitutes an additional torment. Platina offers a picture of the social role of the humanist in a community of scholars. Humanism is seen here as a social activity, a way of assisting one's fellow human beings. This recalls his Ciceronian definition of virtue as a social and civic activity.

Rodrigo's response to Platina's despondent plea is mixed. He first accuses the humanist of indulging in self-pity: "Our religion holds that we should mourn the pain of others as our own. I read your letter and felt no little sorrow, for I see that you are hampered by a stubborn and despairing sadness. It certainly increases your sadness that neither your wisdom and virtue nor my comforts can mitigate, if not eliminate, the things you call misfortunes. Indeed, in lamenting your misfortunes, you seem to have fallen into a hopelessness about life. Some people, Saint John Chrysostom says, are so conquered by sorrow that the more we commiserate with them, the more they abuse our compassion and subsist on our consolation." Such pointed criticism, reminiscent of the accusation in Platina's dialogue of unmanly whining, is meant to snap Platina out of his despair. Rodrigo in this letter, however, then adds insult to injury by questioning Platina's sincerity. "You complain of your afflictions in such elegant rhetoric, in such effective words, and with such groaning that you appear to be the only one of all the living ever to have suffered miseries."[24] Rodrigo raises a key question that still puzzles us today: What are we to make of the fact that the humanists' very real complaints are so eloquently framed, in poems and classically inspired Latin epistles?

The rough, spontaneous writings of the uneducated often hold broader appeal than the studied disquisitions of the learned. The popular form and language of the New Testament, for example, gave it an immediacy and authenticity that many must have found lacking in Plato's polished dialogues. The fact that Platina uses a variety of constructions to express his feelings of despair should not make his sentiments any less authentic than, say, a short description of the humanist's condition in a medical report or trial record. Words can never convey to the fullest extent such powerful feelings as pain and despair. Dante deplored the inadequacy of words to describe the divine. Platina and the other humanists, writers by profession, had at their disposal a much more extensive vocabulary to express their feelings than did some of the other prisoners in the dungeon. The mental and physical suffering of the scholars was undoubtedly real. The humanists saw no contradiction in describing genuine suffering in carefully turned phrases. In fact, they seem to have taken comfort in writing—not just putting words on paper, but also composing artful and persuasive texts. Writing was their tool and their vocation.

Rodrigo next turns to a more troubling part of Platina's lament, in which the humanist claims that he was "born under an unlucky star or an evil fate." He launches into a drawn-out discussion of the difference between pagan fate and Christian providence. He refers to Aristotle and Cicero regarding the ways in which God works through natural causes. Providence will take care of us, as Christ assured his disciples in the Gospel in telling them not to worry about what they would eat. But if divine providence rules all creation, why must Platina suffer? Rodrigo offers a response to this perennial dilemma:

> Believe me, Platina, that man is most fortunate who follows what God has planned, though he knows not the reason. But that man is most unfortunate who chooses to go against it. I thought that by your virtue you could overcome all those miseries, afflictions, and pains. You have always taught that virtue cannot be conquered by adversity. A wise man succumbs to no disaster. For he knows that the strength, wealth, honors, and routines that we call human comforts are fraught and temporary. Of a sudden they take wing and elude their owners. They are fixed in no place or person, but are tossed about by changeable winds. In a sudden reversal, they submerge in the depths of misery those they had raised to great heights. Therefore, Platina, envy not the prosperous, but rather the strongest, who were meant to die but emerged from danger the stronger, for they knew that nothing stood in their way except death, which they willingly embraced. Yield and adapt to circumstances, and bear with a noble heart what you must.[25]

The idea that nothing in life is constant except virtue is a Stoic idea. Beauty, wealth, power, and honor are all fleeting. The wise man can rely only on his virtue. Rodrigo, however, takes this idea one step further and offers a very Christian take on the hollowness of worldly success.

One of the most popular texts in the Renaissance was Boethius' *Consolation of Philosophy* (520 CE). Boethius had held an important position in the government of Emperor Theodoric but fell suddenly from favor when he was accused of treason. He wrote the *Consolation* while in prison awaiting his execution. Rodrigo draws on this book in general, but the image of the sudden reversal of fortune explicitly recalls Boethius' discussion of the Wheel of Fortune. As the wheel turns, the powerful are toppled and the poor raised up, but the wheel keeps turning, and the cycle repeats itself. Nothing in this world endures; all is fleeting. Because of the fickleness of fortune, the only recourse we have in life is to trust in God's providence and mercy. Rodrigo's description of the fortunate accommodating themselves to God's plan and concluding advice to "yield and adapt to circumstances" is an idea that later became central to Niccolò Machiavelli's thought. In *The Prince* (1513), Machiavelli defines virtue as precisely that: knowing how to adjust to one's circumstances. Rodrigo certainly would not have endorsed Machiavelli's secular view of politics, but if we replace fortune with God's plan, the lesson is essentially the same.

Far from following the warden's advice, Platina challenges the classical and Christian tradition of consolation in his next letter:

> It is easy to give advice to the sick when we are healthy, as Terence says. Allow me to speak more freely. You write in your letter that toil, fever, and torments are opportunities for virtue, but it is impossible to help anyone when the body is in excruciating pain. It is likewise difficult, or rather impossible, to advise anyone when you are troubled by mental afflictions, for when a man's mind is disturbed, as we see in many, it lacks all council and reason. Sick oxen are no help to man; sick birds do not delight. You will say that human nature is different. Character and intellect separate us from the beasts. I agree but assert that misery is worse for humans. Man suffers acutely from cold, heat, thirst, and starvation, not to mention the infinite afflictions of the mind. I respect the authority of Augustine, Jerome, Paul, Seneca, the Stoics, the Academics, the Peripatetics and their books about assuaging bodily miseries and mental disturbances, but since most of the Stoics are said to have avoided death and the tribulations of life, I think that it is far safer to philosophize in words than in deeds.[26]

Rodrigo cannot know what it is like to suffer as Platina is suffering. In one sentence, the humanist dismisses all the philosophical and religious authorities on consolation. Experience, not the theories gained from books and contemplation, is the only true guide to life. Humanists immersed themselves in the literature of antiquity, but they did not regard it as an authority to be followed slavishly, as medieval thinkers had often been inclined to regard theology. Rather, the humanists saw the works of Cicero and the poetry of antiquity as repositories of the living word, which also served as a stylistic archetype to be imitated and re-created in dialogue and verse. Unlike the intricate theoretical logic of medieval philosophy and theology, life experience was immediate and authentic. In his desperation, however, Platina rejects the humanist belief in the practical applicability of ancient texts to life's problems.

Despite his protests, Platina claims to find some solace in the warden's advice: "I will nevertheless admit one thing: bearing anything in life with a calm mind makes it seem lighter. I have made my mind stronger to sustain pressing afflictions, for a man's mind cannot be strengthened in virtue without long practice. Perhaps you will say that I have rejected your remedies, but that is not so. I willingly embrace what you have most elegantly written to me about strength and perseverance. But distressed as I am by my recent ordeal, I need time to think it over. I see, as sick people do, that health will follow the bitterness of the medicine. Cheer up and see that your Platina holds his sufferings in contempt and, relying on his innocence, has ceased to be afraid."[27] Human psychology is powerful. Simply by denying or ignoring it, pain loses some of its sting. Platina's favorable response may nevertheless have been conditioned more by the need to please a powerful ally than by the efficacy of his advice.

Saint Augustine himself, Rodrigo writes, complained that he lost his ability to concentrate when he suffered from a toothache. Rodrigo admits that immoderate pain harms the intellect and makes it more difficult to practice virtue. Because of his faith, however, Augustine rose above his pain. This is why we need faith in God: "Saint Paul was so absorbed in loving God that he felt no physical pain. . . . Know for certain that no one who intensely desires the heavenly home is broken by misery and pain. . . . The ills afflicting us bring us closer to God. God afflicts us here so that he may spare us for eternity. Understand then, Platina, that God is punishing you in order to stop your wandering and to speed you along to the home we desire. Stop complaining, and thank God for this sign of your election and for banishing your soul's distractions to strengthen you for divine contemplation."[28] Rodrigo admits the limitations of philosophy and offers religion as the only solace. Faith in God's providence reveals that the afflictions we suffer are given to us for a reason. In loving God and contemplating his truth, we find that our pain turns to pleasure. Christian mysticism taught that through mortification of the body we can paradoxically overcome physical pain and leave the body altogether, in the mystical experience of an ecstatic union between the soul and God. Rather than distracting us and preventing contemplation of the divine, physical discomfort forces the mind to concentrate, to dismiss and transcend the physical. Platina should therefore rejoice in the afflictions God has given him.

Platina admits defeat and praises the warden's persuasive arguments:

> I concede to you, as if admonished by Apollo's oracle. I shall willingly drink this medicine, which soothes but does not cure my illness. But . . . lest you think that I alone am disturbed by anxiety, know that all of my companions in misery are also troubled, not so much while we are being tortured or tormented, but while we are calm and at peace. For if one of us tells an amusing story to entertain us, we distract one another for a little bit. The same happens if we read, write, or converse. We certainly cannot sustain our morale; worry sometimes takes over, and we fall into grief and sadness. You will perhaps say that a remedy for this ailment can be garnered from your letters. I would not disagree, but it is true only in part. . . . You have greatly alleviated the illness, but the thirst and instability plaguing us must be alleviated so that the good foundation that you have built does not perish altogether. By reading, talking, and studying, we can remain strong in mind and spirit.[29]

Rodrigo's consolation could assist individuals in dealing with their grief, but humanists cannot survive alone. Separated from one another, the humanists felt isolated. All their learning, virtue, and faith could not combat loneliness. The greatest consolation lies in community. The Roman humanists felt a need for social interaction and for conversation that was rooted in classical forms and languages, but very much alive. Scholarship was not a solitary activity—they needed to read together, debate, and teach. Dialogue was a fundamental tool and way of life for these devoted intellectuals.

The warden granted Platina's request, and Platina does appear to have gotten progressively better after he was allowed the company of his dear friends in prison. Rodrigo acknowledges the severity of his prisoner's mental anguish but attributes it to original sin. Because of the sin of Adam and Eve, physical and mental passions destroy our stability and preclude complete tranquillity. No one is immune. Even wise men must fight to control powerful emotions. We must put aside negative thoughts and evil temptations: "You do not need a lance, a sword, or armor to defeat them. You have the remedy within you to drive them out. Defeat these weak and destructive thoughts completely by concentrating on a superior, contravening thought."[30] Again, the warden has resorted to positive thinking as a cure for depression.

Pomponio Leto similarly fell into a deep depression over the loss of his freedom and the isolation and loneliness of prison. In his first letter to the warden, he strategically praises the pope:

> If I were to speak of his piety, mercy, clemency, and holiness, my powers and strength of speech would fail, and my mind would be too dull to contemplate so great a pontiff. He remained immovable and undisturbed in the face of great danger, when the threat of high treason had to be investigated. Let Tiberius Caesar yield to him, who spared conspirators, and Trajan yield to him in clemency and mercy. His admirable virtue can easily be recognized in the divine office he holds. He deservedly acts for God on earth and is called the Vicar of Christ, with the power to

Fifteenth-century prison cell in the Castel Sant'Angelo (author photo). "I am surrounded by walls, my liberty taken away, where I cannot see the sky except through little holes and I wander alone in my covered cell" (Pomponio Leto, 1468).

bind and compel that Christ our Lord gave to Peter and his successors. Because of this and innumerable other holy deeds I would easily place him in his most holy judgment before all pontiffs who have lived and will live. Or do you not see him as imitating Christ, who most gently bore a slap in the face?[31]

It is possible to detect an undercurrent of sarcasm in Pomponio's panegyric. "Immovable and undisturbed" could be read negatively, to mean that the pope was unreasonably stubborn. Pomponio emphasizes mercy, of which the pope has shown little enough to the imprisoned humanists. After Sejanus tried to take control of the Roman

Empire, Tiberius Caesar had him arrested and executed. The pagan Roman emperor Trajan was so renowned for his justice and acts of mercy that according to a medieval legend he was allowed into the Christian heaven. Pomponio's discussion of the papacy is a double reminder of Paul's failure. The popes claimed their spiritual authority from a passage in the Gospel of Matthew, which describes how Christ bestowed the power of binding and loosing (condemning and forgiving) on Saint Peter, the first pope. Instead of using the normal verb for loosening *(solvere)*, Pomponio uses the opposite verb, *cogere* (to compel), which was the common word for applying torture. The sarcasm culminates in the comparison of Paul with Christ.

Rodrigo chose to ignore Pomponio's disrespectful tone and convoluted critique of the pope. He praises the humanist's eloquence and learning and confesses that he would like to visit and converse with him. He states, with some sarcasm of his own, "I am most eager for you to enlighten my mind." The warden then offers consolation in the form of his standard meditation on the mysterious workings of providence: "Why does fortune's fury rage against you alone? You who are not rich except in letters, nor pampered in fine cloth at the courts of princes, proud of high honors, a pleasure lover, or an admirer of vanity. But take comfort, Pomponio. Injustice is deceptive. It has made you suffer as much as human nature can; but it can bring good. The harsher the pain, the more your virtue and steadfast spirit become known. You will come out of this battle stronger. It was necessary for you to prove yourself to your fellow men. Virtue is gained in battle."[32] Misfortune builds character. Trials and tribulations are opportunities to practice virtue.

Pomponio respectfully thanked the warden: "I was disturbed and despairing of all hope, but your letter at once brought me back and put me in a better place." The humanist then asked if the warden would provide him with copies of the works of the ancient authors Lactantius and Macrobius. Instead of these books, Rodrigo gave Pomponio his own treatise against the Council of Basel. The Council of Basel, let us recall, attempted to curtail the pope's power by legislating superior authority for a general church council over the pope. After Pope Eugene IV refused to attend and wrote a bull against it, the council elected another pope, Felix V, who had little support. The council finally ended in failure. As a staunch advocate of papal monarchy, Rodrigo condemned the council. He perhaps thought that his arguments in the treatise might persuade Pomponio to think more favorably of the pope. In his letter about the treatise, Pomponio says he prefers Rodrigo's rhetoric to Cicero's eloquence and praises Pope Eugene IV for making his nephew a cardinal, "who [as Paul II] at present guides the papacy with great clemency and more holiness than any pope who has ever been or ever will be on earth."[33] In this obsequious praise we sense that the bitter humanist found little balm in the warden's explanation of the theoretical underpinnings of papal power.

Alone in his cell, Pomponio pined for his friends, his students, and the community of scholars that had regularly gathered at his house on the Quirinal Hill. Prison made his life difficult, but he felt the greatest pain at the loss of community and conversations with friends: "Pliny praises the solitude of a grove for poets, but he means a forest grove, where flocks of birds provide amenity, leafy trees the sweetest shade, and fresh green grass a pleasing primordial bed. A wondrous thing— poets find and compose much here, a true retreat of the Muses. The woods resound with poetic songs; caves echo; all these places seem to recall the Muse Calliope. Would that I had this now! I am surrounded by walls, my liberty taken away, where I cannot see the sky except through little holes and I wander alone in my covered cell. I beg you, please, allow me one cheerful companion to temper my sadness with conversation. If this does not happen, my depression will worsen, and I will die. I beg you—do not deny me someone's conversation."[34] Like Platina, Pomponio emphasizes the social, dialogic character of humanism. These are not antiquarians who spend their time alone reading ancient texts in dark studies. Solitary reading and writing, which might delight in some leafy bower, brings no joy in this bleak place.

Rodrigo disarms the desperation in Pomponio's attack on solitude by presuming it to be a joke:

> You do not think the solitude you are experiencing should be praised, since you are living between walls and, to coin a phrase, seem to be entombed. If I did not think you said this in jest, I would be greatly upset. I pass over the fact that you are contradicting yourself, for in an earlier letter you professed that you desired no earthly success and that you scorned everything except literature and avoided human society. What do you want with all your complaining about solitude? What possible consolation could you get from conversing with vulgar men who were born en masse to prevent the consolation of good men? As Seneca says, "the greater the number of people you mix with, the greater the danger." Have you not forgotten that society impedes and certainly interrupts the progress of our mind toward higher matters? How can a good and learned man like you be alone when he is accompanied by continual thought, crammed with outstanding scholarship, and has divine meditations as his companions? He is never less alone than when he is by himself.
>
> The Greeks say that a wise man can never be alone, since he has with him all the good people who ever lived. When he cannot meet them with his body, he uses his thoughts. And if this connection is lacking, he speaks with God. If the narrow walls constrict his body, he contemplates the divine. The more savagely he is oppressed on earth, the more fervently he longs for the divine. Do not be troubled by your cramped, tight quarters. Valerius Maximus comes to mind: "A humble hut, the tiniest place, holds a great crowd of virtues." Believe me, Pomponio, it is far holier to socialize with a crowd of virtues than of men. The ancient Cynic philosopher Diogenes enjoyed living in a tub on wheels. What can the chatter of men bring you? They are mostly annoying gossips and would not console anyone. Rather, they make you sad. . . . Consider this, Pomponio, that the further anyone is from human conversation, the closer he is to God. Therefore, do not trouble yourself over being alone; rest in the greater consolation of books and literature. Chitchat is not

needed, for the truer and richer consolation of books and literature compensates for [lack of] human contact.[35]

Rodrigo mixes pagan philosophy and the tenets of Christian monasticism. His is an elitist argument for the life of the mind and contemplation of the divine, to oppose the illiterate mob that has failed to rise above the banality of the human condition.

Pomponio corrects the warden with a fine but important distinction:

> Seneca had in mind that solitude obtained in liberty which free men willingly cultivate. But how can captives bear solitude except unwillingly? What can a captive think about besides liberty? Just as fishermen think about fish, sailors about the winds, and ploughmen about cattle, so does everyone concentrate on what he deems necessary. The sick are occupied with no sweeter thought than to be in spring waters or vineyard vaults where they might satisfy their natural desires. You will never find a sick man praising thirst or a healthy man praising excessive drinking. And if anyone deprived of freedom praises solitude, he is not speaking from the heart and should not be trusted. A prisoner is like someone who invents his own religion. After some days, when he sees that he has lost his natural religious fervor, the great loneliness causes him to despair and hang himself. Who except a madman denies himself what kind nature has given? You will never find a beggar who does not revile poverty. If the Cynic philosopher Diogenes had been prevented from crossing certain boundaries, he would have ignored philosophy and spent all his time thinking up a means to liberty. All mortals desire what is denied them and scorn what they have. As Ovid says: "We always strive after the forbidden and desire what is denied."[36]

Like Platina, Pomponio argues that it is virtually impossible for him to think about philosophy when he has lost his freedom. Such thoughts are as natural as a sick man's thirst, and it is futile to try to deny their validity. Pomponio's comparison of the prisoner and the faithless man is odd but telling. Just as natural religion is not enough on its own and

requires the gift of faith from God and the support of organized religion, so is the captive able to survive only with the help of the warden.
The image of suicide further emphasizes Pomponio's desperation. Just
as religion fails without divine aid, so does philosophy without dialogue and a community in which to practice virtue. Society makes
man human, but without the freedom to choose and to live life for
oneself, humanity ultimately collapses.

Pomponio's desperate pleas were answered: the warden allowed the
humanists to reconvene their academy in prison. Pomponio wrote
an impassioned thank-you: "You have gathered us wretches into one
place, so that we might console and encourage each other. Captivity is
nothing amid the conversations of friends. Travel, distance, hunger,
and thirst are not annoying during voyages and fasts if there is pleasant, engaging, and witty discussion. Troubled as we are by one man's
wickedness, the telling of divine and human history cheers us up and
dispels all impending disaster. We all, therefore, thank you for your
kindness and piety."[37] It may seem odd to compare the humanists' suffering to the tedium of a long trip, but travel was physically exhaust-
ing, painful, and fraught with danger in the Renaissance. Whereas
reading philosophy fails to console, discussing it in a group enlivens
and liberates. Conversation serves both to distract the captives from
the monotony of prison life and to foster the kind of learning and
growth that defines human aspiration.

These prison letters are particularly interesting in that they reveal
the effects of consolation, the reaction and response on the part of the
consoled. Most work on consolation focuses on the consoler, on his or
her strategies and philosophical sources.[38] In doing so, it makes us
privy to only one side of the conversation. Rodrigo draws, in his efforts at consolation, on Christian and classical truisms. His pastiche of
sources and trite exhortations to virtue are not remarkable. What
makes the story so compelling is the original responses of the human-

ists to these efforts to console them. The inmates provide a very human reaction in the face of real, excruciating pain, loneliness, and desperation.

In addition to allowing the imprisoned humanists to enjoy each
other's company, Rodrigo provided reading materials, and the letters
he wrote formed the basis for some of their discussions. Platina collected all the letters that Rodrigo and the humanists wrote, "so that
they can be put together in order in a volume, with which we will ren-
der the annoyance of prison lighter, and perhaps produce something
that may help those whom a similar misfortune awaits."[39] Yet it was
not so much the philosophy of the ancients or the theology of the
desert fathers in the letters that consoled them and gave them the will
to endure. It was the community of friends itself.

Loneliness had proved a greater foe than ignorance, but the high
culture of the humanists, though it failed to deal with the harsh reality
of incarceration by offering lasting consolation, did succeed in galva-
nizing group solidarity under threat. Even if classical teachings about
suffering offered the humanists little succor in their isolation, conversations and social interaction based on a common interest in an ancient literary culture gave them moral strength. This vitality, encapsu-
lated in learned conversations, dialogues, and rhetorical disputations,
survived the challenge of incarceration and deprivation. In the end,
the sense of community that Pope Paul II had tried to foster through
his staging of popular festivities was also the attribute that allowed the
humanists to survive his persecution.

Epilogue

[Paul] was considered just and merciful—if it is not a kind of injustice to wear men down with chains for a minor offense. For it is questionable whether death is a greater punishment than lengthy incarceration.

—PLATINA, LIFE OF PAUL (EARLY DRAFT)

*P*LATINA WAS finally released in March 1469, thanks to the intervention of Cardinal Gonzaga. Pomponio and the other humanists had already recovered their freedom. Platina repaid his patron by dedicating the recently completed *History of Mantua* to him. In the dedication, Platina wrote: "By your great authority you liberated me from death; kindly, you continue to bestow favors on me as a free man and help me so much that no one else in the city of Rome enjoys freer life and thought."[1] Life changed significantly for the humanists after Paul died and Sixtus IV became pope in 1471. Platina finally gained the patronage he thought he deserved, when Sixtus put him in charge of the Vatican Library and commissioned him to write a history of the popes.

Under Sixtus the academy was re-formed around Pomponio Leto. Humanist graffiti in the Catacombs of Saint Calixtus dating to 1475 attest to the group's continued existence. "Academia Romana," "Pomponius Pontifex Maximus," and "Pantagathus sacerdos" all appear on the walls. Although the humanist community had been brutally suppressed, it was restored and once again able to thrive. The scholars continued to study pagan authors and to employ mock rituals in their club, as these examples of graffiti attest. Perhaps because Callimachus was absent, the humanists played it safer, though, and in 1478 their academy was officially recognized as a lay Christian fraternity. One member, Pantagathus (a name he adopted, meaning "all holy") was actually a priest, who became bishop of Fermo.[2] Even after the learning of the humanists had been so dramatically called into question, they were able to resume their former playful pagan ways, which they did not seem to consider incompatible with Christianity.

From our standpoint the effeminate intellectuals of the Roman Academy might seem a most improbable threat to the papacy. They hardly fit the bill for would-be assassins of the pope or for serious rebels who would have been able to replace papal power or to rule Rome. Yet the humanists were directly or indirectly associated with all the most pressing issues and threats to the Church during Paul's pontificate. At times the humanists expressed support for a reform movement in favor of a more democratic Church that would drastically curtail the power of the popes. Platina was an outspoken critic of Paul's attempts to reform church administration. As we have seen, when he lost his job as a papal secretary in 1464, Platina tried to call a general church council and have Paul deposed. A similar action was threatened in 1468. The academicians' love of pagan literature and homoerotic culture represented an attack on the core teachings of the Church and threatened to corrupt Christian youth. The humanists were seen as dangerously pagan in the Platonic beliefs they adopted about the soul and in their Epicurean morals. Their appreciation of male beauty and the production of homoerotic poetry accordingly gave rise to charges of sodomy.

Clearly, the humanists' connection with external threats also made the men legitimately suspect. Their curiosity and their correspondence with the East brought them into contact with Islam and linked them to the Ottoman Turks, enemies of Christendom. Callimachus and Pomponio were poor; the Turks could make them rich. Every year the unstoppable Sultan Mehmet II came closer to achieving his ultimate goal of conquering Italy, occupying Rome, and killing the pope. Even the pope's own teacher, George of Trebizond, had fallen under the spell of the sultan. Italian spies, such as Benedetto Dei, had shown the damage that Christians in the East could do to other Christians. Finally, the humanists' love of antiquity and contempt for clerical authority disturbingly called to mind recent rebellions and attempts to replace papal rule in Rome with the glorious republic of Roman antiquity. Two later Renaissance popes, Julius II and Leo X, and the imposing cathedral of Saint Peter's can give the impression that Rome was dominated by the papal power. Such apparent stability, however, was achieved only after a century of constant strife between papal and civic governments. Pope Eugene IV, forced to flee Rome in 1434, remained in exile for nine years; in 1453 Nicholas V faced a serious threat in Stefano Porcari, whose conspiracy might well have succeeded had he not lost the element of surprise. Pius II ceded control of Rome for a good six months in 1460. Paul II, who lived through all these upheavals, did not take rebellion lightly.

Pope Paul II deserves condemnation for subjecting the humanists to torture and confinement in inhuman conditions, which should never be condoned. Far worse punishments were nevertheless regularly meted out by premodern European courts. Criminals were often tortured and executed without trial and sometimes without evidence. Due process, the assumption of innocence, and the rights of the accused are modern inventions. The legal justification for torture was institutionalized in Roman law. Truth had to be obtained by compulsion.[3]

The papal dungeon, though a miserable hellhole, was no worse than other prisons of the day. After Niccolò Machiavelli was arrested and tortured for participating in a conspiracy against the Medici in 1513, he spent a horrifying two months in the Bargello, the prison of Florence.

In a poem to a potential patron, he describes his cell: "Fat and bloated fleas as big as butterflies bounce off the walls; there was not such an awful stench at Roncesvalles or among the trees of Sardinia as at my exquisite lodgings. A clamorous rumbling makes it seem like Jupiter's thunderbolt on earth and Mount Etna. One man is shackled and another is unchained, amid the clanging of keys in keyholes and bolts; yet another screams that they have hoisted him too high on the strappado!"[4] The fleas he mentions are reminiscent of Porcellio's and Benvenuto Cellini's experiences with vermin in the Castel Sant'Angelo (see Chapter 6). The screams of the man being tortured recall Platina's vivid image of the cries of the humanists resounding so loudly that the Castel Sant'Angelo resembled Phalaris' bull.

Paul, the pope who prided himself on never imposing the death penalty, favored lengthy prison sentences. He also condemned murderers to serve as galley slaves, manning the heavy oars on immense ships plying the Mediterranean and the Aegean. The pope's aversion to killing and his respect for life were not limited to human beings: "He would not even allow animals to be mistreated or slaughtered in his presence. He never wanted chickens or other birds killed in front of him; in fact, he snatched them out of his servants' hands and let them escape unharmed. Once from his window in Rome he saw a butcher leading a calf to slaughter, he summoned the man, bought the calf, and paid the butcher to lead it to a herd and allowed it to live. While passing through the city of Sutrina, he saw a man holding a goat down with his hand for slaughter. He paid the man and freed the goat."[5] Of course, Paul ate meat—you could say that he was more squeamish than principled—but taking cruelty toward animals into account at all was unusual in the Renaissance. Paul also had his own pets. He loved parrots, as discussed earlier, and had a favorite little dog.[6] In addition to his domestic animals, the pope also kept a tiger from India on a chain. It would thus not be unreasonable to maintain that Paul's humaneness—his respect for human life as well as his love of animals—was enlightened for his times.

In rejecting the death penalty, Paul proved to be radically different from his predecessors, who had been merciless when it came to any threat to their power, let alone their lives. His uncle, Eugene IV, was notorious for his cruelty, especially toward the Colonna family.[7] Nicholas V had Stefano Porcari and eight other conspirators tortured and executed within three days of their arrest in 1453; and even so, a winged goddess in Orazio Romano's epic about the conspiracy praised Nicholas for his leniency, saying: "Porcari has paid a light penalty and not suffered harsh tortures; for they hung that great and ugly weight of his, when they could have torn his entire body from its members, laid waste to it on the ground, given his entrails to wild dogs, and cursed his name throughout the world forever."[8] After torturing the conspirators in 1460, Pius II boasted of his restraint in executing them rather than using the "specially devised punishments" favored by a senator.[9] Paul may indeed have regarded himself as lenient in having the humanists tortured and incarcerated but not executed.

Paul claimed that life, as a divine gift of God, was precious. One man should not dare to take away what God has given. Platina, after being cruelly tortured and imprisoned, might have argued about Paul's respect for the sanctity of life. Yet it is true that the humanist survived and went on to enjoy fame and prosperity as the librarian of the Vatican Library under Pope Sixtus IV. Platina nevertheless raises a key point about the importance of the quality of life. Platina said that the social deprivation and physical pain of incarceration were worse than death. Is there a point at which a man's life is no longer worthy of being called human?

Platina and his friends offer a peculiarly humanist definition of life. They focus not on the life as opposed to death but on what makes life worth living and what the essential qualities of a full life are. The hu-

Pope Sixtus IV appoints Platina prefect of the Vatican Library, painting by Melozzo da Forli, Pinacoteca, Vatican Museums, Vatican State. © Erich Lessing / Art Resource, New York. The next pope became a much-needed patron. Sixtus commissioned Platina to write a history of the popes, then made him prefect of the Vatican Library.

manists follow Aristotle in viewing man as a social or political animal. Virtue is not a characteristic, but a way of acting. People become prudent, generous, and courageous by acting wisely, helping their fellow beings, and performing brave deeds. Interacting with others is essential to living virtuously. Virtue, according to Aristotle and the Stoics, leads to happiness and the fullest kind of life.

By denying the humanists the right to participate in society, prison has denied them life. The worst aspect of prison, they wrote, was their inability to help their friends and to converse. The agony of torture and their forced captivity made it difficult for them to think of anything beyond their immediate distress. Even if they could have found refuge in contemplation of the divine, though, like monks who have sworn to maintain perpetual silence and dispensed with human contact, their lives would have been incomplete. The classical conception of the human being, which the humanists adopted in opposition to the Christian monastic ideal of solitary contemplation, is based on community. The wise man is no hermit or persecuted saint, but an active member of society.

Paul's lifeless body was found in the early hours of July 26, 1471. Platina attributed the pope's death to a stroke brought on by two very large melons that the pope had eaten the day before.[10] There was a rumor, however, that Paul had been strangled by devils that he kept under lock and key. Another source had it that the strangler was an evil spirit that had been trapped in a ring the pope used to wear.[11] Whatever the cause of his sudden demise, the pope was gone, and a friend wondered whether Platina had forgiven him:

> I would like to know how much Platina is raging now:
> Whether he spares the spirits and pardons the funeral pyre;
> Whether he has dug [the pope's] bones out of the hollow tomb,
> Trampled on them, and scattered them to the wind.
> And who would not forgive Platina, if he were still angry?[12]

Platina was still furious. He would exonerate himself and achieve his revenge in his scathing life of the pope: as Platina had predicted, the biographer had the last word. Paul has been reviled through the centuries as a boorish, uneducated, cruel tyrant.

The plot of 1468 will always remain mysterious. The sources do not definitively prove that there was a conspiracy, nor do they point to a single cause for the pope's reaction. They do, however, reveal the complexity of the situation. The Milanese ambassadors' reports, for example, which seem to be our most objective sources, pile up accusations and attribute a variety of motives to the humanists. This surfeit of explanations may point to an understandable confusion in the immediate aftermath of the arrests, but it also confirms that the humanists had abundant and plausible reasons to murder the pope. If each explanation taken separately is conceivable, then taken together the motives make the presence of a conspiracy probable, even likely. By exploring each accusation in its particular historical context, I have tried to demonstrate that the reason for Pope Paul's reaction can be found not in a single fear but in the coalescence of multiple threats and possibilities. Similarly, no single cause drove the humanists to despise the pope and long for an end to papal tyranny. They had homosexual proclivities, held pagan beliefs, desired a more democratic Church, would have welcomed the reestablishment of the Roman Republic, and might have yearned for the financial stability that the Turkish sultan's patronage would bring.

For the humanists, scholarship was political, and therefore dangerous. The revival of classical thought that characterized the Renaissance was powerful enough to lead the humanists to behave in a way that imperiled their lives, but not powerful enough to offer them consolation in the hour of extremity. Faced with the anguish of torture and incarceration, they found that only communal discussion, debate, and love could save them. Even if we will never know exactly what the humanists were planning during carnival in 1468, the dramatic events that unfolded present a vivid picture for us, in the humanists' own writings, of the Renaissance not as a golden age of learning, but as a time of clashes among the political, sexual, and intellectual cultures in fifteenth-century Rome.

Notes

1. Carnival to Lent

1. Blanchus, 1884, 557. All translations are my own, unless otherwise indicated.
2. Platina, 1913–1932, 380; Egidio, 184.
3. Platina, 1913–1932, 364; discussed with archival evidence in Ian Robertson, "Pietro Barbo—Paul II: Zentihomo de Venecia e Pontificato," in *War, Culture, and Society in Renaissance Venice: Essays in Honour of John Hale* (London: Hambledon, 1993), ed. David Chambers, Cecil H. Clough, and Michael Mallet, 150–151. Pastor, 4:14.
4. Platina, 1913–1932, 366. Gaida supports this report, citing another source, ibid., n. 2.
5. Canensius, 172; Clementi, 58.
6. Niccolò della Tuccia, as cited in Pastor, 4:16.
7. Platina, 1913–1932, 391–392. Gaida, ibid., supports this assertion with additional sources in his notes.
8. Pastor, 4:12.
9. Canensius, 142.
10. Clementi, 59, 65–66. Canensius, 116–117; Platina, 1913–1932, 367. For specific carnival expenditures during Paul's pontificate, see Modigliani, 2003, 159–161; Cruciani, 113–139.
11. John Gage, *Life in Italy at the Time of the Medici* (London: Batsford, 1968), 11, 62, 92, 113; Peter Partner, *Rome, 1500–1559: Portrait of a Society* (Berkeley: University of California Press, 1976), 21.
12. Canensius, 117. On Paul's medals, see Roberto Weiss, *Un umanista veneziano: Papa Paolo II* (Venice: Istituto per la collaborazione culturale, 1958), 49–68; and Modigliani, 2003, 144.

13. Clementi, 70. John M. Najemy, *A History of Florence, 1200–1575* (Oxford: Blackwell, 2006), 337.

14. Infessura, 265; Clementi, 71.

15. Egidio, 184; Platina, 1913–1932, 380.

16. Canensius, 116, n. 1.

17. In Venice broadsheets warned Christians not to attack Jews or enter their synagogues during carnival. The famous plague doctor mask still popular in Venetian tourist shops with its long hooked nose was originally known as the "Jew's mask."

18. Sabellicus, 3r.

19. Blanchus, 1884, 555.

20. Modigliani, 2000, 694.

21. On the serious and sophisticated nature of Renaissance astrology, see Anthony Grafton, *Cardano's Cosmos: The Worlds and Works of a Renaissance Astrologer* (Cambridge: Harvard University Press, 1999).

22. Gaspare Broglio, quoted in Luigi Tonini, *Storia civile e sacra Riminese* (Rimini: Ghigi, 1971 [1882]), 5:314–315.

23. D. S. Chambers, "The Housing Problems of Cardinal Francesco Gonzaga," in *Renaissance Cardinals and Their Worldly Possessions* (Aldershot, U.K.: Ashgate, 1997), 21–58, 23.

24. Blanchus, 1884, 556–557.

25. Canensius, 117. "Rebellious subjects" refers to the rebels in Anguillara (Chapter 3).

26. Pomponio Leto, poem to Platina, in Masotti, 202.

27. "A Giuliano di Lorenzo de' Medici," 1:1–4. Referring to the original Italian, I have modified the translation in De Grazia, 34. Regarding the strappado, see De Grazia, 36.

28. Platina, 1913–1932, 383. Phalaris was a tyrant in the ancient city of Agrigentum in Sicily, who roasted his enemies alive inside a bronze bull. Thanks to its ingenious design, the screams of the victims within sounded like the braying of a bull. Its first victim, of course, was the craftsman who had constructed it for the tyrant.

29. Platina, 1913–1932, xviii–xix.

30. Blanchus, 1884, 557.

2. The Price of Magnificence

The Filelfo letter of September 15, 1464, to Pope Paul is quoted in De Vincentiis, 48, n. 121.

1. Canensius, 96–97.

2. Clementi, 58–73; Roy Strong, *Art and Power: Renaissance Festivals, 1450–1650* (Suffolk, Eng.: Boydell, 1984); Charles L. Stinger, *The Renaissance in Rome* (Bloomington: Indiana University Press, 1985).

3. Pastor, 4:18; Mantuan ambassadorial reports, in Cruciani, 118–119.

4. Niccolò Machiavelli, 7:6.

5. Peter Partner, "Papal Financial Policy in the Renaissance and Counter-Reformation," *Past and Present* no. 88 (1980): 17–62, 41.

6. Canensius, 82, n. 3; Platina, 1913–1932, 368, n. 1; T. Riccardi, *Storia dei Vescovi Vicentini* (Vicenza, 1786), 164–176.

7. Da Verona, 59.

8. De Vincentiis, 96; Roberto Weiss, *Un umanista veneziano: Papa Paolo II* (Venice: Istituto per la collaborazione culturale, 1958).

9. Canensius, 108.

10. Platina, 1913–1932, 392.

11. De Vincentiis, 97–101, and passim.

12. Crivelli, verses 530–533: "Talia de throni decernere Paule supremi / Maiestate videns non ulli aequabile regnum / Condis, et a rubro perductis littore gemmis / Quas habitis ornas; veluti presaga futuri."

13. Reported in Jean Jouffroy, *De dignitate cardinalatus,* quoted and discussed in Miglio, 139, and in De Vincentiis, 98.

14. John Monfasani, "The Fraticelli and Clerical Wealth in Quattrocento Rome," in *Renaissance Society and Culture: Essays in Honor of Eugene Rice, Jr.,* ed. J. Monfasani and R. Musto (New York: Italica, 1991), 177–195.

15. Norman Cohn, *Europe's Inner Demons: The Demonization of Christians in Medieval Christendom* (London: Pimlico, 1993), 61–73. See Flavio Biondo's colorful description of the heresy and an earlier persecution, Biondo Flavio, *Italy Illuminated,* trans. Jeffrey A. White (Cambridge: Harvard University Press, 2005), bk. 3, 5.13.

16. Canensius, 153.

17. On the debate over curial wealth, see Christopher S. Celenza, *Renaissance Humanism and the Papal Curia: Lapo da Castiglionchio's "De curiae commodis"* (Ann Arbor: Michigan University Press, 1999), 71–80.

18. Platina, 2008, 119. For more on Platina's criticism of clerical abuse, see Platina, 2008, xxv–xxvii.

19. Platina, 1913–1932, 388.

20. Platina, 1474, fol. 270r, as discussed in Bauer, 100.

21. Leonardo Bruni, *History of the Florentine People,* ed. and trans. James

Hankins (Cambridge: Harvard University Press, 2001), 1:50. Bauer, 100–101, n. 49, makes the comparison with emperors in Bruni.

22. *Palazzo Venezia: Paolo II e le fabbriche di s. Marco* (Rome: De Luca, 1980), 114–137, and passim; Torgil Magnuson, *Studies in Roman Quattrocento Architecture* (Stockholm: Almquist & Wiksell, 1958), 245–296.

23. Da Verona, 6; Canensius, 82.

24. Magnuson, *Studies in Roman Quattrocento Architecture,* 283.

25. Canensius, 115, editor's note. Modigliani, 2003, 142–143, nevertheless sees the festivities becoming more subdued and private.

26. Canensius, 117–135; Ammannati-Piccolomini, 1984, 11–16.

27. Ammannati-Piccolomini, 1984, 92.

28. Canensius, 135–136, with additional sources in notes; Biblioteca Apostolica Vaticana (henceforth BAV), Barb, Lat. 1991, fols. 22r–v, descriptive sources reproduced by Cruciani, 126–131. Also discussed in Modigliani, 2000, 690; Modigliani, 2003, 143.

29. Campano, *Epistolae,* bk. 5.1. On the context and dating of this letter, see Flavio Di Bernardo, *Un vescovo umanista alla corte Pontificia: Giannantonio Campano, 1429–1477* (Rome: Gregorian University Press, 1975), 190.

30. Ammannati-Piccolomini, 1997, 2:1202–1205. Also quoted in Modigliani, 2003, 139.

31. Clementi, 72–73, quoting Enrico Celani, ed., "La venuta di Borso d'Este a Roma, l'anno 1471," *Archivio della Società romana di storia patria* 13 (1890): 361–450, esp. 399–411.

32. Peter Burke, *Popular Culture in Early Modern Europe* (London: T. Smith, 1978), 182–204.

33. Platina, 1913–1932, 387; Canensius, 165, says 130 Germans were knighted; Pastor, 4:166; Platina, 1998, 22.

34. Platina, 1913–1932, 333.

35. Platina, 1913–1932, 388; Pastor, 4:162.

36. The actual term "Holy Roman Empire" was coined only in the thirteenth century.

37. Crivelli, verses 494–506; De Vincentiis, 94, 105.

38. Patrizi, 1733.

39. The estimate of the number of torches by a person in Frederick's retinue is reported in Pastor, 4:163.

40. Patrizi, 1733, 208; Canensius, 163–166.

41. Canensius, 167–168.

42. Pastor, 4:168.

43. Canensius, 164.

44. Patrizi, 1733, 215.

45. Blanchus, 1884, 559.

46. Pastor, 4:99–103.

47. Modigliani, 2000, 687. Blanchus, 1884, 555.

48. D'Amico, 92–93.

49. Gregorovius, 7.1, 219–220, 221–222; Pastor, 4:7–10.

50. Creighton, 4:6–7; Gregorovius, 7.1, 222.

51. Pastor, 4:25.

52. Platina, 1913–1932, 392; Creighton, 4:7–8; Pastor, 4:28.

53. Platina, 1913–1932, 367.

54. Platina, 1474, fol. 262v, as discussed in Bauer, 98–99.

55. Ammannati-Piccolomini; Pastor, 4:25.

56. Pastor, 4:27; Palermino, 130.

57. Canensius, 141, n. 4.

58. Pastor, 4:25–28; Canensius, 141, n. 4.

59. Platina, 1913–1932, 368.

60. Egidio, 183.

61. Ludwig von Pastor, the nineteenth-century Catholic historian, argued that Paul was a church reformer. Pastor, vol. 4.

62. Platina, 1913–1932, 364; also discussed with archival evidence in Ian Robertson, "Pietro Barbo–Paul II: Zentihomo de Venecia e Pontificato," in *War, Culture, and Society in Renaissance Venice: Essays in Honour of John Hale* (London: Hambledon, 1993), ed. David Chambers, Cecil H. Clough, and Michael Mallet, 150–151.

63. Quoted by Palermino, 128, n. 44.

64. D'Amico, 27–28; Stinger, *Renaissance in Rome*; Denys Hay, *The Church in Italy in the Fifteenth Century* (Cambridge: Cambridge University Press, 1977).

65. Platina, 1913–1932, 369.

66. Palermino, 126; D'Amico, 92.

67. Platina, 1913–1932, 369.

68. Ibid., 370.

69. Platina, 1474, fol. 272v, as discussed in Bauer, 101.

70. Ambassadorial report, quoted and discussed in Pastor, 4:40–41; Palermino, 126; and Bauer, 35.

71. Egidio, 183.

72. D'Amico, 29–30; Palermino, 127–128. De Vincentiis, 151.

73. Platina, 1913–1932, 384.

74. Pastor, 4:103, 105.

75. Masotti, 199.

3. Lessons of Rebellions Past

1. Biondo, 1531, 3.6:481; Biondo, 1963, 26.2–6:770–773; Platina, 1913–1932, 316–317; Bracciolini, 1993, 3.151–165; Gregorovius, 7.1:39–47.

2. Gregorovius, 6.2:476–484; Pastor, 1:111.

3. Gregorovius, 6.2:500–511; Pastor, 1:113–146.

4. Gregorovius, 6.2:642–652; Pastor, 1:194–207.

5. Frittelli, 14–15. Porcellio's nickname was bestowed on him because he apparently preferred the passive position in homosexual intercourse.

6. Maria Grazia Blasio, "Radici di un mito storiografico: Il ritratto umanistico di Martino V," in *Alle origini della nuova Roma: Martino V, 1417–1431*, ed. Maria Chiabò and others (Rome: Istituto storico italiano per il medioevo, 1992), 111–124.

7. See Concetta Bianca, "Dopo Costanza: Classici e umanisti," in Maria Chiabò and others, *Alle origini*, 85–110.

8. Porcellio, 1720, 503; Frittelli, 16–17; Paola Casciano, "Il pontificato di Martino V nei versi degli umanisti," in *Alle origini*, 144–145, 150.

9. Porcellio, 1427–1463, fols. 10r–v: "porrectus et inguina renes concutiens, puro mixtum cum sanguine semen emittit." The poem is quoted and described in Frittelli, 18–19.

10. Casciano, "Il pontificato di Martino V," 151, discusses images of columns in other poems dedicated to Martin V.

11. Bracciolini, 1993, 3.41–67.

12. Charles L. Stinger, *The Renaissance in Rome* (Bloomington: Indiana University Press, 1985), 14–31.

13. Bracciolini, 1993, 3.94–101, 326–339.

14. Gregorovius, 7.1:29; Platina, 1913–1932, 314.

15. Platina, 1913–1932, 316; Bracciolini, 1993, 3.151–155; Biondo, 1963, 26.1–3, 769–771.

16. Biondo, 1963, 26.2:770.

17. Ibid., 26.3:770–771.

18. Creighton, 2:324.

19. Infessura, 32.
20. Latin poem published in Frittelli, 25.
21. Infessura, 33–34.
22. Porcellio, 1720, 517.
23. Frittelli, 26–27.
24. Valla, 2007, 140–141; Infessura, 34. For examples of the bishop's cruelty, see Bracciolini, 1993, 3:616–623.
25. Infessura, 34–36.
26. Pastor, 1:300.
27. Stinger, *Renaissance in Rome*, 248–254; Christopher S. Celenza, *The Lost Italian Renaissance: Humanists, Historians, and Latin's Legacy* (Baltimore: Johns Hopkins University Press, 2004), 89–91.
28. Valla, 2007, 151–153. Manetti, 3:8–18, relates a history of Roman persecution against the popes in order to justify the construction of fortifications. See Miglio, 109–111; Carroll William Westfall, *In This Most Perfect Paradise: Alberti, Nicholas V, and the Invention of Conscious Urban Planning in Rome, 1447–1455* (University Park: Pennsylvania State University Press, 1974), 143–151.
29. Valla, 2007, 145.
30. Robert Black, "The Donation of Constantine: A New Source for the Concept of the Renaissance?" *Language and Images of Renaissance Italy*, ed. Alison Brown (Oxford: Clarendon, 1995), 51–85, esp. 69–70.
31. Charles Trinkaus, "Lorenzo Valla," in *Contemporaries of Erasmus*, ed. P. G. Bietenholz (Toronto: Toronto University Press, 1985), 3:374; Peter Partner, *The Pope's Men: The Papal Civil Service in the Renaissance* (Oxford: Clarendon, 1990), 120–123; Anthony Grafton, *Commerce with the Classics: Ancient Books and Renaissance Readers* (Ann Arbor: University of Michigan Press, 1997), 11–19, 49–52.
32. Stinger, *Renaissance in Rome*, 289–290. Celenza, *Lost Italian Renaissance*, 98.
33. Anna Modigliani, "Pio II e Roma," in *Il sogno di Pio II e il viaggio da Roma a Mantova*, ed. A. Calzona, F. P. Fiore, A. Tenenti, C. Vasoli (Florence: Olschki, 2000), 103–105; Giovanni Antonazzi, *Lorenzo Valla e la polemica sulla Donazione di Costantino* (Rome: Storia e letteratura, 1985), 121–128; Stinger, *Renaissance in Rome*, 248–254; Black, "The Donation of Constantine," 70–77.
34. Egidio, 184; Pastor, 1:306.

35. Platina, 1913–1932, 327; Gregorovius, 7.1:99; 7.2:549–540; D'Amico, 9, 31.

36. Bracciolini, 1993, 3:73–74, 84–90. See also Gregorovius, 7.1:61–62. Platina, 1913–1932, 327.

37. Anna Modigliani, *I Porcari: Storie di una famiglia romana tra Medioevo e Rinascimento* (Rome: Roma nel Rinascimento, 1994), 490; Roberto Cessi, *Saggi romani* (Rome: Storia e letteratura, 1956), 70–72.

38. Modigliani, *I Porcari,* 491–494.

39. Massimo Miglio, "'Viva la libertà et populo de Roma': Oratoria e politica: Stefano Porcari," in *Scritture, scrittori e storia* (Rome: Vecchiarelli, 1993 [1979]), 59–95; Arjo Vanderjagt, "Civic Humanism in Practice: The Case of Stefano Porcari and the Christian Tradition," in *Antiquity Renewed: Late Classical and Early Modern Themes,* ed. Zweder von Martels and Victor M. Schmidt (Leuven: Peeters, 2003), 63–78.

40. Miglio, 61–118, 205–249; Manfredo Tafuri, *Ricerca del Rinascimento: Principi, città, architetti* (Milan: Einaudi, 1992), 47–50, and passim; Anthony Grafton, *Leon Battista Alberti: Master Builder of the Italian Renaissance* (Cambridge: Harvard University Press, 2000), 278–279, 295–330; Westfall, *In This Most Perfect Paradise;* Charles Burroughs, *From Signs to Design: Environmental Process and Reform in Early Renaissance Rome* (Cambridge: MIT University Press, 1990).

41. Pastor, 2:74–105, 138–164, 289–299.

42. Infessura, 45–46; Platina, 1913–1932, 329; Miglio, "'Viva la libertà et populo,'" 86; Modigliani, *I Porcari,* 491.

43. Laurie Nussdorfer, "The Vacant See: Ritual and Protest in Early Modern Rome," *Sixteenth Century Journal* 18 (1987): 172–189.

44. Peter Burke, *Popular Culture in Early Modern Europe* (London: T. Smith, 1978), 182–204; Clementi, 70–205.

45. Cessi, *Saggi romani,* 77–78; Pastor, 2:222.

46. Platina, 1913–1932, 336; Pastor, 2:222.

47. Gregorovius, 7.1:132–133; L. Fumi, "Nuove rivelazioni della congiura di Stefano Porcari," *Archivio della società romana di storia patria* 33 (1910): 490; Tommasini, 105–110, esp. 106.

48. Caccia, 97; Pastor, 2:223–224; Porcari, 1453, 511–512.

49. Anonymous letter, in Tommasini, 106–107.

50. Romano, bk. 1, ll. 239–286. On the *Porcaria,* see Vladimir Zabughin, *Vergilio nel Rinascimento italiano,* ed. S. Carrai and A. Cavarzere (Trent, Italy: Università degli Studi di Trento, 2000 [1921–1929]), 1:293–296. On

Orazio Romano, see Anna Maria Oliva, "Orazio Romano," *Roma nel Rinascimento* (1994): 23–29. See also the similar version of the speech in Alberti, 260–261.

51. Documented in Westfall, *In This Most Perfect Paradise*, 63–84.

52. Cicero, *Tusculan Disputations,* as discussed in Quentin Skinner, *The Foundations of Modern Political Thought*, vol. 1: *The Renaissance* (Cambridge: Cambridge University Press, 1978), 87–101.

53. Romano, 1:260–263.

54. Porcari, 1874, 19, 44.

55. Anonymous letter, in Tommasini, 107.

56. Caccia, 96; Tommasini, 109; Fumi, "Nuove rivelazioni," 492; Pastor, 2:513, 516.

57. Pastor, 2:226–227. On George of Trebizond's prophetic knowledge of the conspiracy, see Monfasani, 83–86.

58. Tommasini, 108; Infessura, 53–54.

59. Caccia, 97–98; Platina, 1913–1932, 336.

60. Pastor, 2:228; Tommasini, 109–110.

61. For a more extensive discussion of these writers and their contradictory accounts, see Anthony F. D'Elia, "Stefano Porcari's Conspiracy against Pope Nicholas V in 1453 and Republican Culture in Papal Rome," *Journal of the History of Ideas* 68, no. 2 (April 2007): 207–231.

62. Alberti; Modigliani, *I Porcari*, 495–497; Tafuri, *Ricerca del Rinascimento*, 44–45; Grafton, *Leon Battista Alberti*, 306–308; Riccardo Fubini, "Papato e storiografia nel Quattrocento: Storia, biografia, e propaganda in un recente studio," *Studi medievali* 3d series, 18, no. 1 (1977): 321–351, 329–331.

63. Miglio, "'Viva la libertà et populo,'" 74–75; Modigliani, *I Porcari*, 495–496. Romano.

64. Romano, 1:281.

65. Machiavelli, bk. 6, section 29. On Machiavelli and Porcari, see A. Modigliani, "Aporie e profezie petrarchesche tra Stefano Porcari e Niccolò Machiavelli," *Roma nel Rinascimento* (1995): 53–67; Marcello Simonetta, *Rinascimento segreto: Il mondo del segretario da Petrarca a Machiavelli* (Milan: FrancoAngeli, 2004), 240–241.

66. Alberti, 261.

67. Infessura, 54; Gregorovius, 7.1:138; Modigliani, *I Porcari*, 492. For positive contemporary assessments of Porcari, see Paola Farenga, "'I Romani sono periculoso populo. . .': Roma nei carteggi diplomatici," in

Roma capitale, 1447–1527, ed. S. Gensini (Pisa: Pacini, 1994), 289–315, esp. 293–296.

68. Godi, 62. On Godi, see Anna Modigliani, "Godi, Pietro," in *Dizionario biografico degli italiani* (2001), 57:515–517.

69. Romano, 1:389–394. See also Platina, 1913–1932, 336.

70. Romano, 1:343–349.

71. Ibid., 496–503; 2:456–469.

72. Cessi, *Saggi romani,* 107–108, and Pastor, 2:235, have also noted this.

73. Manetti, 3:17.

74. Bripio, 330–375.

75. Porcari, 1874, 14–15.

76. Gregorovius, 7.1:137 (on wine and pardon); Caccia, 99 (on leniency); Pastor, 2:510–517; Cessi, *Saggi romani,* 113–128; Platina, 1913–1932, 336.

77. Charles Burroughs, "A Planned Myth and a Myth of Planning: Nicholas V and Rome," in *Rome in the Renaissance: The City and the Myth,* ed. P. A. Ramsey (Binghamton, N.Y.: Center for Medieval and Early Renaissance Studies, 1982), 203–204; Westfall, *In This Most Perfect Paradise,* 101; Burroughs, *From Signs to Design,* 109–110.

78. On the influence of Sallust in the Renaissance, see Patricia J. Osmond, "Princeps Historiae Romanae: Sallust in Renaissance Political Thought," *Memoirs of the American Academy in Rome* 40 (1995): 101–143; Quentin Skinner, "The Vocabulary of Renaissance Republicanism: A Cultural *Longue-Durée*?" *Language and Images of Renaissance Italy,* 87–110.

79. On Pomponio's commentary on Sallust, see *Antiquaria a Roma: Intorno a Pomponio Leto e Paolo II,* ed. Massimo Miglio (Rome: Roma nel Rinascimento, 2003). The commentary was written after 1468 but there is no reason to doubt that Pomponio read and taught the popular Roman author in the 1460s.

80. Quoted and discussed in Massimo Miglio, "Precedenti ed esiti dell'antiquaria romana del quattrocento," ibid., xxxvii. See also Altieri's praise for Pomponio and Platina in his will, "Testamento di Marco Antonio Altieri," in Altieri, 61*–73*, 72*.

81. Altieri, 42. Also discussed in Miglio, "Precedenti ed esiti," xxxvi–xxxviii; Della Torre, 84–86.

82. Zabughin, 2:140–141.

83. Altieri, 138, 140–142.

84. "Testamento," in Altieri, 35*–36*; Miglio, "Precedenti ed esiti," xxxix–xl.
85. Pius, 2007, 4:28.
86. Ibid.
87. Quoted in Della Torre, 128–130, without a date. Gregorovius, 7.1, 187–188, dates the letter to 1460, when Pius was absent from Rome. There is a slight problem with this date because Campano says that he went to Rome to get the pope's blessing. I have decided to follow Gregorovius' dating, since Campano never says that he actually met the pope.
88. Machiavelli would later use this example in his discussion of Roman religion, which, he said, the Romans used to foster a social bond and unite the people against outside threats. In contrast to Campano, Machiavelli criticizes Christianity as promoting disunity and weakness. See Machiavelli, *The Discourses,* ed. Bernard Crick, trans. Leslie J. Walker (London: Penguin, 1998 [1970]), bk. 1, chaps. 11–15, and bk. 2, chap. 2.
89. Pius, 2007, 4.38.
90. Pius, 2007, 4.31.
91. Pius, 1993, 5.2.
92. Jacob Burckhardt, *The Civilisation of the Renaissance in Italy,* trans. S. G. C. Middlemore (London: Penguin, 1990 [1860]), 25.
93. Simonetta, 333: "Jacopo cuius animum immoderata dominandi libido quotidie vexabat." Machiavelli, bk. 7, section 8, 239.
94. Porcellio, 1723 and 1751.
95. Burckhardt was especially impressed by Porcellio's fieldwork, as he mentions in his chapter "War as a Work of Art," in *Civilisation of the Renaissance,* 99–100.
96. Porcellio, 1723, 20:79.
97. Porcellio, 1751, 25:5.
98. Ibid., 59, 33, 50 (quotation); 1723, 20:76.
99. Simonetta, 333; Cristoforo da Soldo, *La cronica di Cristoforo da Soldo,* ed. G. Brizzolara, in Rerum Italicarum Scriptores (Bologna: Zanichelli, 1938), 21, bk. 3, 132.
100. Pius, 2003, 1.31. See also Porcellio, 1723 and 1751, 106.
101. Simonetta, 437 ("atroxissimeque, quantum numquam antea ducum nostrorum memoria").
102. Pius, 2007, 4.39.

103. Compare with the accolades of Nicholas V's rule, discussed in D'Elia, 2007.
104. Pius, 2007, 4.40.
105. Ibid.
106. Ibid., 41.
107. Frittelli, 70.
108. Pius, 1993, 5.2:239. The quotation about the lack of time is from Infessura, 65. On the pope's allies, see Simonetta, 438–440.
109. Pius, 1993, 5.2:239–240.
110. Ibid., 12.10:573.
111. Egidio, 183.
112. Machiavelli, bk. 7, section 8, 286.
113. Blanchus, 1906, 483.
114. Pastor, 4:158–160.
115. As discussed in Platina, 1913–1932, xx, 381; Blanchus, 1884, 557–558; Canensius, 156; Patrizi, 1911, 182; and Egidio, 184.
116. Pastor, 4:52, 58; Blanchus, 1906, 490.

4. A Pagan Renaissance

Patrizi, 1911, 182.
1. Latin poem published in Josef Delz, "Ein unbekannter Brief von Pomponius Laetus," *Italia medioevale e umanistica* 9 (1966): 417–440; poem quoted on 421. On Ganymede and homosexual culture, see James Saslow, *Ganymede in the Renaissance: Homosexuality in Art and Society* (New Haven, Conn.: Yale University Press, 1986).
2. Pomponio Leto, MS: Marc. Lat. Classe XII, n. 210 (4689), fol. 34r, "Ille erit ille felix tenerum cui sydera culum / prestiterint: culo conciliatur Amor, / divitiae culo, culo tribuentur honores / egregio culo fata benigna favent."
3. Pius, 1909, Epistle 78, September 1443, 190–191.
4. On the pope's collecting classically inspired medals, see Roberto Weiss, *Un umanista veneziano: Papa Paolo II* (Venice: Istituto per la collaborazione culturale, 1958), 67. On Paul and printing, see Alison Frazier, *Possible Lives: Authors and Saints in Renaissance Italy* (New York: Columbia University Press, 2004), 239–240; Modigliani, 2000, 691–693. On Paul's luxurious furnishings, see Magnuson, 285. On Paul's restoration of churches, see Canensius, 156–157. Platina, 2008, 16.1.

5. Hankins, 1.213; Concetta Bianca, *Da Bisanzio a Roma: Studi sul cardinale Bessarione* (Rome: Roma nel Rinascimento, 1999); Palermino, 120.

6. Leto, 1894, 191. On Biondo, see De Vincentiis, 48.

7. On Canensius and Gaspare da Verona, see Miglio, 24–30, 121–125, 181–183; and Modigliani, 2000, 687.

8. The Catholic historian Pastor saw Paul as a defender of the true Christian Renaissance against the "heathen Renaissance" of Pomponio Leto and the humanists.

9. Platina, 1913–1932, 389. See also Canensius, 141–142, who says that in conversation Paul usually interspersed his remarks with witticisms.

10. Platina, 1913–1932, 389, 364; MS Florence BNCF, fols. 270v, 262r ("etsi eius rude ingenium esset"), as discussed in Bauer, 97.

11. Creighton, 4:57.

12. Egidio, 184.

13. Platina, 1778, 30–31.

14. Modigliani, 2003, 138–139, quoting a letter to Paul from Ammannati-Piccolomini, who criticizes the pope for the *vanitas* of such displays.

15. Quotations from Blanchus, 1906, 491; also discussed in Pastor, 4:59–60; Palermino, 129; and Dunston, 301.

16. Bracciolini, 1946, 38–41; Bracciolini, 1994, 60.

17. Pius, 2002, 221. Aeneas also recommends Plautus and Terence, ibid., 223. The popular Ferrarese educator, Battista Guarino, 289, further commends Juvenal, Plautus, and Terence as models of Latinity for boys.

18. Canensius, 217 (editor's note). On the popularity of Juvenal, see Eva M. Sanford, "Juvenalis," *Catalogus Translationum et Commentariorum: Mediaeval and Renaissance Latin Translations and Commentaries, Annotated Lists and Guides*, ed. P. O. Kristeller (Washington, D.C.: Catholic University of America Press, 1960), 1:175–238, esp. 210–212, 216–218.

19. Barbaro, 106; Terence, *The Eunuch*, III.6.

20. Augustine, *City of God*, II.7; *Confessions*, XVI.26. On treatments of this passage in the sixteenth century, see Carlo Ginzburg, "Titian, Ovid, and Sixteenth-Century Codes for Erotic Illustrations," in *Clues, Myths, and the Historical Method* (Baltimore: Johns Hopkins University Press, 1989), 77–94.

21. Laurentius de Pensauro, dispatch to Francesco Sforza, quoted in Pastor, 4:61.

22. Giovanni Garzoni, *De christianorum felicitate*, MS 2648, fol. 81r. Bologna University Library. The Latin quoted is in Frazier, *Possible Lives*, 240, n. 92 (my translation).

23. Egidio, 184.

24. Palermino, 121–123.

25. Valla, 1977. See also Franco Cardini and Cesare Vasoli, "Rinascimento e Umanesimo," in *Storia della letteratura italiana*, vol. 3: *Il Quattrocento*, ed. Enrico Malato (Rome: Salerno S. R. L., 1996), 55; Maristella Lorch, preface to Valla, 1977, 33–40.

26. On this issue in general, see Howard Jones, *The Epicurean Tradition* (London: Routledge, 1989), 142; Eugenio Garin, "Ricerche sull'epicureismo del Quattrocento," in *La cultura filosofica del Rinascimento italiano* (Florence: Bompiani-Sansoni, 1994), 72–92.

27. Sabellicus, 2v; Della Torre, 81.

28. Sabellicus, 3r, 2v.

29. Leto, 1894, 191; Giovanni Lovito, *L'Opera e i tempi di Pomponio Leto* (Salerno: Laveglia, 2002), 39; Della Torre, 82–83; Zabughin, 1:26.

30. Dante, *Inferno*, XIX; Boccaccio, *Decamerone*, passim.

31. On anticlericalism in Renaissance literature, see Lauro Martines, "The Italian Renaissance Tale as History," in *Language and Images of Renaissance Italy*, ed. Alison Brown (Oxford: Oxford University Press, 1995), 313–330.

32. Sabellicus, 2v.

33. Zabughin, 1:47–52.

34. Michele Ferno, "Vita" (letter on the death of Pomponio Leto), Latin quoted in Zabughin, 296, n. 151 (my translation). On the letter, see Della Torre, 57–58.

35. Platina, 1778, 37. See also Platina, 1913–1932, 388

36. De' Giudici, 96. On this invective, see Bauer, 49; D'Amico, 95.

37. Platina, 1913–1932, 386.

38. Canensius, 153–155; also quoted in Pastor, 4:48.

39. Della Torre, 124–125. For other examples of the humanists' mentions of pagan gods, see Zabughin, 1:293–295.

40. Patrizi, 1911, 182.

41. Blanchus, 1906, 488.

42. Egidio, 184.

43. Platina, 1913–1932, 388.

44. Della Torre, 126.

45. Monfasani, 1976, 158–160.
46. George of Trebizond, *Comparatio,* quoted and discussed in Monfasani (my translation from the Latin), 158, and passim. See also Hankins, 1:240.
47. Hankins, 1:259–261.
48. Ibid., 210.
49. Monfasani, 188, with quotation from letter at n. 47.
50. John Monfasani, *Fernando of Cordova: A Biographical and Intellectual Profile* (Philadelphia: American Philosophical Association, 1992), 37; preface to Niccolò Palmieri's censorship report, transcribed in Hankins, vol. 2, n. 62.
51. Monfasani, 160.
52. See manuscript at the BAV, http://www.loc.gov/exhibits/vatican/humanism.html.
53. Leto, 1894, 185–187; Lovito, 37–38.
54. Leto, 1894, 187.
55. Quintilian, *Institutes of Oratory,* II.2.
56. Leto, 1894, 187.
57. Latin text published in Delz, "Ein unbekannter Brief," 433 (my translation).
58. Sabellicus, 3r; Della Torre, 86.
59. Michael Rocke, *Forbidden Friendships: Homosexuality and Male Culture in Renaissance Florence* (Oxford: Oxford University Press, 1996), 11.
60. Michael Rocke, "Gender and Sexual Culture in Renaissance Italy," in Judith C. Brown and Robert C. Davis, eds., *Gender and Society in Renaissance Italy* (London: Longman, 1998), 166.
61. Guido Ruggiero, *The Boundaries of Eros: Sex Crimes and Society in Renaissance Venice* (Oxford: Oxford University Press, 1985), 109–145, and the chart of sodomy prosecutions in Venice, 128.
62. Leto, 1894, 187.
63. Zabughin, 2:283–284, nn. 90–93.
64. Deposition for Pomponio, 185.
65. Without pursuing it further, D'Amico writes: "Socrates was a byword for more than wisdom in the Renaissance" (93–94).
66. Blanchus, 1906, 488, 489.
67. On the Roman epigrams, see Kazimierz Kumaniecki, "Il periodo italiano dell'opera poetica di Filippo Buonaccorsi: I suoi epigrammi romani," in *Il mondo antico nel Rinascimento* (Florence: Sansoni, 1958),

65–73; L. Calvelli, "Un umanista italiano in Polonia: Filippo Buonaccorsi da S. Gimignano," *Miscellanea storica della Valdelsa* 23 (1915): 45–65. Kumaniecki does not even mention homoeroticism.

68. Pius, 2002, 222–223.

69. Frank-Rutger Hausmann, "Martialis, Marcus Valerius," *Catalogus Translationum et Commentariorum: Mediaeval and Renaissance Latin Translations and Commentaries, Annotated Lists and Guides*, ed. F. Edward Cranz (Washington, D.C.: Catholic University of America Press, 1980), 4:249–296, esp. 252; Masotti, 191.

70. Callimachus, poem 91. The story of Ganymede and Alexis appears in Martial 5.55, 9.36, 6.68.

71. Calvelli, "Un umanista italiano in Polonia," 60–61; Gioacchino Paparelli, introduction to Callimachi Experientis (Philippi Bonaccorsi), *Carmina*, ed. Francesco Sica (Naples: Fratelli Conte, 1981), 5.

72. Callimachus, poem 90.

73. Callimachus, poem 41.

74. Ibid., poems 37–38, where Callimachus refers to banquets. Platina, 1998; Bauer, 52.

75. Callimachus, poem 28. Callimachus praises male beauty in poems 115 and 125, which are about Glaucus' desire for a boy, "Pamphilius puer." Martial 3.65. The same construction is used in 9.57 and 11.21.

76. Callimachus, poem 109, 117; poem 113 also mention *formosos* and *formosos pueros*—"handsome boys."

77. Martial 10.42.

78. Martial 9.36. See also 1.31 and 12.84.

79. Platina, 1913–1932, 383.

80. Leto, 1468b, fol. 109v.

81. Paolo Marsi, *Bembice*, published by Della Torre, 146–147. Martial's epitaphs to beloved boys are moving and without satire (1.88; 6.28–29, 68).

82. Callimachus, poem 133.

83. Rocke, *Forbidden Friendships*, 1996.

84. See also Callimachus, poems 141–142. On invectives against passive homosexuals in antiquity, see Amy Richlin, *The Garden of Priapus: Sexuality and Aggression in Roman Humor* (New Haven, Conn.: Yale University Press, 1983), 135–139, and passim; J. N. Adams, *The Latin Sexual Vocabulary* (Baltimore: Johns Hopkins University Press, 1982), 118–122.

85. Callimachus, poem 155.

86. Steven E. Ozment, *Ancestors: The Loving Family in Old Europe* (Cam-

bridge: Harvard University Press, 2001); Rudolph Bell, *How to Do It: Guides to Good Living for Renaissance Italians* (Chicago: Chicago University Press, 1999).

87. Martial 12.75, 12.96; Richlin, *Garden of Priapus*, 42; Cf. Juvenal, 6.33–37.

88. Frank-Rutger Hausmann, "Carmina Priapea," *Catalogus Translationum et Commentariorum*, 4:423–450, 426; Hausmann, "Martialis," 252.

89. Da Verona, 57–58, n. 3. The Vatican librarian and publisher Giovanni Andrea Bussi dedicated seven printed editions of classical texts to Paul II, but the author nevertheless remarked that he "did not think that the pope would read them" (quoted in Frazier, *Possible Lives*, 240).

90. Callimachus, poem 105. See also poems 104 and 106.

91. Leto, 1894, 188–189.

92. Platina, 1913–1932, 382.

93. Platina, 1778, 33.

94. Platina, 1998, 9.25. See also Campano's epigram on Callimachus' eyesight, published in Della Torre, 91.

95. Platina, 1913–1932, 386.

96. Bauer, 49; D'Amico, 95.

97. MS Florence BNCF, fol. 267v, as discussed in Bauer, 99; Platina, 1913–1932, 382.

98. Bauer, 46–48; Platina, 1998, 17.

99. Platina, 1998, 17.

100. Campano, Epigrams, bk. 6, fol. 21r.

5. Consorting with the Enemy

1. Babinger, 1978, 428. The epigraph from Seyyid Lokman is quoted and translated ibid., 423–424.

2. Jacopo de Campi, *Governo ed entrate del Gran Turco* (1475), quoted and discussed in ibid., 429–431. On the theme of the cruel Turk, see Paolo Preto, *Venezia e i Turchi* (Florence: Sansoni, 1975), 244–282.

3. For contemporary accounts of the siege, see Robert Schwoebel, *The Shadow of the Crescent: The Renaissance Image of the Turk, 1453–1517* (New York: St. Martin's, 1967), 7–13; and Margaret Meserve, *Empires of Islam in Renaissance Historical Thought* (Cambridge: Harvard University Press, 2008), 65–66.

4. On the Turks as descendants of Trojans, see Meserve, *Empires of Islam*, 22–64; James Hankins, "Renaissance Crusaders: Humanist Cru-

sade Literature in the Age of Mehmed II," *Dumbarton Oaks Papers* 49 (1995): 111–207, esp. 136–144; and Agostino Pertusi, "I primi studi in Occidente sull'origine e la potenza dei Turchi," *Studi veneziani* 12 (1970): 465–552.

5. Critoboulos, 181–182; Meserve, *Empires of Islam,* 43–44; Hankins, "Renaissance Crusaders," 139–140.

6. Filippo da Rimini, as reported in Hankins, "Renaissance Crusaders," 139; Filelfo, 3:566–576.

7. *Europa,* in Pius, 1551, 387–471, 394. Pertusi, "I primi studi in Occidente," 482; Meserve, *Empires of Islam,* 68–84, esp. 79–80; Hankins, "Renaissance Crusaders," 137–138.

8. *Oratio ad Calixtum Papam,* in Pius, 1551, 926; F. Arnaldi, L. G. Rosa, and L. Monti Sabiam, 156–158; *Oratio Aeneae de Constantinopolitana clade et bello contra Turcos congregando,* in Pius, 1551, 680.

9. Kenneth M. Setton, *The Papacy and the Levant, 1204–1571* (Philadelphia: American Philosophical Association, 1978), 272–275.

10. Preto, *Venezia e i Turchi,* 25–32.

11. Pastor, 4:96–97.

12. Preto, *Venezia e i Turchi,* 25.

13. Dei, 159–160.

14. Ibid., 160; Maria Pisani, "Un avventuriero del '400: La vita di Benedetto Dei," *La Rassegna* 29 (1921): 177–178. Benedetto similarly intercepted Venetian correspondence in 1466. See Dei, 164.

15. Babinger, 1963, 311; Babinger, 1951, 492.

16. Paolo Preto, *I servizi segreti di Venezia* (Milan: Il Saggiatore, 1994), 25.

17. R. Barducci, "Dei, Benedetto," in *Dizionario biografico degli italiani* (1971), 252–257; Paolo Orvieto, "Un esperto orientalista del '400: Benedetto Dei," *Rinascimento* 9 (1969): 209–213.

18. Dei, 136, 154, 157, 158, 160.

19. Pius, 1959, 13:351–352. I have modified the translation and taken only selected sentences from the two-page speech.

20. Ibid., 352–364.

21. Dei, quoted in Babinger, 1963, 312–313; Dei, 115.

22. Dei, 161.

23. Babinger, 1951, 492.

24. W. Miller, *Essays on the Latin Orient* (Amsterdam: Hakkert, 1964), 488–490; Orvieto, "Un esperto orientalista," 212.

25. Dei, 127–128.

26. Ibid., 128.

27. Ibid., 128–129.

28. Ibid., 163; Babinger, 1951, 493.

29. Dei, 162–165; Orvieto, 211–213; Babinger, 1951, 478–479.

30. Quoted in Babinger, 1963, 313.

31. Niccolò Sagundino, quoted in Babinger, 1951, 485.

32. Babinger, 1951, 485; Babinger, 1978, 494–495.

33. Preto, *I servizi segreti di Venezia*, 95–109, esp. 96–97; Babinger, 1951, 491.

34. Setton, *The Papacy and the Levant*, 282–283; and letter dated July 1467, Latin quoted in 289, n. 74.

35. Ibid., 291.

36. Canensius, 158–159; Pastor, 4:154–156.

37. Letter in Canensius, 197–198.

38. De Rubeis, 484.

39. Dante, *Inferno*, XXVIII:28–63.

40. In general, see R. W. Southern, *Western Views of Islam in the Middle Ages* (Cambridge: Harvard University Press, 1962); Schwoebel, 1–77, and passim. For fifteenth-century humanist rhetoric against the Turk, see Hankins, "Renaissance Crusaders."

41. On the social and religious appeal of the Ottoman Empire in the sixteenth century, see Preto, *Venezia e i Turchi*, 163–232, esp. 221–226.

42. Monfasani, 189.

43. Blanchus, 1906, 490–491.

44. Zabughin, 1:29, 282, n. 83.

45. Leto, 1894, 190; Zabughin, 1:25–29; Masotti, 197.

46. Hankins, "Renaissance Crusaders," 119, 121–122; Preto, *Venezia e i Turchi*, 237; Norman Daniel, *Islam and the West: The Making of an Image* (Edinburgh: University of Edinburgh Press, 1960).

47. Babinger, 1951, 482–483.

48. Giacomo Languischi-Dolfin, fol. 313, quoted on 363, n. 61, Marios Philippides, "The Fall of Constantinople 1453: Classical Comparisons and the Circle of Cardinal Isidore," *Viator: Medieval and Renaissance Studies* 38 (2007): 349–383. On these readings of history, see also Julian Raby, "Cyriacus of Ancona and the Ottoman Sultan Mehmed II," *Journal of the Warburg and Courtauld Institutes* 43 (1980): 242–246, esp. 245.

49. Philippides, "Fall of Constantinople," 363–365; Niccolò Sagundino, letter to Alfonso of Aragon, 1454, quoted in Babinger, 1951, 478.

50. Julian Raby, "A Sultan of Paradox: Mehmed the Conqueror as a Patron of the Arts," *Oxford Art Journal* 5, no. 1 (1982): 3–4.

51. Preto, *Venezia e i Turchi*, 246–250.

52. Raby, "A Sultan of Paradox," 3–8. On Mehmet's patronage of Italian artists, see also *Bellini and the East*, ed. Caroline Campbell and Alan Chong (New Haven, Conn.: Yale University Press, 2005).

53. Babinger, 1978, 78, 80–82.

54. Raby, "A Sultan of Paradox," 5–6. Babinger, 1978, 410–411. Critoboulos, 177.

55. On this, see John Monfasani, "The 'Lost' Final Part of George Amiroutzes' *Dialogus de fide in Christum* and Zanobi Acciaiuoli," in *Humanism and Creativity in the Renaissance: Essays in Honor of Ronald G. Witt*, ed. C. Celenza and K. Gouwens (Leiden: Brill, 2006), 197–229.

56. Quotations are taken from Nancy Bishaha, *Creating East and West: Renaissance Humanists and the Ottoman Turks* (Philadelphia: University of Pennsylvania Press, 2004), 147–152; I have adapted the English translation from Pius, 1990, 167, 122.

57. Monfasani, 131–136; Bishaha, *Creating East and West*, 153–155.

58. Discussed and translated in Monfasani, 158–159; Bishaha, *Creating East and West*, 155.

59. Quoted and translated in Bishaha, *Creating East and West*, 155–156; Monfasani, 188.

60. De Rubeis, quoted in both Masotti, 197–198; and Monfasani, 192, n. 74.

61. Monfasani, 189–194, and, for George's letter of defense, app. 9, 355–359; Palermino, 126.

62. Quoted, translated, and paraphrased in Monfasani, 133.

63. *Liber de sceleribus et infelicitate perfidi Turchi*, BAV Ms. Vat Lat. 971; Monfasani, 191; Trame, 186–187; Masotti, 198.

64. Babinger, 1958, 433–449, esp. 434–435.

65. Raby, "A Sultan of Paradox," 5; Preto, *Venezia e i Turchi*, 247.

66. Platina, 1913–1932, 384.

67. Pius, 1959, 185. On Pius and Sigismondo, see P. J. Jones, *The Malatesta of Rimini and the Papal State: A Political History* (Cambridge: Cambridge University Press, 1974), 220–234.

68. Pius, 1959, 184. On these charges, see Jones, 176–178.

69. Pius, 2003, 1.31.

70. Masotti, 196–197.
71. Raby, "A Sultan of Paradox," 4.
72. Valturio, fols. 283v–284r. This may have been the presentation copy seized by the Venetians.
73. Blanchus, 1884, 559; Da Verona, 48–49; Platina, 1913–1932, 384; Pastor, 4:50.
74. Platina, 1999, 8. The warden actually gives this description, but Platina was the author.
75. Platina, 2008, 30.6. In his brief account of Muhammad in the *Lives*, Platina, 1913–1932, 102–103, also decries Christian inaction in the face of the imminent Turkish threat.
76. Canensius, 149–150; Pastor 4:81–82.
77. Babinger, 1978, 359. See also Jerry H. Bentley, *Politics and Culture in Renaissance Naples* (Princeton: Princeton University Press, 1987), 171; and Franz Babinger, "Sechs unbekannte aragonische Sendschreiben im Grossherrlichen Seraj zu Stambul," in *Studi in onore di Riccardo Filangieri* (Naples: L'arte tipografica, 1959), 2:107–128.
78. D. Caccamo, "Buonaccorsi, Filippo," in *Dizionario biografico degli italiani* (1971), 15:79.
79. Miller, *Essays on the Latin Orient*, 298–313.
80. Masotti, 195, dates these events to 1460, whereas Caccamo, "Buonaccorsi" (79), and Babinger, 1978 (278), date them to 1469. The historical context makes 1469 a much more probable date. Cf. Gioacchino Paparelli, *Callimaco Esperiente (Filippo Buonaccorsi)* (Salerno: Beta, 1971), 80–85.
81. Ian Robertson, "Pietro Barbo—Paul II: Zentihomo de Venecia e Pontificato," in *War, Culture, and Society in Renaissance Venice: Essays in Honour of John Hale* (London: Hambledon, 1993), ed. David Chambers, Cecil H. Clough, and Michael Mallet, 147–159.
82. Pastor, 4:12, 19–20, 154–157; Platina, 1996, 101. Egidio, 183, says that the pope supported the attack on Florence.
83. Dei, 166.

6. The Emperor's Tomb

Platina, 1999, 83.

1. Gregorovius, 6.2, 512–517.
2. Latin poem in Frittelli, 26–27.

3. Latin poems, ibid., 27, 28.
4. Latin poem, ibid., 29.
5. Cellini, 63–76 (chaps. 34–39).
6. Ibid., 191–212 (chaps. 101–111).
7. Ibid., 218 (chap. 15).
8. Ibid., 218–238 (chaps. 116–128).
9. Trame, 167–168.
10. Platina, 1999, xci–xciii.
11. David Marsh, *The Quattrocento Dialogue: Classical Tradition and Humanist Innovation* (Cambridge: Harvard University Press, 1980).
12. On Valla and Erasmus, see Maristella de Panizza Lorch, *A Defense of Life: Lorenzo Valla's Theory of Pleasure* (Munich: Wilhelm Fink Verlag, 1985); and *Erasmus and His Catholic Critics,* ed. Erika Rummel (Nieuwkoop, The Netherlands: De Graaf, 1989).
13. Platina, 1999, 3–4, 5–8, 9–12.
14. Ibid., 14–17.
15. Ibid., 23, 28–29.
16. Ibid., 29–34. To cut down on repetition, I have translated selected sentences to distill Rodrigo's lengthy discourse.
17. Ibid., 1999, 35–36.
18. Isaiah Berlin, *Four Essays on Liberty* (Oxford: Oxford University Press, 1969); Quentin Skinner, "The Idea of Negative Liberty: Machiavellian and Modern Perspectives," in Skinner, *Visions of Politics* (Cambridge: Cambridge University Press, 2002), 2:186–212.
19. Platina, 1999, 40, 44–45.
20. Ibid., 52–56.
21. Platina, 1999, 69–71. On Phalaris' bull, see Chapter 1.
22. Platina, 1999, 71–76.
23. Ibid., 81–104.
24. Ibid., 109.
25. Ibid., 105; see also 4, 79.

7. Humanism Imprisoned

Patrizi, 1911, 182.

1. Canensius, 104, which includes notes on other sources.
2. As Platina says at the beginning of his dialogue *De amore*, quoted and discussed in Bauer, 47.

3. Platina, 1913–1932, 385.

4. Platina, 1778, 33–34; a similar passage appears in his letter to Pomponio, 38.

5. Ibid., 30–31. A similar threat appears on 32.

6. Ibid., 31–32, 34.

7. Platina, 1778, 32, 34.

8. Ibid., 32, 33–34.

9. Ibid., 35–36.

10. Steven Ozment, *Ancestors: The Loving Family in Old Europe* (Cambridge: Harvard University Press, 2001), 54–76.

11. The story appears in Jacopo's lament to his mother, Tolomei, fols. 31r–v, published in Paola Medioli Masotti, "Per la biografia di Jacopo Tolomei," *Italia medioevale e umanistica* 227–228, 230–231, 237; Carlo Dionisotti, "Jacopo Tolomei fra umanisti e rimatori," *Italia medioevale e umanistica* 6 (1963): 137–176; De Vincentiis, 2002, 41.

12. Dionisotti, "Jacopo Tolomei," 142, 156 (for quotation from Jacopo Tolomei, London BL MS. Add. 19908, fols. 51–52v).

13. Ibid., 153. The ancient Roman Cato was a famous champion of republicanism who chose to commit suicide by stabbing himself in the chest rather than live under Caesar's tyranny.

14. Ibid., 155–156.

15. Platina, 1778, 38–39.

16. Trame, 177–179.

17. Platina, 1913–1932, 383; Dionisotti, "Jacopo Tolomei," 155; Palermino, 127.

18. Quoted by Flavio Di Bernardo, *Un vescovo umanista alla corte Pontificia: Giannantonio Campano, 1429–1477* (Rome: Gregorian University Press, 1975), 220.

19. By contrast, Platina refers to the patience of the biblical Job and the constancy of the Christian martyrs. See the humanist's letter to the Count of Anguillara, Platina, 1778, 41, 43–44; and the previously discussed letter to Pope Paul, 30–34.

20. Ibid., 45–46.

21. Ibid., 47.

22. Ibid., 47. Cf. Platina, 1999, 85, where the interlocutor criticizes Platina's lamentations as befitting a woman.

23. Platina, 1778, 51–53.

24. Ibid., 50.

25. Ibid., 52–53.
26. Ibid., 54–55.
27. Ibid., 54–56.
28. Ibid.
29. Ibid., 57–60.
30. Ibid.
31. Pomponio to Rodrigo, March 28, in Leto, 1901, 318–319 (my translations are given here of the Latin letters in Creighton's appendix).
32. Rodrigo to Pomponio, ibid., 319–320.
33. Ibid., 321–323. Rodrigo also gave him his treatise on whether one should flee the plague. See Pomponio's praise for this work in Leto, 1468b, fols. 97r–98r.
34. Leto, 1901, 323–324.
35. Ibid., 324–325.
36. Ibid., 326.
37. Ibid.
38. See, for example, George W. McClure, *Sorrow and Consolation in Italian Humanism* (Princeton, N.J.: Princeton University Press, 1990); and Margaret L. King, *Death of the Child Valerio Marcello* (Chicago: Chicago University Press, 1994).
39. Platina, 1778, 37–38.

Epilogue

Platina, 1913–1932, 397; MS Florence, fol. 272r, as discussed in Bauer, 101.

1. Platina, 1731, 617.
2. Dunston, 288–289, makes these points. He criticizes Creighton and Pastor for using the graffiti to justify Paul's reaction to the 1468 conspiracy.
3. When a hermit was accused of plotting to kill Lorenzo de' Medici in 1480, the Florentine police "stripped the soles from his feet, which were then put over a fire . . . so that the fat ran. Then they stood him up and made him walk over coarse crushed salt, so that he died of this." His guilt was never determined. Landucci, quoted and translated in John Gage, *Life in Italy at the Time of the Medici* (London: Batsford, 1968), 109–110.
4. Roncesvalles was the site of the famous massacre of Charlemagne's army in the *Song of Roland*. Sardinia was a place outside the walls

of Florence where dead horses and mules were left to rot. Niccolò Machiavelli, "A Giuliano di Lorenzo de' Medici," *Il Teatro e tutti gli altri scritti letterari,* ed. Franco Gaeta (Milan: Fetrinelli, 1965), 1.5–14:362. On this poem, see De Grazia, 34–36.

5. Canensius, 105.

6. The pope was so fond of the dog, in fact, that it became the subject of ridicule. The humanist Campano composed a lament on its death: "To me the white puppy's name was Sweetie. / I believed it surpassed Scythian snow in whiteness. / It was nurtured under the roof of Pope Paul II, / Worthy of sacred food and holy housing. / I caressed the troubles from its tail and back, / and brought happiness to its feet, ears, and mouth. / It died of old age; I could not save it from dying, / nor were the hands of Christopher the doctor able to." Campano, 8.3.

7. Duchesne, 2:556; Bracciolini, 1993, 3:326–339.

8. Romano, 1:11–54.

9. Pius, 1993, 5.2.

10. Platina, 1913–1932, 397.

11. Di Benedetto, 104, with additional references in n. 3.

12. Campano, 6.1. On this poem, see Flavio Di Bernardo, *Un vescovo umanista alla corte pontificia: Giannantonio Campano, 1429–1477* (Rome: Gregoriana, 1975), 221.

Acknowledgments

This book began on a dark, cold, foggy December evening in 2002 in Venice. I had finished transcribing a fifteenth-century Latin oration in the Marciana Library and was looking through some manuscripts that had caught my eye in the library catalogue. I found the prison letters of Bartolomeo Platina and Pomponio Leto in the Castel Sant'Angelo contained in manuscript, Marc. Lat. Classe XI 103 (4361). I was translating *Lives of the Popes* (ITRL 30) by Platina at the time and had always been puzzled by his alleged involvement in a conspiracy to murder the pope. The letters, written in an eloquent, polished classical Latin, were deeply moving in their descriptions of pain, torture, and loneliness. I wondered how the lives of these humanists could have taken such a nasty turn and what, if any, consolation their classical erudition could have provided in the midst of such suffering. The conspiracy itself remains shrouded in mystery. Historians have wondered whether it ever really existed and have offered various quite disparate explanations for the pope's brutal reaction against the humanists. As my research progressed, I discovered hitherto unnoticed connections. No explanation, however, made sense on its own. The answers concerning the reality of the conspiracy and the pope's reaction, I concluded, could be found not in one clear-cut explanation but in the dizzyingly complex historical context of 1468.

I have explored specific aspects of the story in numerous papers I presented at the Renaissance Society of America Conference, the Sixteenth Century Studies Conference, and more specialized conferences and invited talks at the University of Texas, Austin; the University of Toronto; and the

University of California, Los Angeles. My research was made possible through a generous grant from the Canadian government, a Social Sciences and Humanities Research Council of Canada Standard Research Grant, which included a partial release from teaching obligations. I have also benefited from the liberal and enlightened parental leave policy at Queen's University, which permitted me to continue my research while enjoying my newborn daughter, Zoe. My colleagues here at Queen's, especially Jeff Collins, Ana Siljak, Andrew Jainchill, Rebecca Manley, Jim Stayer, Richard Greenfield, Christopher Fanning, Pierre Du Prey, David McTavish, and Sebastian Schutze offered helpful suggestions. John Monfasani, Chris Celenza, Margaret King, Paul Grendler, Jim Hankins, Alison Frazier, Lou Waldmann, Ken Gouwens, Margaret Meserve, Emily O'Brien, David Marsh, and two anonymous readers for Harvard University Press have given me great feedback on either individual chapters or the entire manuscript. Susan Abel at Harvard University Press has done an amazing job at copyediting. Her close reading and suggested revisions transformed my prose and helped me express my ideas more clearly. Ron Witt provided line-by-line corrections, which saved me a lot of embarrassment. Father Reginald Foster started me on the Latin adventure of my life. His dedication, enthusiasm, and willingness to grapple with the mind-boggling intricacies of a difficult language and culture first ignited my curiosity and will always inspire me. This book is dedicated with much thanks to Reginald, a modern-day abbreviator at the Vatican, who lives antiquity and personifies the Genius of Rome as much as Platina and Pomponio did. My parents, Donald and Margaret, introduced me to the majesty and mystery of the papacy, not only by taking me to Rome and Saint Peter's several times when I was a child but by including me in a private audience with Pope John Paul II in 1986. As a historian and avid traveler, my father, along with my mother, taught me to see beyond the local in geography and time. My wife, Una Roman D'Elia, an art historian, read through numerous drafts, helped me figure out the structure of the book, and offered rewrites of particular sentences when I was stumped. Her encouragement is constant and generous, no matter how absurd my ideas sometimes are. My two beautiful daughters, Lucy and Zoe, fill my life with joy. Nothing tops a giggle with my girls.

Select Bibliography

Archival Sources

Deposition for Pomponio Leto. 1468. Consiglio dei Dieci, Misti, reg. 17, c. 47 B. Archivio Segreto, Venice. Published in Giuseppe Zippel, ed. *Le vite di Paolo II di Gaspare da Verona e Michele Canensi.* 3.16:184–185. Rerum Italicarum Scriptores. Città di Castello: Lapi, 1911.

Leto, Pomponio. 1467. Poems. Marc. Lat. Classe XII, n. 210 (4689). Biblioteca Marciana, Venice.

———. 1468a. Defense. Vat. Lat. 2934. Biblioteca Apostolica Vaticana, Vatican City.

———. 1468b. Prison letters. Marc. Lat. Classe XI 103 (4361). Biblioteca Marciana, Venice.

Platina, Bartolomeo. 1474. *Liber de vita Christi ac omnium pontificum,* first version with corrections. Conventi soppressi, C.4.797. Biblioteca Nazionale Centrale, Florence.

Porcellio. 1427–1463. Poems. Magliabechiano J IX. Biblioteca Nazionale Centrale, Florence.

Tolomei, Jacopo. 1464–1471. Poems. Marc. It. IX 212 (6644). Biblioteca Marciana, Venice.

Valturio, Roberto. 1460. *De re militari.* Marc. Lat. Classe VIII 29 (2498). Biblioteca Marciana, Venice.

Published Sources

Alberti, Leon Battista. 1890. "De Porcaria coniuratione" (1453). *Opera inedita et pauca separatim Impressa.* Ed. G. Mancini. 257–266. Florence.

Altieri, Marco Antonio. 1995. *Li nuptiali di Marco Antonio Altieri pubblicati da Enrico Narducci* (ca. 1502). Ed. Massimo Miglio. Rome: Roma nel Rinascimento.

Ammannati-Piccolomini, Iacopo. 1984. *L'Eversana Deiectio di Iacopo Ammannati Piccolomini* (1465). Ed. Rossella Bianchi. Rome: Storia e letteratura.

————. 1997. *Lettere, 1444–1479.* 3 vols. Ed. P. Cherubini. Rome: Ministero per i beni culturali e ambientali.

Arnaldi, F., L. G. Rosa, and L. Monti Sabiam, eds. 1964. *Poeti latini del quattrocento.* Milan: Riccardo Ricciardi.

Babinger, Franz. 1951. "Maometto, il Conquistatore e l'Italia." *Rivista storica italiana* 63:469–505.

————. 1958. "Maometto il conquistatore e gli umanisti d'Italia." In *Il mondo antico nel Rinascimento: Atti del V convegno internazionale di studi sul Rinascimento.* 433–449. Florence: Sansoni.

————. 1963. "Lorenzo de' Medici e la Corte ottomana." *Archivio storico italiano* 121:305–361.

————. 1978 [1953]. *Mehmed the Conqueror and His Time.* Rev. ed. Trans. Ralph Manheim. Princeton, N.J.: Princeton University Press.

Barbaro, Ermolao il Vecchio. 1972. *Orationes contra poetas, epistolae* (1455). Ed. Giorgio Ronconi. Florence: Sansoni.

Bauer, Stefan. 2006. *The Censorship and Fortuna of Platina's Lives of the Popes in the Sixteenth Century.* Turnhout, Belgium: Brepols.

Biondo, Flavio. 1531. *Historiarum ab inclinatione Romanorum imperii decades* (1453). Basel: Froben.

————. 1963. *Le decadi* (1453). Trans. A. Crespi. Forlì, Italy: Zauli.

Blanchus, Johannes. 1884. Ambassador's Reports to Duke of Milan (1468). In Emilio Motta, "Bartolomeo Platina e Papa Paolo II." *Archivio della società romana di storia patria* 7:555–559.

————. 1906. Ambassador's Reports to Duke of Milan (1468). In Ludwig von Pastor, *The History of the Popes from the Close of the Middle Ages,* ed. F. I. Antrobus. 4:483, 488–492 (apps. 19, 21). Saint Louis: Herder.

Bracciolini, Poggio. 1946. *Contro l'ipocrisia* (1447–48). Ed. G. Vallese. Naples: R. Pironti.

————. 1993. *De varietate fortunae* (1448). Ed. Outi Merisalo. Helsinki: Suomalainen Tiedeakatemia.

————. 1994. *Facezie* (1438–1452). Ed. Marcello Ciccuto. Milan: Biblioteca Universale Rizzoli.

Bripio, Giuseppe. 1880. "Conformatio Curie Romane . . ." (1453). Transcribed in O. Tommasini, "Documenti relativi a Stefano Porcari." *Archivio della reale società romana di storia patria* 3:111–123.

Caccia. Stefano. 1883. Letter (1453). In *A. Piccolomini senesis opera inedita,* ed. G. Cugnoni. Rome: Salviucci.

Callimachus (Filippo Buonaccorsi). 1963. *Philippi Callimachi Epigrammatum libri duo* (1462–1472). Ed. Casimir Felix Kumaniecki. Bratislava: Zaklad Narodowy im. Ossolinskich.

Campano, Giannantonio. 1520. *Omnia Campani opera* (1477). Venice. Available online at http://diglib.hab.de.

Canensius, Michelis. 1911. *De vita ac pontificatu Pauli Secundi* (1471). In *Le vite di Paolo II di Gaspare da Verona e Michele Canensi,* ed. Giuseppe Zippel. 3.16:65–176. Rerum Italicarum Scriptores. Città di Castello: Lapi.

Cellini, Benvenuto. 1966. *The Autobiography of Benvenuto Cellini* (1562–1566). Trans. George Bull. London: Folio Society.

Clementi, Filippo. 1939. *Il Carnevale romano nelle cronache contemporanee dalle origini al secolo XVII.* Città di Castello: RORE.

Creighton, Mandell. 1901. *A History of the Papacy from the Great Schism to the Sack of Rome.* 6 vols. London: Longmans.

Critoboulos. 1954. *History of Mehmed the Conqueror* (1468). Trans. C. T. Riggs. Princeton, N.J.: Princeton University Press.

Crivelli, Leodrisio. 2002. *De regno* (1466). In *Battaglie di Memoria,* ed. Amedeo de Vincentiis. 165–178. Rome: Roma nel Rinascimento.

Cruciani, Fabrizio. 1983. *Teatro nel Rinascimento: Roma 1450–1550.* Rome: Buzoni.

D'Amico, John F. 1983. *Renaissance Humanism in Papal Rome: Humanists and Churchmen on the Eve of the Reformation.* Baltimore: Johns Hopkins University Press.

Da Verona, Gaspare. 1911. "Vita Pauli Secondi" (1471). In *Le vite di Paolo II di Gaspare da Verona e Michele Canensi,* ed. Giuseppe Zippel. 3.16:3–64. Rerum Italicarum Scriptores. Città di Castello: Lapi.

De' Giudici, Battista. 1987. *Apologia Iudaeorum, Invectiva contra Platinam* (1477). Ed. Diego Quaglioni. Rome: Roma nel Rinascimento.

De Grazia, Sebastian. 1989. *Machiavelli in Hell.* Princeton, N.J.: Princeton University Press.

Dei, Benedetto. 1985. *La cronica dall'anno 1400 all'anno 1500* (1473). Ed. Roberto Barducci. Florence: Francesco Papafava.

Della Torre, Arnaldo. 1903. *Paolo Marsi da Pescina: Contributo alla storia dell'Accademia pomponiana.* G. Mazzoni.

De Rubeis, Augustinus. 1906. Ambassador's Reports to Duke of Milan

(1468). In Ludwig von Pastor, *The History of the Popes from the Close of the Middle Ages,* ed. F. I. Antrobus. 4:484–487, 492–493 (apps. 20, 22). Saint Louis: Herder.

De Vincentiis, Amedeo. 2002. *Battaglie di Memoria.* Rome: Roma nel Rinascimento.

Di Benedetto, Paolo. 1893. "Il memoriale di Paolo di Benedetto di Cola dello Mastro dello rione di Ponte" (1484). Ed. Mario Pelaez. *Archivio della società romana di storia patria* 16:80–106.

Dizionario biografico degli italiani (DBI). 1960–. Rome: Istituto della enciclopedia italiana.

Duchesne, L., ed. 1892. *Liber Pontificalis.* (4th–15th c.). Paris: Ernest Thorin.

Dunston, A. J. 1973. "Pope Paul II and the Humanists." *Journal of Religious History* 7 (4): 287–306.

Egidio da Viterbo. 1911. *Historia XX Seculorum* (1513–1518). In *Le vite di Paolo II di Gaspare da Verona e Michele Canensi,* ed. Giuseppe Zippel. 3.16:182–184. Rerum Italicarum Scriptores. Città di Castello: Lapi.

Filelfo, Giovanni Mario. 1978. *Amyris* (1471). Ed. Aldo Manetti. Bologna: Pàtron.

Frittelli, Ugo. 1900. *Giannantonio de'Pandoni detto il "Porcellio": Studio critico.* Florence: Paravia.

Godi, Pietro. 1906. "De coniuratione Porcaria dialogus" (1453). In *Horatii Romani Porcaria,* ed. M. Lehnerdt. 57–75. Leipzig: Teubner.

Gregorovius, Ferdinand. 1898–1906. *History of the City of Rome in the Middle Ages.* 8 vols. London: G. Bell & Sons.

Guarino, Battista. 2002. *A Program for Teaching and Learning* (1459). In *Humanist Educational Treatises,* ed. and trans. Craig Kallendorf. 260–309. I Tatti Renaissance Library. Cambridge: Harvard University Press.

Hankins, James. 1990. *Plato in the Italian Renaissance.* 2 vols. Leiden: Brill.

Infessura, Stefano. 1890. *Diario della città di Roma di Stefano Infessura* (ca. 1493). Ed. O. Tommasini. Rome: Forzani.

Leto, Pomponio. 1894. "Defensio Pomponii Leti in carceribus et confessio" (1468). Ed. I. Carini. Bergamo.

———. 1901. *Letters* (1468). In Mandel Creighton, *A History of the Papacy from the Great Schism to the Sack of Rome.* 4:318–326. London: Longmans, Green.

Machiavelli, Niccolò. 1988. *Florentine Histories* (1520–1525). Trans. Laura F. Banfield and Harvey Mansfield, Jr. Princeton, N.J.: Princeton University Press.

Manetti, Giannozzo. 2006. *Life of Nicholas V* (1455). Latin text and translation in Christine Smith and Joseph F. O'Connor, *Building the Kingdom: Giannozzo Manetti on the Material and Spiritual Edifice*. 305–483. Tempe, Ariz.: Brepols.

Masotti, Paola Medioli. 1982. "L'Accademia romana e la congiura del 1468." *Italia medioevale e umanistica* 25:189–204.

Miglio, Massimo. 1975. *Storiografia pontificia del quattrocento*. Bologna: Pàtron.

Modigliani, Anna. 2000. "Paolo II." *Enciclopedia dei papi*. 685–701. Rome: Treccani.

———. 2003. "Paolo II e il sogno abbandonato di una Piazza imperiale." In *Antiquaria a Roma: Intorno a Pomponio Leto e Paolo II*. 125–161. Rome: Roma nel rinascimento.

Monfasani, John. 1976. *George of Trebizond: A Biography and a Study of His Rhetoric and Logic*. Leiden: Brill.

Palermino, R. J. 1980. "The Roman Academy, the Catacombs and the Conspiracy of 1468." *Archivum Historiae Pontificiae* 18:117–155.

Pastor, Ludwig von. 1906. *The History of the Popes from the Close of the Middle Ages*. 40 vols. Ed. F. I. Antrobus. Saint Louis: Herder.

Patrizi, Agostino. 1733. *De adventu Friderici III Imperatoris* (1468). Ed. Ludovico Muratori. 23:205–216. Rerum Italicarum Scriptores. Milan: Palatine.

———. 1911. Letter to Antonio Monelli (1468). In *Le vite di Paolo II di Gaspare da Verona e Michele Canensi*, ed. Giuseppe Zippel. 3.16:181–182. Rerum Italicarum Scriptores. Città di Castello: Lapi.

Pius II. 1551/1967. *Opera omnia*. Basel: Henrichum Petri. Facsimile edition, Frankfurt: Minerva.

———. 1909. *Der Briefwechsel des Eneas Silvius Piccolomini* (1463). Ed. Rudolf Wolkan. Vol. 1 in Fontes Rerum Austriacarum. Vienna: A. Holder.

———. 1959. *Memoirs of a Renaissance Pope: The Commentaries of Pius II* (1463). Trans. F. A. Gragg. New York: Capricorn.

———. 1990. *Epistola ad Mahometam II (Epistle to Mohammed II)* (1461). Ed. and trans. Albert R. Baca. New York: Peter Lang.

———. 1993. *Pii Secundi Pontificis Maximi Commentarii* (1463). Ed. Ibolya Boronkai and Ivan Boronkai. Budapest: Balassi Kiado.

———. 2002. *The Education of Boys* (1450). In *Humanist Educational Treatises*, ed. and trans. Craig Kallendorf. 126–259. I Tatti Renaissance Library. Cambridge: Harvard University Press.

———. 2003 and 2007. *Commentaries* (1463). Vols. 1 and 2. Ed. and trans. Margaret Meserve. I Tatti Renaissance Library. Cambridge: Harvard University Press.

Platina, Bartolomeo. 1731. *Historia urbis Mantuae Gonziacaeque Familiae.* Ed. Ludovico Muratori. 20:617–862. Rerum Italicarum Scriptores. Milan: Palatine.

———. 1778. Prison Letters (1468–69). In *Cremonensium monumenta Romae extantia,* ed. Tommaso Agostino Vairani. 29–66. 2 parts in 1 vol. Rome: Salomeni.

———. 1913–1932. *Liber de vita Christi ac omnium pontificum* (1474). Ed. G. Gaida. 3:1. Rerum Italicarum Scriptores. Bologna: Zanichelli.

———. 1996. "De pace Italiae componenda atque de bello Turcis indicendo oratio" (1468). In *Zur Theorie von Krieg und Frieden in der italienischen Renaissance,* ed. Wolfram Benziger. 97–105. Frankfurt: Peter Lang.

———. 1998. *On Right Pleasure and Good Health: A Critical Edition and Translation of* De honesta voluptate et valetudine (1466–67?). Ed. and trans. Mary Ella Milham. Tempe, Ariz.: Medieval and Renaissance Texts and Studies.

———. 1999. *De falso et vero bono* (1466). Ed. Maria Grazia Blasio. Rome: Storia e letteratura.

———. 2008. *Lives of the Popes* (1474). Ed. and trans. A. F. D'Elia. Vol. 1. I Tatti Renaissance Library. Cambridge: Harvard University Press.

Porcari, Stefano. 1874. *Orations* (1427–28). In *Prose del Giovane Buonaccorso da Montemagno,* ed. G. B. C. Giuliari. Bologna: G. Romagnoli.

———. 1906. "Confession" (1453). In Ludwig von Pastor, *The History of the Popes from the Close of the Middle Ages,* ed. F. I. Antrobus. 2:510–517 (app.). Saint Louis: Herder.

Porcellio. 1720. Poems (1427–1463). In *Carmina illustrium poetarum.* 7:497–519. Florence: Typus regiae celsitudinis.

———. 1723 and 1751. *Porcellii Commentaria comitis Jacobi Picinini* (1452–53). Ed. Ludovico Muratori. Vols. 20 and 25. Rerum italicarum scriptores. Milan: Palatine.

Romano, Orazio. 1906. *Horatii Romani Porcaria* (1453). Ed. M. Lehnerdt. 4–34. Leipzig: Teubner.

Sabellicus. 1500. *Life of Pomponio Laeto.* In Pomponius Laetus, *Romanae historiae compendium,* fols. 1r–4r. Venice: Bernardinus Venetus.

Simonetta, Giovanni. 1932–1934. *Rerum gestarum Francisci Sfortiae, Medio-*

lanensium ducis commentarii (1477). Ed. Giovanni Soranzo. 21:2. Rerum Italicarum Scriptores. Bologna: Zanichelli.

Tommasini, O. 1880. "Documenti relativi a Stefano Porcari." *Archivio della reale società romana di storia patria* 3:63–127.

Trame, Richard H. 1958. *Rodrigo Sánchez de Arévalo, 1404–1470: Spanish Diplomat and Champion of the Papacy.* Washington, D.C.: Catholic University Press.

Valla, Lorenzo. 1977. *De voluptate* (1431). Ed. and trans. A. Kent Hieatt and Maristella Lorch. New York: Abaris.

———. 2007. *On the Donation of Constantine* (1440). Trans. G. W. Bowersock. I Tatti Renaissance Library. Cambridge: Harvard University Press.

Zabughin, Vladimiro. 1909. *Giulio Pomponio Leto: Saggio critico.* 2 vols. Rome: La Vita Letteraria.

Index

Aaron (biblical prophet), 21

Academics, 172

Aeneid (Virgil), 80

"Against Mehmet, the Wicked King of the Turks" (Pius II), 107

Agnadello, battle of, 108

Alain of Avignon, Cardinal, 34

Albania, 118

Alberti, Leon Battista, 57, 60

Alexander the Great, 12, 114, 115, 121, 126; exemplary literature and, 148; Mehmet II compared with, 129; in records of historians and poets, 154

Alexander VI, Pope, 37, 107

Alfonso of Aragon, king of Naples, 50, 68, 75

Altieri, Marcantonio, 62–63, 65

Amiroutzes, George, 123, 126

Ammannati-Piccolomini, Cardinal, 24, 26–27, 36, 87, 132

Amyris (Filelfo), 105

Anacletus, Pope, 23

Andreas of Chios, 120

Anguillara, counts of, 24

Anjou, Jean d', 66, 68, 72

Antherus, Pope, 22

Anti-Semitism, 5

Arabic language, 13, 115, 120, 121

Argyropoulos, John, 88–89

Aristotelian ethics, 148, 152

Aristotle, 79, 88, 149, 154, 170–171, 189

Astrology, 10–11

Augustine, Saint, 88, 90, 147, 163, 172; on dangers of lust, 82, 83–84; on suffering and virtue, 173

Augustus (Roman emperor), 43

Avignon, papacy in, 42

Barbaro, Bishop Ermolao, 83, 84

Barbo, Cardinal Marco, 154, 158

Barbo, Pietro. *See* Paul II, Pope

Battista, Giovanni, 27

Bayezid II, Sultan, 126

Beccadelli, Antonio, 99

Beccafumi, Domenico, 16

Bellano, Bartolomeo, 20, 122

Bellini, Gentile, 106, 122, 126

Benedictine order, 40, 48

Bessarion, Cardinal, 2, 30, 90, 91; Callimachus protected by, 95; Election Capitulation and, 34; humanists at house of, 80; as patron of Platina, 101, 160–161; Platina and, 133; as Platonist, 89, 124–125; Porcari conspiracy and, 56

Biondo, Flavio, 52, 80

Bishops, 22–23, 33

Bisticci, Vespasiano da, 40

Boccaccio, Giovanni, 86